MONTY'S NORTHERN LEGIONS

50th NORTHUMBRIAN and 15th SCOTTISH DIVISIONS AT WAR 1939–1945

PATRICK DELAFORCE

SUTTON PUBLISHING

First published in the United Kingdom in 2004 by
Sutton Publishing Limited · Phoenix Mill
Thrupp · Stroud · Gloucestershire · GL5 2BU

British Library Cataloguing in Publication Data
A catalogue record for this book is available from the British Library.

ISBN 0-7509-3556-1

Typeset in 10/12pt Plantin.
Typesetting and origination by
Sutton Publishing Limited.
Printed and bound in England by
J.H. Haynes & Co. Ltd, Sparkford.

Contents

Acknowledgements

This is the story of two infantry divisions whose gallant role in the Second World War deserves to be much better known. My grateful thanks go to four individuals – Dave Sclater, Andrew Black, Ron Sheather and Gerry Briscoe – who lent me vital books (some of them fifty years out of print) so that 50th Northumbrian (Tyne-Tees) Division, with its four Victoria Crosses, and 15th Scottish Division, with its record of four assault crossings of the Seine, Escaut, Rhine and Elbe, will take their place in history.

Very many thanks to the various historians Ewart Clay, David Rissik, B.S. Barnes, Lt-Gen H.G. Martin, Robert Woollcombe, C.R. MacLellan, D. Fenner, Geoffrey Picot, W.L. McElwee and of course Alan Moorehead, the famous journalist, and many others. The Imperial War Museum Photographic Archives have as usual produced a wonderful range of photographs for both of Monty's Northern Legions.

To the reader of this book it will be horrifying how many times the huge hideous casualty figures appear. '6th DLI lost over 100 casualties . . . the bitter defence caused losses of twenty officers and 200 men – 9th DLI was torn apart.' '15th Scottish Division had been torn apart. . . . Five battalions suffered over 300 casualties each . . .' From North Africa, Sicily and D-Day to the Rhine and the Baltic, these two superb British infantry divisions between them suffered over 30,000 casualties – almost on a First World War scale. Nowadays, when the British Army loses a man or two in Kosovo or Basra or Liberia (which of course is regrettable), it should be seen in the context of the dreadful losses of the Second World War. Immaculate, dignified British war cemeteries, beautifully tended – rose bushes in front of white gravestones – rank on rank of them: there lie the young men of 'Monty's Northern Legions' who fought so bravely, and died.

PART 1

50TH NORTHUMBRIAN DIVISION

CHAPTER 1

Introduction

The northern British 50th Division had a long and distinguished history. Its First World War history by Everard Wyrall tells the tragic story of its 34,000 casualties in four years. In April 1915 at St Julien it suffered in the first German gas attack, then in the appalling battles of the Somme, the Scarpe, Passchendaele, Lys and Aisne.

In the Second World War it fought in 1940 with the British Expeditionary Force (BEF), in many North African campaigns and in Sicily. Gen Bernard Montgomery selected it for the dangerous honour of being one of the two British infantry divisions to land on D-Day in Normandy. It fought in Operations 'Overlord' and 'Market Garden' before Montgomery decreed that because of casualties and Python/LILOP (a decision that veterans with long years of service outside UK would be repatriated), 50th Northumbrian Division would be disbanded as a fighting unit and become a training division in the UK. Prime Minister Winston Churchill was furious. He wrote on 3 December 1944 to the First Lord, Secretary of State for War, to Gen Ismay and to the CIGS and Chief of Staff committee:

> I am much distressed by the impending cannibalisation of the 50th Division. We cannot afford at this stage to reduce our stake in the Western line of battle. We must examine all possibilities which are open. The 50th Division might close its three brigades into two and add a third Royal Marine brigade . . . Finally on no account is the breaking up of the 50th Division to proceed any further until these matters have been thrashed out between us and decisions upon them given by the War Office.

Even the powerful Prime Minister could not win this battle.

In Sicily and north-west Europe the 'Fifty Div' suffered 9,000 casualties, and over 12,000 more with the BEF and in North Africa. No division in the British Army won more than its four Victoria Crosses: Pte Eric Anderson, Pte Adam Wakenshaw, Lt-Col Derek Seagrim and CSM Stan Hollis. Gen Horrocks, Commander of XXX Corps, described it as the 'most experienced battle fighting division in the British Army'.

There had been two excellent histories published about 'Fifty Div', by Maj Ewart Clay, MBE, in 1950, which has been out of print for many years, and by Barrie Barnes in 1999 about the Sicilian and north-west Europe campaigns.

In September 1939, 50th (Northumbrian) Division, included infantry battalions of the Durham Light Infantry (DLI) (6th, 8th and 9th), the Green Howards (4th and 5th Battalions from North Yorkshire and the Yorkshire coast) and the East Yorkshires (4th Battalion from Hull and the East Riding). The Artillery Regiments (72nd, 74th Field and 65th Anti-tank) came mainly from Tynecastle, the RASC from Hull and the Reconnaissance Regiment was the 4th Royal Northumberland Fusiliers. It was a new motorised formation, with its own transport for dismounted personnel, capable of close support to armoured formations. The badge of two superimposed T's, red on a black background, stood for Tyne and Tees. If it was looked at sideways, an H appeared for Humber.

The GOC was Maj-Gen Sir G. Le Q. Martel. Brig C.W. Haydon commanded 150th Infantry Brigade (4th East Yorks, 4th and 5th Green Howards). Brig J.A. Churchill commanded 151st Infantry Brigade (6th, 8th and 9th Durham Light Infantry). The CRA was Brig C.W. Massy, and the CRE was Lt-Col W.M. Spires. From October 1939 to January 1940 the division trained in the Cotswolds and was inspected by King George VI at Broadway in Oxfordshire just before it left for France to take its place with the BEF.

CHAPTER 2

With the BEF in France: 'Last out of Dunkirk'

The division disembarked at Cherbourg on 19 January and moved to the Le Mans area, with Divisional HQ at Evron. Lt-Gen Alan Brooke commanded II Corps, which had five divisions including the 50th. On 30 January Maj-Gen Martel, his GSO1 Col M. Everett and his Divisional HQ staff visited Alan Brooke, who commented, 'Martel and his staff came in. He was wondering why we were not more concerned with preparing offensive measures to attack the Siegfried Line and seemed oblivious of the fact that, instead of attacking this spring, we are far more likely to be hanging on by our eyelids in trying to check the German attacks.' The only way the BEF, now a quarter of a million strong, so ill equipped for mobile war, could hope to defeat the Germans was by awaiting their attack in the fortified lines it had worked so hard to construct.

The Allied High Command had decided on Plan D. The moment the Germans attacked, the British and French forces on the left should leave their defences (the BEF had built 400 concrete pillboxes, made forty miles of anti-tank obstacles and constructed fifty-nine airfields) and hurry forward across sixty or seventy miles of unknown and refugee-crammed roads to take up a new position on the right of the Belgian Army on the River Dyle. On 27 January the division arrived at Lens with Divisional HQ at Billy Montigny. Two weeks later it moved to a training area near Amiens with Divisional HQ at Que-vau-Villiers. A month later it moved up to the Lille–Loos area to work on the defences of II Corps and reserve defence lines from Loos to Seclin and Wavrin. On 11 May, 25 Infantry Brigade joined the division under Brig Haydon with 7th Battalion the Queen's Royal Regiment, 2nd Battalion the Essex Regiment and 1st Battalion the Royal Irish Fusiliers. The senior chaplain, Revd R.T. Newcombe, with a team of unit padres, started a system of hostels in every village where men were billeted. In the 'padre's house' men could visit, talk, write letters and pray in the chapel. No alcoholic drink was sold!

The codeword 'Birch' was to be used to put the division on six hours' notice for action under Plan D. There was a false alarm on 11 April, but at 6.30 a.m. on 10 May it was the real thing. The Germans had invaded Belgium and Holland. Lt-Gen Alan Brooke placed Maj-Gen Montgomery's 3rd Division to

Green Howards land in France as part of the British Expeditionary Force, 28 January 1940.

guard a sector of the River Dyle, east of Brussels, with 4th Division behind 50th Division in reserve. Brig Massy, the CRA, was in charge of II Corps Road Control Centre with 4th Royal Northumberland Fusiliers and their motor cycles and eleven scout cars supervising all the 'centre line traffic'.

Most of Holland was quickly over-run and paralysed by savage Luftwaffe bombing. The Belgian Army along the Albert Canal covering Liege and Maastricht was under severe pressure. It suited the enemy for the BEF to drive as far into Belgium as possible. The seven German Panzer divisions were hurrying through the Ardennes and Luxembourg to cut off the BEF, the Belgian Army and much of the French Army. Behind them came thirty-seven infantry divisions of von Runstedt's German Army Group A. On the 16th Lord Gort, the BEF GOC, received orders for a withdrawal and 50th Division in GHQ reserve was sent to take up a defensive position from Ath to Ninove along the River Dendre behind and west of Brussels. On the 28th the division withdrew to the line of the River Escaut, where divisional engineers had prepared all bridges for demolition. However, the British Cabinet sent Gen Ironside, the CIGS, to meet Lord Gort with the message 'Send the BEF south towards Amiens and attack all forces it met.' So Gens Billotte (French), Ironside and Gort ordered two British divisions (the 5th and 50th) to attack from Arras towards Bapaume. At the same time two of Billotte's divisions would attack across the River Sensée towards Cambrai.

The British attack would be supported by the 1st Army Tank Brigade of 4th and 7th Royal Tank Regiments (RTRs). They had between them fifty-eight Mark I tanks with heavy armour but equipped only with a machine gun, and sixteen Matilda tanks with a 2-pounder gun. The objective was to smash into the flank of the 39th Panzer Corps, more specifically onto Gen Rommel's SS Death's Head Division. On 20 May Gen Martel went to Arras and immediately reinforced a Welsh Guards battalion there with a battalion from 150 Brigade, an anti-tank battery and a field company RE. The rest of 150 Brigade reached Vimy just north of Arras at noon. The GOC of 5th Division, Maj-Gen Franklyn, was senior to Martel and would therefore take charge of what became known as the 'Battle of Arras'. Two columns, each on a narrow front, mainly of the Durham Light Infantry of 151 Infantry Brigade, preceded by 4th RTR and 7th RTR, would be launched from the Arras–Saint-Pol road, westwards in a sweep round the south of Arras to clear an area about ten miles deep and four miles wide. It was planned for two phases, the first up to the River Cojeul and the second to the River Sensée. A brigade of 5th Division and a French division with seventy Somoa tanks would take part in the second phase.

After an approach march of eight miles the attack started at 1430 hours on 21 May. Lt-Col Miller's 6th DLI and 4th RTR were in the left column and Lt-Col Beart's 8th DLI with 7th RTR, in the right column. 9th DLI was in reserve. The 6th DLI/4th RTR column rapidly took Danville, Achicourt and Beaurains. The tanks shot up transport, anti-tank guns and tanks and the Durhams mopped up, taking 400 prisoners. The 8th DLI/7th RTR column took Duisans and, after a hard fight, Warlus, using the same tank/infantry tactics. Gen Martel then decided to make Beaurains, Duisans and Warlus 'tank-proof' localities.

However, predictably the superior German forces counter-attacked heavily. The Luftwaffe launched more than 100 Stuka dive-bombers in concentrated twenty-minute attacks on the three defence points. Then came fierce attacks by Panzer Mark III and IV tanks. Maj Forrester's anti-tank gun battery had a field-day and knocked out more than twenty Panzers with their 2-pounder guns. Both the RTR tank commanders, Lt-Cols Heyland and Fitzmaurice, were killed in the one-day battle. Maj P.J. Jeffreys, 2 i/c 6th DLI, extricated his troops skilfully from Beaurains. Gen Rommel in Wailly was very nearly captured and wrote in his 'Papers': 'In the village and around it the situation was critical. Our troops had been thrown into a terrible confusion. Carried away by retreating infantry, gun-layers in one battery abandoned their guns. The anti-tank guns which we hastily brought into action proved too light to pierce the thickly armoured [Matilda] tanks. These guns were knocked out by artillery and then overrun by the tanks. A great number of vehicles were set on fire.' The German 6th Fusiliers were almost destroyed and the SS Death's Head Division broke up and withdrew in disorder towards the south.

It looked as through the division would have to defend the Arras salient. 'There is no doubt', said Gen Martel, 'that those North Countrymen would

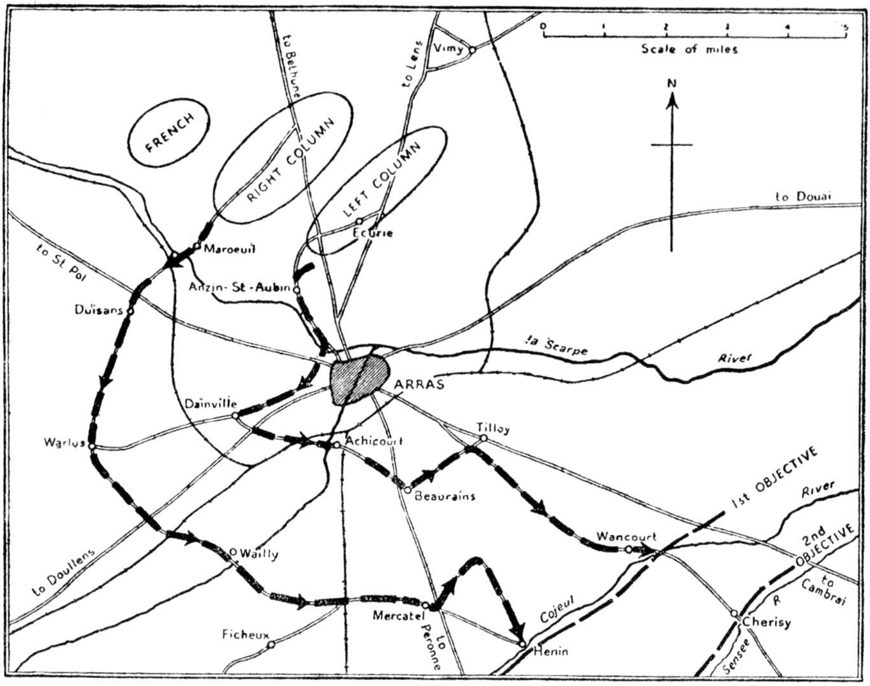

Operations with the British Expeditionary Force around Arras.

have fought to the last man and this might have set a standard which we badly needed on one or two occasions later on in the war'. However, during the night of the 23rd, the division moved northwards through the corridor to rejoin the main body of the BEF, at the canal on the upper Deule.

Gunner Stonard's 72nd Regiment RA of 25-pounder field guns supported 150 Brigade. Stonard wrote:

> Our role was to be a GHQ reserve, ready to rush to any part of the battle that needed rapid reinforcement. The 50th was to spend two or three weeks after the first German attack swanning backwards and forwards, getting hopelessly enmeshed with tens of thousands of refugees who blocked most of the route along which the BEF was ordered to move. Our battery arrived at Bailleul, a small village [on 26 May]. The gun position was between a 1914–18 German cemetery and a small British war cemetery. Our 50th Division was considered by the Germans to have been one of the most determined they had encountered during the campaign.

151 Brigade, holding positions in the Provin–Carvin area, was being shelled and bombed on the 25th and 26th. 6th DLI was moved back to Herrin, 9th DLI had been badly shot up and was in close contact with the enemy and 8th DLI was counter-attacking enemy patrols that had crossed the canal at Carvin. Brig Churchill phoned Gen Martel to say that the

Germans had broken through the French in front and were then engaging 8th DLI at Camphin, and that afternoon recaptured Carvin. 9th DLI was then firmly established at Provin. Gen Martel next received orders via Lt-Gen Alan Brooke, the Corps Commander, that Ypres was to be defended. So Brig Haydon was ordered to take his 150 Brigade there with 72nd Field Regiment RA, 150th Field Ambulance, plus 6th DLI. The move was planned for dawn on the 27th.

Henri Braem, a Belgian living in Zillebeke, a small village between Ypres and Menin, recalled:

> Both the British 5th and 50th Divisions had been in our area. They had been in the bitter fighting around Arras and arrived in the Zillebeke–Hollebeke–Houthem area of Ypres during 25/26 May and were attacked by elements of German 6th Army. Rifle fire we heard was between British recce patrols and the Germans. The British used the natural defence lines in our area, Hill 60, Hill 62, the Ypres–Comines railway line and the canal alongside it. The main German assault on Monday, 27 May went in under a heavy barrage; they advanced from Zillebeke village green and Hill 60 against the railway line. The British slaughtered them and each time the German attack was renewed the British shot them down from their good defensive positions. Although they were outnumbered, exhausted and without food, they held to the last.

The churches in England were packed with worshippers and a special Service of Intercession was held on the 26th for the safety of the BEF. Winston Churchill was in Westminster Abbey, and wrote, 'I could feel the pent-up passionate emotion and also the fear of the congregation, not of death or wounds or material loss, but of defeat and the final ruin of Britain.' Lord Gort had been given permission to withdraw the BEF to Dunkirk 'in conjunction with the French and Belgian armies'. The Admiralty rather pessimistically started to organise Operation 'Dynamo' to rescue perhaps 45,000 soldiers in the course of the next two nights.

Lt-Gen Alan Brooke, II Corps GOC, recorded:

> 27 May my next visit was to 50th Division on outskirts of Ypres where I found Martel who informed me that [Brig] Haydon with the 150th Brigade was in position . . . He had come up quickly with his division, the other brigade was not far off [Poperinghe] and it was tremendous relief to see this dangerous gap filling. I placed Martel in command of the French Division Lourde Motorisée, of the MG battalion of 4th Division and of course of his own two infantry brigades. We were only just in time. The western approaches to Ypres were already being shelled.

King Leopold of the Belgians asked for an armistice and capitulated his country at midnight on 28 May. On the 28th Gen Alan Brooke ordered Martel to send 4th Northumberland Fusiliers to plug the gap between 50th and 5th Divisions, which were now the main BEF rearguard. For Churchill, the CIGS and the War Cabinet, the terrible dilemmas occurred almost daily. 51st Highland Division at Saint-Valéry was under the command of the French Army and could not be seen to escape and leave the French in the lurch. In Calais the Rifle Brigade and 3rd RTR fought to the last and gained time for Dynamo.

Back at Ypres the division was shelled and attacked on the 27th and 28th. Lt-Col C.N. Littleboy, a powerfully built man, was CO 4th Green Howards, who were heavily engaged, but Brig Haydon handled 150 Brigade very efficiently in a dangerous situation. By the next day the division was holding a line between Poperinghe and Elverdinghe. II Corps was holding the eastern portion of the BEF bridgehead, with Gen Bernard Montgomery's 'Ironsides' 3rd Division on the left, 50th Division in the centre and 5th Division in reserve.

Lt-Gen Alan Brooke's diary recorded: '28 May I returned to 50th Division and instructed Martel to throw back his right flank from the Canal to rest at Poperinghe where it should come into contact with 1st Division. He was to retain this covering position throughout the next day to allow 5th and 4th Divisions to retire through his division and to cover their retirement.' During the 29th the division retired into the bridghead position along the Bergues–Fournes Canal. Some of the motor transport was destroyed, as were guns when supplies of ammunition ran out. Divisional HQ was sited at Adinkerke, 150 Brigade on the right near the frontier, and 151 Brigade on the left near Bulscamp. The enemy closed up on the 30th and made a few light attacks. The Royal Northumberland Fusiliers and the machine guns of 4th Gordon Highlanders were also put under command and fought splendidly. On 31 May the division had to pivot to the right and occupy the Franco-Belgian frontier with 5th Division on the left, and casualties mounted rapidly in 151 Brigade. During the night of 1 June the division withdrew to south of Bray Dunes, with 150 Brigade holding off the enemy and 151 Brigade dug in on the sea shore behind them. The RASC and gunners were the first to be embarked. In many places troops had to wade through deep water, but, with rifles and all their machine guns to hand, 150 Brigade embarked from the beaches at Malo Les Bains and the remainder from the Dunkirk mole.

The 50th Division was the last division to leave Dunkirk. Lt-Gen Alan Brooke said farewell on the afternoon of 30 May to his four divisional commanders. He estimated that Montgomery's 3rd Division was still 13,000 strong and 4th Division 12,000 strong, that 5th Division (with two brigades) had only about 600 per brigade, and that 50th Division (also with two brigades) had a total of 2,400.

Alan Brooke described the bridgehead at Dunkirk.

> The Navy were working wonders to produce the craft they had but measured in relation to the numbers that had to be evacuated and the limited time available for this process, it all seemed painfully inadequate. We were watching the slow process of the embarkation, a heavy [Luftwaffe] bombing raid came over. It was a most awe-inspiring sight. The beaches crowded with men were being plastered with bombs. A black cloud of smoke soon shrouded the whole beach and was punctuated by vivid flashes as new bombs burst and threw up jets of sand and what appeared like human bodies but luckily turned out to be greatcoats and clothing abandoned by men who had already embarked. I then went down to the

Operation Dynamo and the Dunkirk evacuation: the bombing raid was 'a most awe-inspiring sight'.

> beach expecting to find a regular shambles. To my surprise, I found only a few men who had been seriously wounded. The bulk of them were smothered with sand which they were busy extracting from their ears, eyes, noses, necks and sleeves. The men had all flattened themselves on the beach. We also watched another raid directed against the shipping lying off the beaches and this time the results were far more serious. One destroyer was hit amidships by a dive-bomber. As the smoke cleared, the destroyer had entirely disappeared.

Brooke went on to describe the

> quality of detachment and staunchness of the British soldier. He can sympathise with misery, he can rub shoulders with demoralised allies and suffer on their account. He can be subjected to untold fatigues and hardships in the face of disaster, and yet none of these factors affect his balance. It is this factor more than any other that has saved us from many disasters and has contributed to the successes of the British Army. Never have I had greater admiration, respect and affection for the British soldiers than during those anxious days of our retirement from Louvain to Dunkirk.

During the retreat, for that is what it was, to Dunkirk, the names of the young commanders cropped up who were eventually to help lead to final victory some five years after: Montgomery, Alan Brooke, Alexander, Horrocks, Lumsden, Anderson, Barker, Ritchie and others.

Lt E.W. Clay was a young infantry officer who later wrote about key individuals in the division: the gunners under the CRA, Brig Massy, his brigade major (Priestman) and staff; Capt (Gibson) and Lt-Col R.M. Graham, who commanded 72nd Field Regiment, 'had a splendid team and were in the thick of the fighting during the BEF withdrawal'; Lt-Col Spiers, CRE 'of the robust body of Sappers, well skilled in their role'; Lt-Col Sheffield, OC Signals; the RASC under Lt-Col Divers; the field ambulances under Col Errington and Maj McCracken.

CHAPTER 3

The Nomads

The division reassembled after its various Channel crossings at Knutsford in Cheshire. Brig Massy, the CRA, set up a report centre at the entrance to the park to guide the many individuals rejoining the Northumbrian Division. Gen Martel went round every unit to tell them of the main lessons to be learned from the brief BEF campaign. The next move was south to Dorset to help defend the coastline against a possible invasion. Gen Bernard Montgomery, promoted after the BEF Campaign to V Corps Commander, visited Gen Martel's 50th Division and subsequently noted:

> The standard of training in the division is low. All energies have been directed to work on defence. The net result is that all the finer arts of how to compete with the Germans in battle have been put in the background. There are men who have never in their lives fired more than five rounds with the rifle, there are men who have never fired the Bren gun; the use of carriers is not practised; the Headquarters of formations and units are untrained; the techniques of observation and sniping as learnt from the Germans; and so on. I met companies who had been in the same place for one month doing nothing but dig and work on defences. The men had done no drill, no PT, no training. The men did not seem to be on their toes. I did not see the light of battle in their eyes.

Monty knew that the 50th had performed well in the Battle of France, perhaps as well as his own 3rd British Division. He knew that the risk of invasion was a possibility. He knew that the current orders for the 50th were to man and prepare excellent defensive positions. Perhaps he was a little bit unfair!

At the end of June, 69 Infantry Brigade joined to make the division's third brigade, with 5th East Yorkshires and 6th and 7th Green Howards. Divisional HQ was at Blandford. Sport and training took place and concrete, shell-proof machine-gun posts were built and manned from Lyme Regis to Christchurch. After two years as GOC, Maj-Gen Martel left to become commander of the Royal Armoured Corps. Part of his last 'Special Order of the Day' ran: 'Never before have I been so sorry to leave such an appointment, but never before have I felt so sure of the future well-being of a command. Nothing can stand against the deep-spirited determination of this division.' He was succeeded by Maj-Gen W.H.C. Ramsden, who had commanded 25 Brigade, which had fought alongside the Northumbrians in the Battle of France. The division next moved to the north coast of Somerset, still in an anti-invasion role. Detailed plans were made to repel nearly twenty possible enemy landings. Orders came to mobilise for overseas, and the quartermaster's stores began to fill up with tropical kit. Embarkation leave was given about Christmas 1940, but in the New Year Lt-Gen Franklyn, VIII Corps GOC (he had commanded 5th Division so ably with the BEF), ordered intensive exercises on the bleak moors of Somerset and Devon. Fifteen soldiers lost their lives gassed in a troop carrier on one exercise. In March 1941 embarkation leave was again granted and the division received a visit from King George VI. On 21 April, 150 Brigade Group and Divisional HQ sailed from Liverpool in the two Canadian Pacific liners *Empress of Asia* and *Empress of Russia*. The huge naval convoy consisted of HMS *Repulse*, fourteen destroyers and an armed merchantman. The voyage via Freetown took six weeks to round the Cape of Good Hope, calling at Cape Town and Durban. The rest of the division followed a few weeks later.

There were adventures on the way – the worst storm for sixty years; most of the stokers on the *Empress of Asia* deserted in Cape Town and troops had to stoke the ship through the fiery heat of the Red Sea. The Victoria League in Durban produced wonderful hospitality, with food and wine not seen in Britain for a couple of years. The convoys sailed on to Port Tewfik near Suez, where 150 Brigade disembarked on 13 June and almost immediately was sent into the Western Desert with Divisional HQ at Mena to plan defensive positions around Alamein.

The Prime Minister wrote, 'By long persistence I had at last succeeded in having the 50th British Division brought to Egypt. I was sensitive to the hostile propaganda which asserted that it was the British policy to fight with any other troops [Australian, New Zealand, Indian and South African] but our own and thus avoid the shedding of United Kingdom blood.' Churchill noted that British casualties in the Middle East, including the Greece and Crete campaigns, had in fact been greater than those of all other forces put together. The German press and radio taunted with their propaganda and provoked unfavourable comments in the USA and Australia. All the armoured and artillery units were British and the Indian division had a British brigade. 'I had looked forward to the arrival of the 50th Division as an effective means of countering these disparaging currents. Gen Auchinleck's decision to pick this Division . . . a magnificent body of men . . . for Cyprus certainly seemed unfortunate.' So Churchill sent a strong message to Gen Auchinleck on 19 July 1941. 'The Defence Committee were concerned to see the 50th Division, your one, complete, fresh British division, locked up in Cyprus in what appeared to be a purely defensive role and wonder whether other troops might not have been found.' Auchinleck thought a German offensive against Syria through Anatolia might develop in September.

During July 1941 the division duly moved to garrison Cyprus, since the German success in Greece and Crete threatened the Eastern Mediterranean. Auchinleck told Maj-Gen Ramsden, 'Hold the island for HM Government.' Defensive positions for three brigades were allocated

(150 Brigade had not yet rejoined), and a vast labour directorate was set up employing almost 23,000 locals building airfields and railways and reorganising the dockyards. Supplies of food, water, petrol and ammunition for three months had to be brought in, for a garrison including RAF squadrons of 31,000 troops. Churchill had to be kept informed of the date of completion of the first pillbox. Some of the lessons of the ferocious airborne conquest of Crete by German paratroops meant that defensive plans for 'box' warfare were undertaken. They were little fortresses with infantry, supporting arms and artillery, to be held to the last man. A mobile force was created with tanks of part of 3rd Hussars, 74th Field Regiment RA, 1st Sherwood Foresters and the Cyprus Regiment – all based around the capital, Nicosia. Lt-Cols Kennedy and Bickford organised the huge engineering and building works in key places on the island. On 31 August Gen Auchinleck visited and inspected the defences. 150 Brigade rejoined after a peaceful month in the Western Desert. The whole division enjoyed its three months in such a beautiful island with warm seas to bathe in, magnificent mountains to climb, an abundance of wines and exotic fruits, and Cypriots, in the main, friendly and amusing. On 3 November 5th Indian Division arrived to take over the defences and the division sailed away at night, heading for Palestine and Iraq to fight side by side with the Russians in the Caucasus. Winston Churchill noted to the CIGS, '31 Oct 1941, I am very glad to see the 50th Division moving out of Cyprus, relieved by the Indian division. No decision has however yet been taken about moving the 50th Divison to the Caucasus. Where will it wait in the interval?' And on 5 November, Churchill to the Chiefs of Staff Committee, 'We do not know when the Germans will arrive in the Caucasus. It is quite certain that if the Germans press hard neither the 50th nor the 18th British Division could be on the spot in time.'

There were five Russian divisions crowded into Northern Persia protecting Russian interests. Churchill promised Stalin that 50th and 18th Divisions could move there, to relieve them to return to the Caspian basin, promising 'the faith of Britain that no rightful interest shall suffer in Persia'. The German Plan Orient was for a Panzer corps to drive southwards through Persia in the winter of 1941–2 if the Russian defences in the Caucasus were defeated. The division concentrated around Haifa. Re-equipping with serviceable vehicles was very difficult, so 150 Brigade was stripped of most of its transport to make 69 and 151 Brigades up to strength. They moved across the desert via Baghdad to Kirkuk in Iraq. No maps were available, so the march across the Transjordan desert was their first experience of desert driving. On arrival a defensive position was dug at two rivers north and west of Kirkuk. In April and May the German coup to seize the oil wells had been defeated, mainly by the RAF around Habbaniya. Stalin and Churchill had every reason to protect their various oil interests in Iraq. The winter weather was very bad, with cold torrents of rain; nearly all the troops were living in tents and bivouacs. On Christmas Day the concert party under Lt Stringer Davis put on a pantomime in a wet marquee for a theatre, lit by oil-lamps. They would continue to put on shows in seventeen different countries. 69 Brigade was then ordered to Baalbek in Syria to relieve the 6th Australian Division, needed back at home to prepare against a possible Japanese invasion. The tragic fall of Singapore had altered the balance of power in the Far East and ripples came into the Middle East Command. In January 1942 the three brigades met up in the Western Desert: 69 came from Syria, 151 came from Iraq, and 150 Brigade was already there from Palestine – and had already been in action. Suddenly on 19 November 150 Brigade was recalled from Haifa to rejoin the Eighth Army. It trained for three weeks at Baggush and then on 22 December moved to Bir Thalata, the desert railhead. There the tempo of training for both day and night operations increased. Maj-Gen Ramsden visited the brigade on 3 January 1942. Three weeks later it set off for Bir Harmat in Libya, 120 miles to the west, much of it through a vicious 'Khamseen' sandstorm. In Harmat it received its first anti-tank guns, not 2-pounders nor the new 6-pounders, but captured – eight of them – 50mm German weapons. Its next area, sixty miles on, was Garet el Auda, so desolate and forbidding that the troops named it 'Land of the Moon' or more simply 'The Bloodiness'. 4th Green Howards were sent fifteen miles west to Bir Tengeder. Their Capt Kirkby captured a Volkswagen with a German sergeant-major plus mail and rations – their first prisoner in the desert war. The next move was to Bir Hacheim, the southern 'box' fortress in what became known as the Gazala line. Mines were laid and wire erected and infantry and gunners dug in as fast they could. South of Bir Hacheim was desert patrolled by armoured cars and the obvious place for an enemy flank attack. High command now ordered 150 Brigade to exchange places with the Free French Brigade, and on 15 February a move was made north, twenty-five miles to Bir Naghia, with 4th East Yorks in the centre and 4th Green Howards on the left at Alem Hamza.

The main body of the division, 69 and 151 Brigades coming up from the east, took over a 25-mile line held by 4th Indian Division and south of 1st South African Division around Gazala. Lt-Col R.H.L. Wheeler, divisional GSO1, wrote in April, 'The contention was that this position would be a secure base, holding fast in spite of enemy break-through and giving to our armoured forces a point of manoeuvre. It is evident that this policy gave the Germans the initiative from the outset. It is hard to see what else could have been done with the resources then available.' At the time, 50th Division was the only British infantry division in contact with the enemy in any part of the world. Their three brigade boxes, like the Guards at 'Knightsbridge' and the French at Bir Hacheim, were little fortresses with all positions dug flush with the ground without parapet and very hard to see. Overhead cover was provided nearly everywhere. Around the box was a minefield covered by supporting arms and artillery. Anti-tank guns were in short supply, 151 and 69 Brigades each having a dozen 2-pounders. The ubiquitous 25-pounder

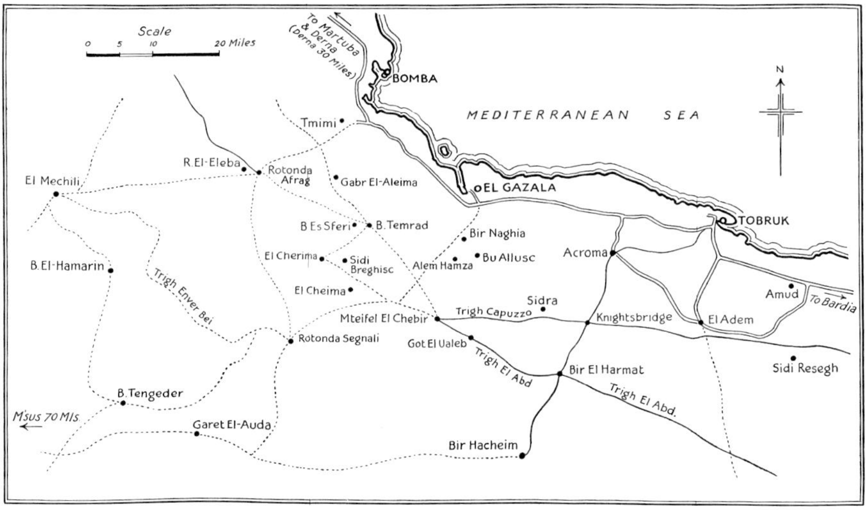

The El Gazala battleground. 150 Brigade was destroyed at Got El Ualeb.

field guns were frequently used in an anti-tank role. Italian 47mm guns were salvaged and deployed, but were useless against the Panzer Mark III and IV tanks. Brigades took it in turn to provide flying columns of a half, or whole, battalion with supporting arms, all motorised. They ranged the desert 'No Man's Land', shelled enemy positions and sent out fighting patrols at night. One such operation, codenamed 'Fullsize', took place at the end of March. Brig J.S. Nichols, commander of 151 Brigade, was in charge. Three columns would harass the Luftwaffe landing grounds at Martuba and Tmimi, respectively about twenty and thirty miles north-west of Gazala. 4th East Yorkshires provided the infantry for the Martuba attack, plus mortars, Bofors anti-aircraft guns, anti-tank guns, 25-pounders and Bren-gun carriers. In broad daylight they got within two miles of Martuba aerodrome and opened fire. The second column of DLI captured 150 prisoners at Gabr el Aleima before going on to harass Tmimi aerodrome. The third smaller column was right-flank protection, in action at Ras el Eleba. The Luftwaffe was predictably very annoyed and dive-bombed and machine-gunned the Northumbrian columns, destroying forty vehicles. The main purpose of Fullsize was to distract the Luftwaffe from bombing an important convoy to Malta, then besieged and under intense pressure.

Yet another move was made at the end of April. 150 Brigade was ordered to relieve 201 Guards Brigade, south of the main desert track Trigh Capuzzo at Ualeb. It had a huge perimeter of twenty miles and was separated from 69 Brigade by six miles and to the south by ten miles from the Free French in Bir Hacheim. Moreover, it was very hard to defend from the rear (east) and was far too large for three battalions to defend. The weak patch in the defensive minefields was on the Trigh Capuzzo. So the Northumbrian Division was holding three boxes, 151 in Alem Hamza/Gabriel, 69 in Fachri and 150 Trigh Capuzzo/Ualeb.

All the desert battles (except Alamein) began by swift turning movements of armour on the southern desert flank. Gen Rommel launched the German Afrika Korps attack on the evening of 26 May. He swept round Bir Hacheim intending to engage the British armour and seize the key El Adem–Sidi Rezegh position by nightfall on the 28th and then to take the Gazala line defences from the rear. At the northern end Italian divisions put in a diversionary attack against the South African Division. Rommel's Panzers smashed up 7 Motor Brigade and 3 Indian Motor Brigade. After several days of hard and bitter fighting Rommel realised that he had to bring up all his supplies by a wide detour round Bir Hacheim. He instructed his engineers to clear two short cuts through the British minefields. Winston Churchill noted, 'These passages were continually broadened, lay on each side of the box held with devoted tenacity by 150 Brigade of the 50th (Northumbrian) Division.' Two Panzer divisions, 15th and 21st, were now in the area between Trigh Capuzzo and Trigh el Abd known as 'the Cauldron', a depression in the desert, four miles by two, five miles south-west of Knightsbridge box.

The two boxes held by 69 and 151 Brigades were only lightly attacked by Italian troops of Ariete and Trieste Divisions. The Northumbrian Divisional HQ moved into the 151 Brigade position. The 150 Brigade box was surrounded, although the Divisional Mobile Reserve tried hard to protect the weak rear and eastern flanks. The Reserve consisted of 6th Green Howards (Lt-Col Cooke-Collis), a squadron of 42nd RTR, a squadron of South African armoured cars, a battery of 124th Field Regiment (Maj Bransom) and a machine-gun company of 2nd Cheshires and the entire 44th RTR. Brig Haydon commanded the 150 Brigade garrison. Ewart Clay noted some of the actions by the defenders. 4th East Yorkshires destroyed thirteen Italian tanks on the 27th, and Capt Mitchell, 4th Green Howards, established a fighting patrol on the disputed ridge about a mile ahead on the Capuzzo Gap. Confused fighting took place on the 28th around Aslagh. Trucks sent by the defenders to Tobruk for ammunition supplies never returned. On the 29th the enemy edged forward and pushed back 4th East Yorkshires and gained control of the disputed ridge. Gen Cruewell, GOC Afrika Korps, was shot down and his Fieseler Storch landed in the 4th Green Howards' area. Night patrolling was carried out by all three battalions. Lt Hopkins, 5th Green Howards, inflicted heavy casualties on an enemy working party. On 31 May heavy fighting took place on the 4th Green Howards' front and Maj Jackson was mortally wounded. 232nd Field Company RE on the eastern flank was overrun. Maj Peter Fox, 5th Green Howards, led a carrier counter-attack to repulse one attack, but he was wounded and captured. Capt Good, who was killed in action, commanded B Company, 4th East Yorkshires, in the north-east corner before it was overwhelmed, as was F troop, 286 Battery RA. 2/Lt Farmiloe of 25 Light Anti-Aircraft Regiment helped pump Bofors shells into Mark IV Panzers. At the south-east corner, the junction of the East Yorkshires and 5th Green Howards, the enemy made a breakthrough until halted by Maj Jack Brewer and HQ Company of the East Yorkshires.

Capt P.B. Watson, 4th Green Howards, relaid mines under heavy fire where the enemy had breached the minefield in front. He later received the DSO. By nightfall on 31 May the defenders had only thirteen tanks, twelve 25-pounders and six medium guns battle-worthy. Most of the 2-pounder anti-tank guns had been destroyed and the infantry battalions had little ammunition left. No outside help was forthcoming. At first light on 1 June the enemy renewed its intense pressure from all four sides, and, platoon by platoon, the brigade was overrun and captured. Capt Bert Dennis of 5th Green Howards was probably the last to go down. Brig Haydon, who had commanded the brigade in France and the desert, was killed in action.

Winston Churchill wrote, 'During the first week of June the battle was focused on Bir Hacheim and the bridgehead [the Cauldron Corridors]. Within the latter was the stubborn 150th Northumbrian Brigade. Rommel was in dire need of supplies and water. If the whole battle were not to be lost he must eliminate the brigade so that his convoys might pass. It was set upon and destroyed on 1 June.' This is Rommel's account in his own words, 'Yard by yard the German and Italian units fought their way forward against the toughest resistance imaginable. The British defence was conducted with considerable skill. As usual the British fought to the last round of ammunition.'

CHAPTER 4

Abandon the Gazala Line: The Two Break-outs

The Eighth Army now suffered two great blows in the month of June. The French garrison at Bir Hacheim, the most southern box, under Gen Koenig had endured ferocious attack by land and air for ten days. Eventually Gen Ritchie ordered the French troops to break out on the night of 10/11 June. Rommel was then able to roll up the British Gazala line as far as Knightsbridge, which was evacuated on the evening of the 13th.

For two weeks the 69 and 151 Brigade boxes were not under great pressure, although many sharp small actions were fought. 7th Green Howards, as part of the divisional mobile reserve, took part in several attacks, with 44th RTR on enemy established in the Cauldron. 151 Brigade in one raid brought back an Italian battalion as prisoners and 9th DLI destroyed an enemy convoy. The 2nd Cheshire anti-tank guns and machine guns were in action every day. On 13 June a major armoured battle took place and about 120 British tanks were destroyed, mainly by the superior 88mm anti-tank guns the Germans were now deploying. Early on the 14th Gen Ritchie ordered XXX Corps to retreat eastwards to the frontier. 50th Division and 1st South African Division were now isolated. Maj-Gen Ramsden told his Corps Commander, Gen Gott, 'This is a bitter blow, a very great disappointment,' as the two boxes were abandoned – undefeated and indeed unchallenged. Gen Ritchie gave his order, 'Abandon the Gazala line. Get out, and get out before it is too late.' The brilliant journalist Alan Moorehead summed up the mood of the troops.

> On Gazala the British 50th Division to the south heard the news with black dismay. Immediate retreat. This was the dismal end to their high hopes, to all the weeks and months of planning and working and preparing. They had stood ready to advance, not retreat, to blast through westwards along the coast and take Derna. The men felt thwarted, restless and angry. They cursed as they dug out their guns and gathered their equipment. They cursed still more when they were ordered to blow up some of those priceless guns and demolish the dumps of fuel and food and ammunition which they had dragged with such effort to high crannies in the rocks. It seemed to them there was no sense in this waste. Why couldn't they fight?'

The Guards Brigade with the same discipline smashed their guns and equipment. They had survived two weeks of intense fighting. One by one each box was emptied and the men got away. The coast road and the desert south of it were just adequate for Maj-Gen Pienaar to take his 10,000 South Africans to relative safety eastwards.

The Northumbrian Division was ordered to give the South Africans twelve hours' start. To withdraw due east would bring them into the path of Rommel's rampant Panzer divisions and moving due south would be the same. Transport was a problem. To lift the division 180 three-ton lorries would be needed, but only half that number were available. Rations and water for three days, weapons and wireless were taken; everything else was abandoned. A dust storm blew up on the afternoon of 14 June.

Alan Moorehead described the break-out.

> There remained only the English 50th Division south of Gazala. It was too late now for them to follow the South Africans eastwards down the coast road . . . the Germans were already swarming there. They had three alternatives – they could surrender, they could try to find their way through the desert to the east, or they could go west. They chose the last. It was the one stroke of leadership and imagination that lightened the whole of this stage of the campaign – a forced march straight into the heart of the enemy. By going west they were turning their backs on Tobruk and the British lines: they were taking a chance of one in a hundred that they would be able to burst clean through the Axis line and then wheel south and east through the open desert right round Bir Hacheim and so on back to the Egyptian border.
>
> This plan had something in it that stirred the men. With the feeling of high adventure they got to work. The whole Divison was split into small groups of a few vehicles each. Each group was composed as a commando and told to fight like one – silently, swiftly, and to kill and get away. Rations were carefully measured out – water was the main thing. All lights, all smoking, was forbidden. Even talking was stopped. Then they sallied out into the darkness against the Italians, each man for himself.
>
> An indescribable confusion broke out in the enemy lines as the British threaded or blundered their way through the minefields. An attack westward was the last thing that the enemy had expected at this moment. The attackers seemed to be coming at them from half a dozen directions at once. Italian commanders who sent reinforcements to a threatened area suddenly found themselves under fire and with what strength and with what objective they did not know. Italian prisoners were taken as they lay sleeping on the ground. Convoys of enemy supply vehicles were ambushed and overwhelmed. Guns were put out of action before they could open fire. Dumps of food and petrol were pilfered before the guards could understand what was happening.
>
> The 50th burst clean through the enemy defences leaving a trail of burning vehicles, panic-stricken men, bemused commanders and confusion everywhere. Had they been on an organised and supported offensive, they might have scattered the enemy in this sector in a single night and cleared the road to Bomba and Derna. As it was, they were alone and with many extraordinary adventures they came around Bir Hacheim and reached the British lines almost intact.

The columns broke out in two brigade groups with the initial objectives of establishing bridgeheads on the ridges two to three miles west of their

Gazala boxes. 5th East Yorkshires led 69 Brigade and 8th DLI, 151 Brigade. Besides their artillery they shared one squadron of tanks under Maj Lindsay. The bridgehead troops stayed in their position until 0400 hours on 15 June, when they themselves moved off. The eventual objective after rounding Bir Hacheim was a further 120 miles to the frontier at Fort Maddalena. For various reasons Lt-Col Percy, CO, and Maj J.C. Slight, 2 i/c 9th DLI, were given the option of following 151 Brigade Group or turning about and retiring along the coast road towards Tobruk. They chose the coast-road option, and, moving in two parallel groups, despite the chaos of the South African rearguards, attacks by Stukas, minefields and attacks by enemy tanks, bombarded by enemy guns, they passed through Tobruk and reached the frontier wire on 16 June. Some of the many heroes were Pte Albert Robinson, 5th East Yorkshires, and CSM Thomas Mattock and Maj Ferens, 6th DLI. Lt-Col Kennedy, the Commander RE, was killed leading a column, and Maj Slight, 9th DLI, won the DSO.

The Divisional Intelligence Officer, Lt E.H. Moss, gives an account of the long trek.

> The enemy in the bridgeheads were Italians stiffened by a few German gunners. They were very much taken by surprise. It was late at night before they realised that a whole division was passing straight through their lines. Some vehicles went up on mines, others were shot-up, but on the whole we had very few casualties and both attacking battalions did their jobs successfully. The infantry went in with the bayonet and the Italians departed, often leaving all their arms and equipment lying about the trenches. It was a black night, with brilliant stars but not a wisp of moon. We started grinding and jolting off through the darkness at four or five miles an hour, nose to tail . . . It was a curiously beautiful scene with the little fireworks of tracer bullets, red, green and purple; occasional anti-tank shells cracked past and over our heads; the dots of blazes of smoking light ahead of us and the long dark column of vehicles, all drowned in an enormous glittering night.

Maj Bill Watson, 2 i/c 6th DLI, noted:

> Of course trucks got mislaid but everyone knew the compass bearings and by now most of us had become experts at moving in the desert. I never stopped that night. We passed Italian positions, trucks and gun emplacements in the first few miles. Under cover of darkness we travelled about forty miles. As daylight came I found most of my column had left me but we travelled on for another hundred miles and halted for the night. I had picked up many other stragglers. Next morning over the first rise I found to my joy most of the rest of the column making breakfast . . . it was quite apparent that our casualties were very, very few.

Eventually the division in scores of scattered groups and parties concentrated in an area known as 'The Kennels' near Bir Thalata and then back to the area of Mersa Matruh to reorganise.

That was the story of the first break-out. A week later Gen Klopper surrendered Tobruk. Of the 32,000 prisoners, no fewer than 19,000 were

British and the remainder South African. Winston Churchill and the Eighth Army were devastated.

Gen Ritchie now planned to hold Egypt on a line pivoted on the coastal resort of Mersa Matruh, with delaying actions being fought on the frontier to enable Eighth Army to prepare the Matruh line. The defences were similar to those at Gazala and relied on minefields, barbed wire and defensive boxes stretching south for about thirty miles. As usual an outflanking move in the southern open desert would isolate and roll up the boxes. Rommel reached Sidi Barrani on 24 June, having covered 100 miles in twenty-four hours. By nightfall on the 25th the Desert Fox and his Panzer army had arrived in front of the Matruh defences. Gen Auchinleck relieved Ritchie and took command and control of the Eighth Army. Bardia, Solum, Halfaya and the Omars had fallen without a fight. The Northumbrian Division was part of the rearguard from the 22nd onwards, falling back steadily in contact with the enemy, using delaying tactics and shelling his forward troops. At the same time its engineers had to demolish stores and water supplies. The stores depot at Sidi Barrani yielded tinned pineapples, pears and other delicacies before the dumps were soaked in petrol and set on fire. 10th Indian Division garrisoned Matruh port and 50th Division a defensive position south-east of the town. By the 27th the German Panzers had cut the road east of Matruh and the two divisions were isolated. Most of the heaviest fighting fell on 151 Brigade, and Pte Adam Wakenshaw, 9th DLI, won the Victoria Cross, manning a 2-pounder anti-tank gun on a forward slope against two tracked vehicles with light guns. Wakenshaw's left arm was blown off at the shoulder but he loaded the DLI gun and fired five more rounds, damaging both enemy vehicles and guns before a direct hit on the ammunition destroyed his gun and killed him.

Maj David Rissik, the DLI historian, wrote:

> At 5.15 in the morning the Germans launched an all-out attack with overwhelming numbers of infantry supported by tanks and artillery. They seemed determined to destroy the Battalion [9th DLI] and seemed oblivious of the casualties they suffered in doing so. Fierce hand-to-hand fighting lasted for some hours but the Germans kept renewing their attacks and as time went on the Battalion's resistance began to lessen. The battle raged on and surged around the Battalion positions. By 7.30 a.m. the three forward companies were completely isolated; and as time passed one by one they were over-run. At 9 a.m. the rest of the Battalion – mainly HQ and HQ company – was ordered to withdraw and ultimately reached Division. The loss of the 9th Battalion was a grievous blow to the Brigade.

At 0530 hours 8th DLI was attacked from the south-west by captured Stuart tanks, which were driven off with the loss of five. 6th DLI had a two-hour pitched battle against enemy self-propelled guns and armoured cars and suffered eighty-one casualties including fifty-three missing. Lt-Col Guy Stansfield and 5th East Yorkshires took part in a night battle with heavy casualties on both sides. X Corps, of which 50th Division was part, was

Pte Adam Herbert Wakenshaw, VC, 9 Durham Light Infantry, Western Desert, 27 June 1942.

ordered to fight its way out of the trap and rally further east near Fuka. On 29 June the situation of the division was becoming desperate. The troops were exhausted, short of weapons and serviceable transport. The enemy this time were Germans, not Italians; not infantry but armour supported by 88mm guns. Instead of a dark night there was now a full moon. The ground was unfavourable, with steep ravines and wadis to be crossed. Columns each of about thirty vehicles formed up at 2100 hours.

The DLI brigade set out after dark and 6th DLI made a successful withdrawal, but 8th DLI ran into a German ambush, as Maj David Rissik relates.

> The columns moved through a wadi on their climb up the escarpment. Up went enemy flares and soon all hell seemed let loose. Some troop carriers burst into flames as men jumped out and returned the fire; the rest pushed ahead over the top of the escarpment where they had to run the gauntlet of German MG fire. One troop carrier stuck and blocked the way. Somehow it was pushed over the top. The CO and Adjutant acted as traffic policemen; RSM Jennings soon had the situation in the wadi under control. He got Bren guns positioned. He mounted a 2-inch mortar and sent bomb after bomb to fall with amazing accuracy into the German gun crews out in the open. But of those who received the full force of the initial German fire, few survived and most of 'D' company were either killed or captured. Maj W. Urton, DAQMG at Divisional HQ, remained behind to bring along survivors and strays. By the morning, after many nightmare journeys the columns turned east and those which went to Fuka (later orders had altered the RV) found the Germans already there. The GSO1, Lt-Col R. Wheeler, the AQ Lt-Col Steele and the senior Padre, Reverend Harlow, and many others were captured. By the time the main columns were back behind the Alamein defence lines casualties were much heavier than the break-out from the Gazala line. But for five more days the survivors fought in battlegroups on the Ruweisat Ridge, ten miles south of Alamein.

On 4 July, 50th Division – what was left of it – was relieved in the line and withdrew to Mareopolis south-west of Alexandria to reorganise. Since the start of the battle of Gazala on 27 May, in five weeks of severe attritional fighting, the division had lost almost 9,000 casualties. 150 Brigade in its entirety went first; then the Gazala break-out and finally the Matruh break-out were the main causes of the appalling losses.

CHAPTER 5

Slow Recovery: Operation Manhood

Maj-Gen Ramsden was promoted to command XXX Corps, and Maj-Gen J.S. Nichols, DSO, MC, became on 11 July the new divisional GOC. July 1942 was probably the nadir of the Eighth Army's fortunes. Only one barrier lay between Rommel's German and Italian army and the Delta – the Alamein line, 150 miles from Cairo, sixty miles from Alexandria. Winston Churchill was in Washington with President Roosevelt when Tobruk fell, and realised that the whole British position in the Middle East was in danger of immediate collapse. It promised to be the greatest disaster since the fall of France in 1940. The loss of Egypt would precipitate a chain of misfortune almost too disastrous to contemplate. The Suez Canal would be lost, Malta would fall, Suez, Port Said, Alexandria, Beirut and Syrian Tripoli might go and the Germans might capture the vital oil wells. The British Fleet had left Alexandria. Long convoys were setting out for Palestine. The wives and families of British soldiers were warned to get ready for immediate evacuation, some to be sent to Palestine, others to South Africa. The British Embassy by the Nile and GHQ were burning secret documents. In Cairo there was a curfew. King Farouk was preparing to leave. The journalist Alan Moorehead drove out past Mena House and the Pyramids, 'when we came on a sight that bore the marks of a full-scale retreat. Guns of all sorts, RAF wagons, recovery vehicles, armoured cars and countless lorries crammed with exhausted and sleeping men were pouring up the desert road into Cairo.'

Rommel's first attack on the El Alamein line on 1 July was blunted by 1st South African and 8th Indian Divisions, and the German 90th *Leicht* Division was brought to a bloody standstill. And Auchinleck handled his forces more skilfully than Ritchie. Then followed three days of mainly tank-*versus*-tank fighting, with the British tanks in dug-in positions in a defensive role. The Desert Air Force flew about 900 missions and by the end of the first week in July the Afrika Korps strength was down to twenty-six runners. Rommel signalled the German High Command, *Oberkommand Wehrmacht* (*OKW*), in Berlin that he would have to go on the defensive for at least five weeks. During this period Auchinleck deliberately targeted the Italian formations, forcing Rommel to move German troops to bolster the Ariete,

Pavia and Brescia Divisions. Much of the fighting took place on and around the Ruweisat Ridge.

The Northumbrian Division when it reached the Delta was not in good shape. The average infantry battalion strength in 69 and 151 Brigades was only about 300, or less than half establishment. They had little or no transport. The artillery had not only lost 72nd Field Regiment RA in the Gazala box defeat, but almost 40 per cent of its normal strength. Instead of seventy-two 25-pounder guns supporting a divisional attack, they were down to fewer than thirty. Engineers, machine-gunners, signals, RASC, ordnance and medical services – all had had heavy losses. In mid-July reinforcements brought the average infantry battalion up to the 400–500 level and training took place in the Amiriya area and the artillery reorganised at the School of Artillery at Almaza. But for a three-day period the whole of 69 Brigade and the sappers worked as 'navvies', urgently constructing reserve defences east of the Ruweisat Ridge. It was dull, arduous, vital work under a merciless sun and flies. Then Operation 'Manhood' was launched with elements of XIII and XXX Corps to seize the Miteiriya Ridge. Brig Cooke-Collis was now given orders for 69 Brigade to come under command of 7th Armoured Division in the deep south. 7th Green Howards lent platoons to 5th East Yorkshires and 6th Green Howards to bring them up to fighting strength, together with a battalion from 201 Guards Brigade (of Knightsbridge fame), with 2nd Cheshire machine-gunners and 233rd Field Company RE.

There were three phases for the attack planned for the night of 21/22 July, involving the capture of Taqa Plateau, then the capture of Jebel Kalakh, and finally 4th Light Armoured Brigade with its fast Stuart tanks would pass through the gap created and cause havoc behind the enemy's lines. All three phases would be supported by the divisional artillery. Detailed reconnaissance of the area was impossible by day. Brig Cooke-Collis realised that the whole operation was difficult. The Guards battalion was much under strength; the two composite Northumbrian battalions had no time to train together. The light-tank support and armoured cars were no match for the heavier Panzer tanks – and there had been no reconnaissance. And ammunition for the gunners was short, so no preliminary bombardment. The Guards were to tackle Phase 1, the capture of the east end of the Taqa Plateau and Naqb el Khadin. On completion, in Phase 2, the Green Howards and East Yorkshires would attack Taqa Plateau from the south. Little was known of the enemy's defences or locations. The final target was Garet el Himeimat. At sunset the whole brigade moved up to the start line some six miles south of Taqa. All went well to start with, and the Guards reached their objectives by 2300 hours and Phase 2 was completed successfully. By dawn 6th Green Howards had two companies firmly established on the plateau, but at daylight came under heavy mortar and machine-gun fire. On their left 5th East Yorkshires reached the southern flank of the plateau but could make no more headway. During the 22nd both battalions were under considerable fire, which caused many casualties, and men suffered from heat exhaustion. At 1600 hours the expected counter-attack with infantry and armoured cars came in but was repulsed. Patrols during the night reported a strengthening of the enemy's forces so Brig Cooke-Collis asked Maj-Gen Renton, GOC 7th Armoured Division, for permission to withdraw during the night of 23/24 July. The last day on the plateau was very difficult. The enemy counter-attacked twice, mainly against 5th East Yorkshires, and was beaten back. Heavy artillery and mortar fire rained down all day.

> Lt-Col Sammy Battiscombe with a composite DLI battalion, with one company from each battalion, took part in the night attack. In the moonlight they advanced 5,000 yards, but the Germans let them pass and then cut off their line of retreat and communication. When daylight came promised tank support failed to materialise and the composite battalion found itself isolated, hemmed in on all sides and after a vigorous resistance, the survivors including the CO were captured. Most of the East Yorkshires and the Australians suffered a similar fate. It was a sad end to months of hard fighting.

So wrote Maj David Rissik, the DLI historian. The whole three-day probing raid was a feint to draw enemy forces from the north, where XXX Corps was putting in a larger attack to seize the Miteiriya ridge.

In late July and throughout August, Maj-Gen Nichols and the Northumbrian brigades were part of Northern Delta defence force with 26 Indian Infantry Brigade, 1 Greek Brigade, 2 Free French Brigade, Guides cavalry (armoured cars) and the Alexandria Garrison. It was a huge area stretching from the sea to Halfway House (fifty miles south of Alexandria on the road to Cairo) and including all the Delta behind that line. The GS03, Capt Parker, took over responsibility for staff work, as both GSO1 and GSO2 were in hospital. This international command freed up X Corps to resume its place in the Alamein defences. The divisional artillery moved from Almaza to reinforce XIII Corps. Instead, Brig Fowler CRA had under command the French Brigade's 75mm guns, a Greek Brigade 25-pounder battery, some HAA batteries around Alexandria, and the coastal defence batteries, which could fire inland as well as out to sea. The key defences were boxes on the commanding hill features around Amiriya, west of Alexandria.

Far-reaching changes now took place in the Eighth Army command. On 9 August Gen Alexander replaced Auchinleck, who returned to India, and three days later Gen Bernard Montgomery arrived to change the face of history.

CHAPTER 6

Operations Lightfoot and Supercharge and 'the unpleasant smells of battle'

'What was wrong? Why were the British armies consistently forced to retreat? Why had Norway, Dunkirk, Greece, Crete, Singapore, Burma and Egypt followed so closely upon one another? Was it the generals, the equipment, the men, the War Cabinet, the unpreparedness, the structure of the army, or just bad luck?' asked Alan Moorehead in his brilliant *African Trilogy*.

In the chapter 'August – in Conclusion', he puts all the pros and cons and the comparisons. Perhaps his two most significant conclusions were:

> If there had been any genius at all on the Axis side it had been the genius of the average German soldier for organisation. In all its branches the German war machine appeared to have a better and tighter control than our army. Many believed that this was because the Germans had been so long in training for this war. Time and again one would note the steady rhythm of a German attack – first the Stukas, then the artillery, then the infantry, then the tanks, then the Stukas following up again.

And secondly:

> It was in the control of tanks that the Germans revealed their greatest gifts. They were tank technicians pure and simple. They were the elite of the Afrika Korps, as compact, as neat and efficient as a team of acrobats. They were self contained. Stukas, tanks, recovery vehicles, petrol wagons, anti-tank gunners, all went forward together and their senior officers were often in the van . . . The co-operation between the tanks and the anti-tank gunners was their best achievement. The Germans no longer used tanks to attack equal enemy armoured forces. Let me repeat that – they did not attack with tanks.

What Moorehead wrote in 1942 was equally true in 1943, 1944 and 1945. When Lt-Gen Bernard Montgomery arrived in the Delta in August 1942, he almost immediately started to raise the morale and the confidence of the badly bruised Eighth Army. New divisions appeared – 51st Highland, 44th Home Counties, 1st, 8th and 20th Armoured Divisions. New Corps

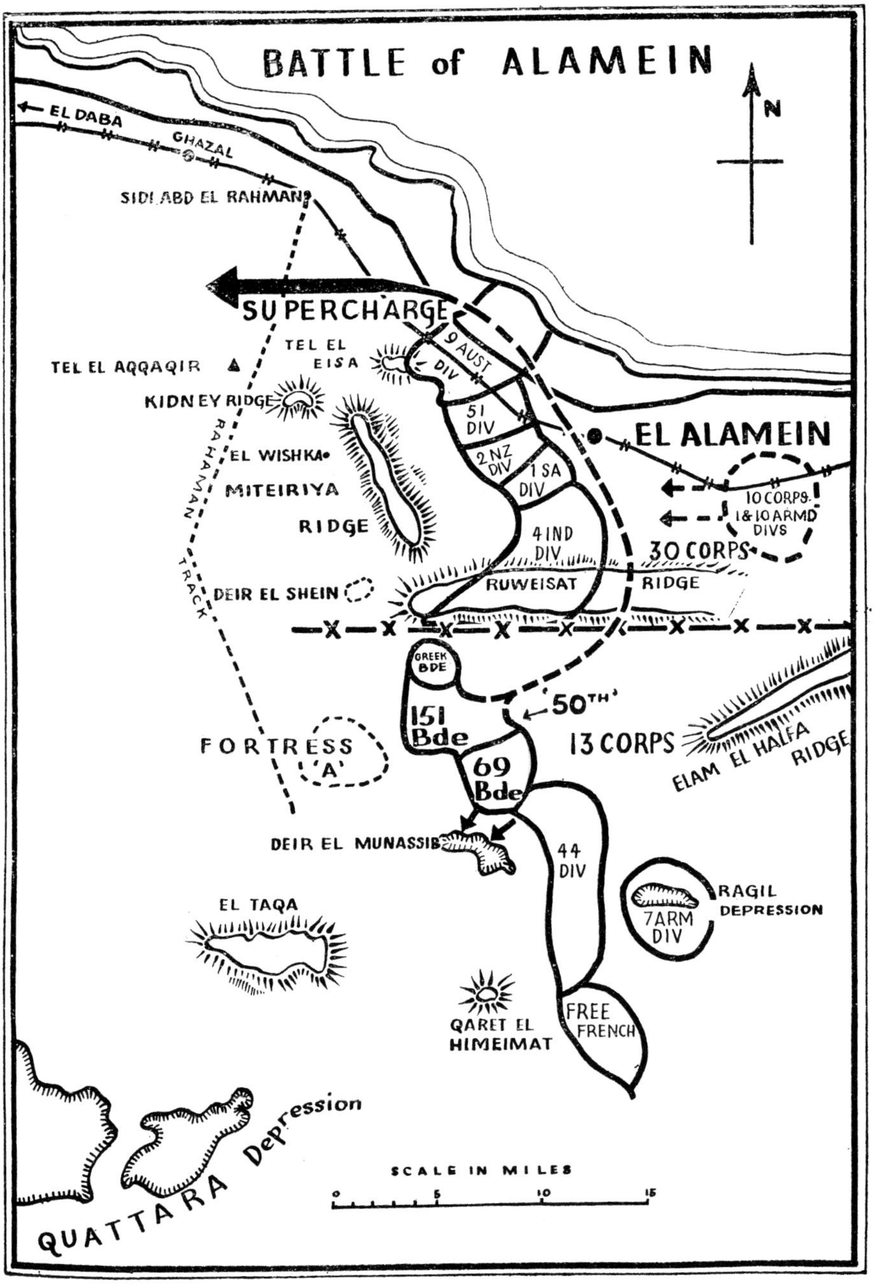

Operation Lightfoot and the Battle of Alamein. Operation Supercharge was the final 'break-in'.

Commanders were appointed, Horrocks and Leese. Many hundreds of new Sherman tanks and new 6-pounder anti-tank guns appeared. Artillery strengths were increased. The Desert Air Force was also reinforced and additional US Army Air Force units arrived. Montgomery wrote 'I had decided that in building up the Eighth Army . . . I would concentrate on three essentials, leadership, equipment and training.' Starting with the successful defensive battle at Alam el Halfa, the second battle of Alamein on 30/31 August, Montgomery's armies were never defeated. Some battles were not won. His many detractors said that he was too slow, deliberate and cautious, but quite soon nearly all his troops, and most of his officers, were certain he would lead them to victory. The Eighth Army had suffered 80,000 casualties since its formation in 1941. The battered Northumbrian Division had borne more than its fair share, with over 9,000 casualties.

151 Brigade was still operational and at the beginning of September came under command of the New Zealand Division and took over part of the line in the NZ box. At the end of the month it came under command of 44th Division south of Ruweisat Ridge around Alam Nayil. It sent out patrols on a daily basis and dominated No Man's Land, and at night retrieved carriers and other vehicles abandoned in previous actions. It found the parachute Folgore Division patrols worthy opponents. Recce patrols of the Durhams under Capt Lindrea, Lt Lawrence and Lt Galloway engaged Italian and German patrols near the 'Jarrow' gap in the 'Don' minefield. On 10 October 151 Brigade reverted to the reconstituted 50th Division once again with 69 Brigade. The latter was supported by 124th Regiment RA, 102nd Anti-Tank Regiment (Northumberland Hussars) and 233rd Field Company RE. They took up positions in the Munassib Depression area, 69 on the left, adjacent to 44th Division, 151 Brigade in the centre and a newcomer, 1st Greek Brigade (under Col Katsotos), as the third brigade in Maj-Gen Nichols' Northumbrians.

Lt-Col R.G.B. Innes was the new GSO1; Capt Ewart Clay, GSO3, described the desert front.

> The Munassib Depression was formidably held and was not unlike a deep wide river bed of very irregular shape. Worn away by the wind and sand of many ages, it had high and precipitous sides which dropped abruptly below the level of the surrounding desert. Within the Depression the enemy was well concealed. It was quite impossible to look down on to the sandy floor. A vast network of defences protected by broad minefields had been dug along the lip of the depression whose occupants were safe from artillery and mortar fire.

A great deal of work had gone into training the divisional staff and the many hundreds of reinforcements and welding them together into one team. But morale had distinctly improved in the last three months. XIII Corps held the southern sector of the Alamein line with 50th, 44th (Home Counties) and 4th Indian Divisions, a Free French Brigade, the Greek Brigade and, behind, the Desert Rats, 7th Armoured Division. The first attack in

Lightfoot was to drive a hole through the enemy defences at its weakest point between Himeimat and the Munassib Depression, with the main object of persuading Rommel that the major attack was being made in the southern sector. This would draw the powerful Panzer divisions, 15th and 21st, down from the north, where Montgomery's main thrust would occur. The eventual role of the Northumbrians was rather different from the original plan. 69 Brigade would make a night attack, supported by all the XIII Corps artillery, to seize two enemy strong-points in the Depression called 'The Moor' and 'The Cape', followed in the next phase by penetration of a line of defences 300 yards to the rear (west). 5th East Yorkshires on the left and 6th Green Howards on the right started their attack on the third night, 25 October, of Lightfoot. Lt-Col Lance led his Green Howards through minefields, reaching their objectives and securing the east end of 'The Moor', and by the morning of the 26th had secured two-thirds of his final objective, but suffered 100 casualties in the process. On the other flank, Maj Edgar's East Yorkshires were unable to clear the deep minefields, and at one stage were surrounded by booby-trapped barbed wire and a belt of anti-personnel mines. After a third attempt had failed, Maj-Gen Nichols ordered Brig Cooke-Collis to withdraw the hapless East Yorkshires, who lost 150 all ranks. But worse was to follow in the afternoon: the Green Howards renewed their attack and were beaten back by enemy mortar and artillery defensive fire and lost a further sixty men. Like many of Gen Montgomery's 'crumbling' tactics, this attritional infantry warfare achieved very little except brave men's lives. During the next few days, 7th Green Howards under Lt-Col Seagrim carried out daily programmes of intensive mortar harassing fire, which accounted for an Italian corps commander among other heavy enemy casualties.

On the night of the 28th, 151 Brigade was taken out of the line to join XXX Corps in the break-out Operation Supercharge. They moved to a concentration area, Tel el Eisa, a few miles west of Alamein railway station. In support were 505th Field Company RE, 149th Field Ambulance and an anti-tank battery. Their place in the line was taken by 2nd Free French Brigade. Gen Freyberg's experienced New Zealand Division took temporary command of two British infantry brigades, who in parallel were tasked with forcing a bridgehead west to the desert route, the Rahman track. Clearly marked by a line of telegraph poles, it ran for forty miles due south from the coast down to the Qattara Depression. 152 Brigade was borrowed from 51st Highland Division and would provide the left flank attack, and on the right was 151 Brigade. The Northumbrians were supported by 8th RTR Shermans and 28th Maori Battalion. The opposition were the experienced German 90th Light Division, 164th Infantry Division and the Italian Trento and Littoria armoured divisions. Bofors guns would fire red tracer along the brigade boundaries. 9th DLI would attack on the left flank and 8th DLI on the right, with 6th DLI moving in the rear to mop up isolated enemy posts. Then 6th DLI would move into the advance for a further 2,500 yards, before making a complete right wheel during a lull in the barrage, when it should have reached a line of dug-in tanks, self-propelled (SP) guns and 88mm anti-tank guns. Brig J. Percy's brigade had Lt-Col W. Watson, CO 6th DLI; Lt-Col M. Jackson, CO 8th DLI, and Lt-Col A. Clark, CO 9th DLI. The immense artillery support comprised thirteen field (including 65th, 74th, 111th and 124th from 50th Division) and two medium regiments. Gen Montgomery knew the value of shattering barrages and fireplans from the First World War. Capt Ewart Clay, GSO3, described the battlefield.

> The countryside was flat and open, almost imperceptibly rising on a stony, barren waste to the track itself. The Germans had been laying mines with all speed, but the fields were incomplete and unidentified. So the infantry were ordered to advance straight through, risking casualties [the anti-tank, round, heavy, Teller mines did not normally blow up under the pressure of a marching infantryman]. Then the Royal Engineers would make two gaps for the follow-up vehicles, including tanks. A study of the air photograph over-prints showed there was a row of dug-in tanks or SPs and a box position with 88mm guns. The march was long and dusty and the night seemed warm and sticky There were the usual unpleasant smells of battle, of burnt explosive and rotting corpses. The New Zealand gunner crews were stripped to the waist, their sweating bodies shining in the flashes of their guns.

The barrage opened promptly at 0055 hours, and ten minutes later the leading battalions crossed the start line dead on time. Visibility was down to fifty yards and the partial moon was hidden in gun smoke and dust. After a 500-yard advance, dazed and scattered German mine-laying parties, stunned by the barrage, quickly surrendered. The enemy sent up numerous flares and Spandau fire opened up in front of 8th DLI.

The lead battalions broke into the enemy's main defences and moved through the heart of the lines, past the advanced ambulance posts, the HQ and finally through the gun lines. Meanwhile 6th DLI, after a 1,000-yard advance, came under fixed line machine-gun fire from the right hand (northern) flank. RSM Page took out one position before he was killed that night. Maj Teddy Worrall kept excellent control of his 9th DLI company with a hunting horn. Sgt Albert Dunn demolished one post and its five defenders with his bayonet. The leading battalions kept close to the barrage, and, when it halted on the first objective, they were in the midst of tanks and guns, many smashed by gunfire, others full of fight, who were dealt with by furious, determined Durhams. 6th DLI duly made the right flanking movement northwards. At 0200 hours the last-phase attack went in, and two hours later, on their objectives, they started to dig in the difficult rocky outcrops.

Maj David Rissik, DLI historian, wrote:

> As each succeeding small post was rushed, the pace of the attack increased. In the almost uncanny light, not unlike a thick pea-souper fog, figures could be seen moving about whom it was impossible to identify as friend or foe. At 4 a.m. the barrage stopped and everyone dug madly in order to be well below ground level by dawn, when a German counter-attack was anticipated. By a quarter to six, when

> the first flush of dawn could be seen in the eastern sky, the British armour could be heard moving up towards the gaps in the minefields. The desert tracks so recently crowded with marching infantry were now jammed with long lines of tanks nose to tail. In the opposite direction went the ambulances one after another crammed with wounded. Long processions of bedraggled and dejected Axis prisoners shuffled away into captivity.

By 0500 hours the 'A' Echelon transport came up through the sapper-created gaps bringing rations and ammunition. During the day Supercharge developed into a large-scale tank battle in which Brig Curry's 9th Armoured Brigade lost seventy tanks to 76mm self-propelled and 88mm anti-tank guns. At least one enemy tank was knocked out by the DLI. Shelling and mortar fire occurred most of the day. In the early hours of the next day, the 3rd, as the enemy in front was starting to pull out, the brigade, relieved and very weary, marched back seven miles to its original concentration areas. It had done very well, had taken more than 400 prisoners, and severely damaged many more, but had inevitably suffered itself. Almost 400 of all ranks had been killed or wounded, with 8th DLI suffering the worst. It had captured the CO and ninety of his Panzer Grenadiers from elements of 15th Panzer Division.

Down south, 69 Brigade, the Greeks and Free French were in action and tasked with clearing from the Ruweisat Ridge the vast minefields on the way to the Rahman track, with several strong-points at Bab el Qattara known as 'Fortress A'. During the 4th, 5th and 6th, British, French and Greek troops slowly and surely cleared the minefields and defences in front of them. Corps HQ decided that 50th Division would form a mobile brigade column and strike hard due west early on 7 November and cross the Rahman track. Every available vehicle was sent to 69 Brigade. Gen Nichols's orders to Brig Cooke-Collis were: 'Advance as fast as possible; accept big risks and attack the enemy with the utmost dash.' Rommel had made the decision on the evening of 2 November – five days earlier – to pull back sixty miles to Fuka what he could save of Panzer Army Afrika. His troops in the southern sector were withdrawn to the Qaret el Abd–Gebel Kalakh line. For four enjoyable days the motorised infantry, with anti-tank guns, drove and shot up minor defence posts and collected several thousand weary and disillusioned Italian prisoners, including the HQ of the Brescia Division. When it reached the Matruh–Siwa track, seventy miles west of Alamein, and level with the leading troops of X Corps armour, a halt was called. On 12 November the mobile column returned and was reunited with 151 Brigade. They spent the next two weeks clearing the huge battle area and collecting the spoils of war and still more thousands of Italian prisoners abandoned by Rommel's retreat along the coast road.

In twelve days of fighting the Eighth Army in Lightfoot and Supercharge had lost more than 13,500 casualties. Winston Churchill wrote, 'The Battle of Alamein will ever make a glorious page in British military annals. It may almost be said, before Alamein we never had victory. After Alamein we never had a defeat.'

CHAPTER 7

Operation Pugilist: The Mareth Disaster

Rommel's retreat along the coast road was disciplined, and very heavy rainfall on the night of 6 and 7 November turned the desert south of Matruh into a quagmire, so X Corps in the pursuit was bogged down. By the 11th, Egypt was clear of the enemy and Montgomery's Cherry Pickers pushed into Libya, an advance of 270 miles from Alamein. South African troops entered Tobruk on 12 November. At Gazala, Rommel fought a delaying action. Both the Italians and Germans were now skilful at mine laying and booby traps. The Martuba landing grounds were found undefended and in good condition, and Benghazi fell on the 20th, although the harbour installations had been wrecked.

The Northumbrian Division's future hung in the balance, as the manpower situation in the Middle East was acute. 1st South African and 9th Australian Divisions had been withdrawn from the Eighth Army. Nevertheless 50th Field Regiment RA, 102nd Anti-Tank Regiment and 25th Light Anti-Aircraft RA joined the division, which consolidated around El Adem, sixteen miles south of Tobruk. Their next move was to Regina, fifteen miles east of Benghazi, and all units of X Corps improvised transport platoons to carry rations, patrol and ammunition from Tobruk to the army railhead in the 'Marble Arch' area.

Capt Ewart Clay, GSO3, wrote:

> As the enemy was chased in turn from Agheila and Buerat positions and then out of Tripoli, it became clear that his next stand would be on the Mareth line in Tunisia. Accordingly X Corps started discussions to study the conditions of an attack on such a position. A detailed divisional drill was produced for an attack through enemy minefields and across obstacles. A rehearsal of this, combined with training attacks against the rocky escarpment in which the Division was bivouacked, did much to prepare the troops for the forthcoming battle.

A street-fighting school was opened in Benghazi and intensive training took place in January and February 1943. The divisional sappers were sent off to open up ports, repair damaged docks and improve roads, mainly in the Sirte area. The 25th LAA Regiment was also detached forward to protect the newly freed air landing grounds. All the carrier platoons were in Sirte – by mistake – where they spent two lonely months. Lt Stringer-Davis directed the divisional concert party, which produced an entertaining pantomime with a personable female impersonator. Several changes were made to the divisional staff: Lt-Col R. Batten became AAQMG, Brig R. Hall became CRA, Lt-Col C. Brownrigg became CRE; Col Melvin became ADMS and Maj James took command of 5th East Yorkshires. In the last week of February the division moved forward 700 miles to a concentration area south of Tripoli. Although it still had only two infantry brigades, 69 and 151, it was once more a formidable fighting force.

Montgomery's next battle was on 6 March at Medenine, when for some strange reason Rommel sent three Panzer divisions down from high ground head-on against Montgomery's forces dug-in with massive anti-tank defences. Three times the Panzers attacked and each time were thrown back, leaving fifty tanks brewed up on the battlefield. The Eighth Army had few casualties and lost no tanks. The Northumbrian Division was represented at Medenine by 2nd Cheshire machine guns and mortars and 102nd (Northumbrian Hussars) Anti-Tank Regiment.

The French had built a twelve-mile defensive line from the coast at Mareth, eighteen miles north-west of Medenine, westwards inland into the Matmata Hills. The Wadi Zigzaou ran parallel in front of the line, making a natural anti-tank ditch. The Germans had also constructed more concrete blockhouses and steel gun cupolas, and laid wire and minefields. The French told Montgomery's staff that the desert west of the Matmata Hills was an impassable sand sea, apparently making any outflanking movement impossible.

Rommel left Tunisia on 9 March to try to persuade Hitler and Mussolini to agree that the Axis lines should be shortened by a withdrawal some forty miles back to the defences at Wadi Akarit. The Italian Gen Messe took Rommel's place and at Mareth deployed four Italian divisions, two German (90th Light and 164th Light) with three Panzer divisions lurking behind in reserve (15th, 21st and 10th).

Operation 'Pugilist' was planned for 20 March, with the main attack in the coastal area by 50th Northumbrian Division. They would create the initial bridgehead, pushing inland for three miles before 4th Indian Division passed through them. Capt Paul Mezan, an officer in a Tunisian rifle battalion, provided valuable information about the complex defences. He had helped to plan and build part of the Mareth line, which 50th Division was tasked with attacking. The sandy coastal plain had scattered clumps of palms, small ridges and lateral wadis, which were deep inland but shallow near the coast.

Capt Ewart Clay, GSO3, described the situation:

> The defences which the 50th now faced were a series of forts along the north-west bank of the Wadi Zigzaou, each containing some six pillboxes. A second line of forts in the rear were on top of a ridge covering the other positions and protecting their rear. Most pillboxes were surrounded by a maze of tunnels and trenches, many of them concreted. As the division faced the Mareth line, the forward enemy redoubts were, from right to left, Ksiba Est, Ksiba Ouest, Ouerzi, Zarat Sudest and the

Bastion (of great strength forward of the Wadi on high ground). Behind them were an enemy locality marked X on the map, Ouerzi Est, and Ouerzi Ouest. Still further back was the village of Zarat, and nearer the sea a mansion called Maison Triolet.

The defenders manning this section of the Mareth line were the Italian Young Fascisti Division and 164th German Infantry Division. Prior to D-Day an enemy outpost line along the Wadi Zeuss three miles in front of Wadi Zigzaou had to be taken. On the nights of the 16/17th and 17/18th, 6th and 7th Green Howards and 5th East Yorkshires with clockwork precision gained possession of a low ridge facing the Bastion and took control of the Chet Meskine, a more or less covered approach to Wadi Zigzaou. Each battalion was led by a picked fighting patrol known as 'The Thugs', with an experienced officer and sappers who could deal with minefields. They advanced in darkness to the edge of the minefield, waited for the artillery fire to come down, at once made gaps in the minefield and, when the fire lifted, raced through the gaps and attacked the nearest enemy posts. Lt Watney led a 5th East Yorkshires patrol and captured an enemy post without loss. Lt-Col 'Bunny' Seagrim led 7th Green Howards on the left flank and in heavy fighting took all his objectives. The sector chosen for attack was between Ksiba Ouest and Ouerzi, a one-and-a-half-mile frontage with two old crossing places, but overlooked on the left flank by the powerful Bastion. 151 Brigade would make the main assault on the right, supported by 50th RTR tanks, and 69 Brigade on the left would take on the defenders in the Bastion.

Patrols on the night of 18/19 March examined the bed of the wadi, crossed it and made a recce of the anti-tank ditch on the other side. The wadi itself and its slopes were found to be mined. The wadi had some water in it but had a firm bottom. The Corps Commander sent special congratulations to the leaders of these daring patrols. Short wooden ladders, made to cross the anti-tank ditches, and fascines, to be rolled off the front of the tanks into the trenches and wadis, plus a squadron of Scorpion mine-flailing tanks, were three methods of helping the 'Forlorn Hopes' (reminiscent of Wellington's Peninsular sieges). The plan was for an attack in three phases. At H-hour, 2200 hours, 7th Green Howards were to assault the Bastion. Half an hour later 151 Brigade, forming up on the right in the Chet Meskine, was to capture an initial bridgehead from Ksiba Ouest to Ouerzi with two battalions. The third phase, shortly after midnight, would task the third battalion to attack the defences at the top of the ridge, from locality X to Ouerzi Ouest. Massive artillery fire by thirteen field and three medium regiments and RAF and USAAF would bomb and strafe the defences.

The sappers had a difficult task, with one field company gapping minefields, helping to cross anti-tank ditches and assisting as assault engineers. The other sapper company would concentrate on making two vehicle crossings over the wadi for Scorpions, the 50th RTR tanks and the infantry carriers.

At H-hour on the night of the 20/21 March, Pugilist started as 7th Green Howards advanced in two columns. The right-hand 'Thug' patrol reached

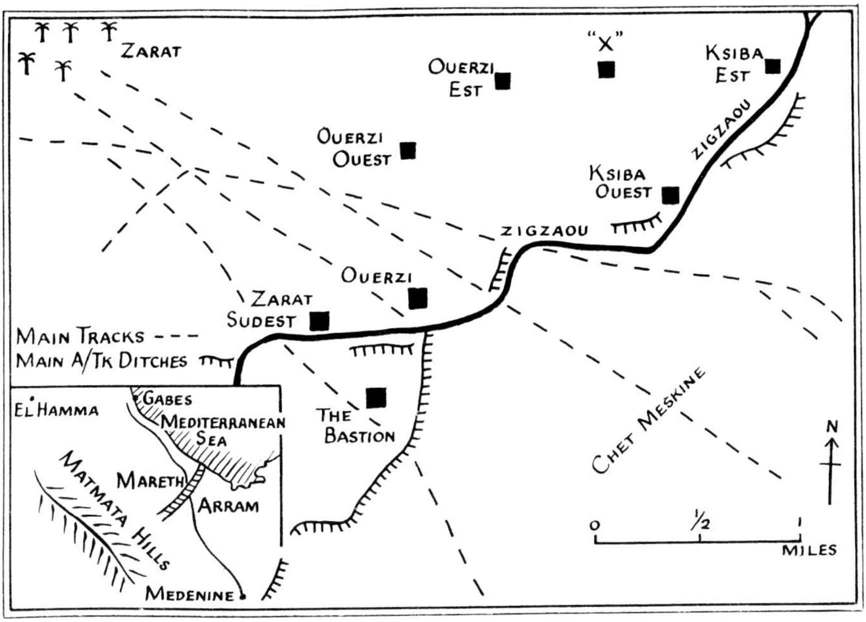

Operation Pugilist and the Mareth battle, where Lt-Col Seagrim won his VC.

the anti-tank ditch and minefield and was halted by enfilade fire from a strong-point. At this stage their CO, Lt-Col D.A. Seagrim,

> realising the seriousness of the situation, pushed to the front and took personal charge of the team attempting to place a scaling ladder over the twelve-foot-wide anti-tank ditch. The first man across, he attacked two machine-gun posts with his pistol and grenades, killing or wounding ten or a dozen Germans. It was largely due to Seagrim's inspired courage that the 7th Battalion captured the Bastion and held it throughout the following day against a succession of counter-attacks.

This was part of the citation for the colonel's Victoria Cross, the second won in North Africa. The Green Howards captured 200 prisoners and patrolled ahead into and across the Wadi Zigzaou. Meanwhile the three Durham battalions launched the main attack on the right flank from the Chet Meskine. 9th DLI under Lt-Col A. Clark followed the rumbling Scorpions and the gapping parties through the minefields, crossed the anti-tank ditch by the ladders, waded across the wadi and then encountered the young Fascisti in hand-to-hand fighting. Maj Worrall led the follow-up company, and, trying to scale the steep bank, came under heavy fire from Ksiba Ouest. Some of the men formed a human ladder against the bank, and the remainder scrambled up and out on the top. Despite his wounds, Worrall led the way into the strong-point, cheering them on with his hunting horn. He recalled:

Lt-Col Derek Anthony Seagrim, VC, 7th Green Howards, Mareth Battle, Tunisia, 20–21 March 1943.

> Here the fire was quite bloody. I told Cpl Bell to crawl forward and cut the wire, while Scotty White, Sgt Randall, Cpl Daly and myself lay beside two palm trees and tried to cover him. We couldn't have taken those pillboxes unless somebody had cut that wire, and the bullets were missing by inches here. A lot of the Company had temporarily stuck and slowed down crossing the wadi and getting up the anti-tank ditch. At last Bell said, 'I've cut the wire, Sir'. We made a dash for it and by sheer luck got into their trenches fifty yards beyond the wire. We went up these. When we got near the pillboxes, I put Randall and Daly with two Brens to fire at the slits, while White and I led a party up the trench towards them, throwing Mk 36 Mills grenades at each corner. To my joy, suddenly about fifty Italians appeared with their hands up. I then saw that the Bren guns had set the pillboxes on fire, at least the two left-hand ones. More Italians then surrendered, among them a major and a captain.

Maj Worrall and his men then tackled the right-hand pillbox with the same tactics. 'The Italians came rushing out in our faces. I tried to make one put his hands up but found I was unarmed.' Worrall had lost his revolver and his hunting horn. 'We swarmed over all three strong-points quickly. We took about eighty prisoners and pushed them out of the fort along the trench to the road.' So Ksiba Ouest was taken. 8th DLI on the left under Lt-Col M. Jackson had to tackle the Ouerzi strong-point. The CO was killed in the wadi, and the 2 i/c Maj Kidwell did well to capture Ouerzi by 0200 hours, despite heavy losses. The leading support tanks of 50th RTR tried to cross the wadi at midnight. The first crossed, stalled and stuck fast. Sappers made another crossing with fascines and by dawn four tanks were across. Gen Nichols, unfortunately out of wireless touch with the true position, postponed the third phase. During the next day, the 21st, a few anti-tank guns were manhandled across the wadi and the Cheshires manhandled their machine guns across, as did two troops of light anti-aircraft (LAA) Bofors guns. The enemy still held the commanding ground, but three strong-points had been captured, with several hundred prisoners. Gen Nichols changed the plans to Phase 3 for the night of 21/22nd. 51st Highland Division would take over responsibility for the Bastion, 69 Brigade would relieve 9th DLI in Ksiba Ouest and then attack Ksiba Est, and 151 Brigade would tackle locality X, Ouerzi Est, Ouerzi Ouest and Zarat Sudest.

The battalions of 151 Brigade were all under strength, since their losses at Alamein had not been fully made up. In the Mareth battle they fought on a three-company basis. Brig Beake, VC, DSO, commanding 151 Brigade, sent his own 6th DLI, under Lt-Col Watson, and 5th East Yorkshires from 69 Brigade into the bridgehead. The latter took Ksiba Est and found it to be a huge labyrinth of fortifications with a length of 1,200 yards and a depth of 400 yards – a battalion locality. In the centre, 9th DLI spent much of the day in hand-to-hand fighting, lost casualties and took prisoners. On the left, 6th DLI secured Ouerzi Ouest and Zarat fairly easily, which was also a huge defensive network. During the day 50th RTR managed to get a total of fifty Valentine tanks into the bridgehead; however, only eight of them were fitted with 6-pounder guns, the remainder with inadequate 2-pounders. During the day hundreds of Italian soldiers surrendered, and thus the actual Northumbrian attack had gone fairly well.

But the situation deteriorated on the 22nd. The Valentine tanks had badly damaged the crossing point, which was under constant harassing fire, and snipers took toll of the engineers. As a direct result there were far too few anti-tank guns over the wadi in the bridgehead, and the infantry battalions were running short of ammunition. Many of the minefields strewn across the bridgehead could not be cleared because of heavy defensive fire. The RAF reported to Corps, who reported to Divisional HQ that the enemy was – of course – preparing around the woods at Zarat for a substantial counter-attack. Considerable numbers of guns, tanks and transport had obviously been moved south from Gabes. Gen Montgomery, Corps and Division knew that a heavy counter-attack was inevitable. The divisional and corps artillery could possibly, even probably, halt a counter-attack, depending on its strength. Also there were scores of RAF fighter-bombers on airfields within range.

And then it rained heavily and caused the water level in the wadi to rise. Unfortunately it was deemed sufficient to ground the RAF and USAAF planes. At noon on the 22nd the XXX Corps Commander, Lt-Gen Oliver Leese, visited Maj-Gen Nichols. They were presumably unaware that the RAF were not available to deter a counter-attack and unaware that there were insufficient anti-tank guns in the bridgehead.

An hour later the enemy launched its counter-attack. Rommel would have been proud of it. Three columns formed up around Zarat, each with about ten or a dozen Mark IV tanks from 15th Panzer Division, backed by anti-tank guns and large numbers of infantry. Under a heavy artillery bombardment backed by Luftwaffe aircraft, the columns set off from the north, one directed on Ouerzi Est, the second on the gap between Ouerzi Est and Ouerzi Ouest, and the third in the shallow valley between Ouerzi Ouest and Ouerzi. By about 1700 hours thirty of the 50th RTR Valentines had been knocked out, and their CO, Lt-Col Cairns, killed. The surviving fifteen tanks rallied back to cover the wadi crossing, where they remained in action until nightfall. The enemy coordinated tanks with infantry and forced the Northumbrian defenders out of Ouerzi Est and locality X; Zarat, of course, went first, but Ouerzi Ouest garrison held firm. The situation was very serious, and ammunition was extremely low. Capt Ewart Clay, GSO3, wrote:

> By the evening a bloody and desperate battle was being fought out west of the Wadi Zigzaou, and slowly but surely the infantry were driven back to the wadi edge, until by midnight except for the East Yorkshire Regiment holding out in Ksiba Ouest there was no depth whatever in the bridgehead. Though tremendous casualties had been inflicted by the supporting artillery, whose concentration had been kept going ceaselessly in support of the infantry, they failed to stop the enemy attack. Later in the evening even this support flagged, as wireless sets with the forward troops were gradually knocked out or failed due to exhausted batteries. The men of the 6th, 8th and 9th DLI were inextricably mixed up, many without commanders, all hungry, tired and desperately short of ammunition. The whole area was lit up by the twenty-seven derelict burning Valentine tanks of 50th RTR fought to a standstill by superior enemy armour.

Maj-Gen 'Crasher' Nichols, GOC 50th Division, Mareth line, 28–29 March 1943.

Gen Nichols had no option but to withdraw the remnants of the three DLI battalions across the wadi to rest and refit.

> The fighting of those three days in March tore grievous holes in the ranks of the Durham brigade. Three rifle companies of 6th DLI were reduced from 300 all ranks to sixty-five, and the other two battalions' losses were similar. The gallant stand north of the Wadi Zigzaou against overwhelming odds drew the German armour out of position and directly facilitated the success of the New Zealanders' flanking attack.

Thus wrote Maj David Rissik. Gen Montgomery afterwards wrote that the Mareth line battle was a significant battle honour for the Durhams.

On the night of 23/24 March the gallant 5th East Yorkshires were withdrawn to the east side of the wadi, and eventually the whole division was withdrawn into reserve to rest. Monty won the battle of Mareth brilliantly with his famous and daring left hook round Wilders Gap, and on through the Tebaga Gap, with 8 Armoured Brigade combining superbly with Gen Freyburg's 2nd New Zealand Division. Then 1st Armoured Division took over and raced for El Hamma and Gabes. Fortunately it had not rained and the Desert Air Forces gave good support, although many planes were grounded by a fierce Khamsin dust-storm. So the Eighth Army marched on from Alamein, Medenine and Mareth, with Wadi Akarit still to come.

Alan Moorehead described Monty's switch to the left, using all available armour and aircraft in support of the New Zealanders, as 'possibly the boldest thing Montgomery ever did'. Had the left hook been delivered earlier, the Tunisian campaign might well have been shortened.

Battle of Wadi Akarit: Anderson's VC

The division relieved the Desert Rats on 25 March in a quiet sector astride the Mareth–Medenine road. Patrols reported Mareth unoccupied, so the 50th spent several days clearing up the devastated battlefields, burying the dead and recovering much lost equipment. Brig R. Senior relieved Brig Beake, the commander of 151 Brigade, and Brig Hill became the new CRA. Most of the divisional transport was removed to help the Eighth Army build-up of supplies forward at Gabes, and for an all-out attack on Wadi Akarit some twenty miles north of Mareth. Most of the Afrika Korps had been drawn off to the north-west to fend off Patton's US II Corps attack. Montgomery planned to make a direct attack on the Wadi Akarit line before the new moon and therefore before the enemy expected it. The wadi ran from the sea to the salt marshes inland, called Sebket el Hamma, known to be impassable to all transport. The most easterly of the hills between the wadi and the German positions astride the Gafsa road was Djebel Roumana. Maj-Gen Nichols was only told on 2 April at his HQ in Zaret that a brigade would be needed for the next battle.

The general plan was for 7th Armoured to hold the coastal plain between the sea and the hill Djebel Roumana, but with no attack planned. 51st Highland Division would attack Djebel Roumana and the enemy positions between the hill and the coast road, using two brigades. On the far left flank, 4th Indian Division with its only two brigades would seize the Fatnassa Hills

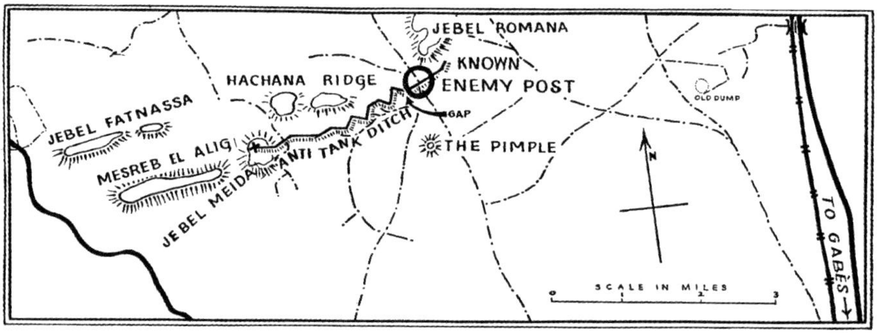

The battle of Wadi Akarit. Hachana Ridge, where Pte Anderson won his VC.

and the Djebel Meida. Maj-Gen Tuker was confident his Gurkhas would take the rocky massif in their stride. In the centre the Northumbrian 69 Brigade would capture the anti-tank ditch between Roumana and Fatnassa, specifically the Hachana Ridge and an enemy post guarding a track that crossed into the plains of southern Tunisia.

All the division's transport and artillery were completely grounded and not available. Artillery support would come only from the Highland Division gunners. A shallow open valley lay in front of the hills of the Akarit position, so all movements for three or four miles could be seen by the enemy. The troops in position on forward slopes could not move during the day. The Eighth Army's guns opened fire at 0415 hours on 6 April to support the three battalions, but the Indians climbed the Tebaga Fatnassa and Mesreb el Alig in deadly silence.

Brig Cooke-Collis sent 69 Brigade off with supporting arms, with Lt-Col James's 5th East Yorkshires on the left and Lt-Col Seagrim's 7th Green Howards on the right flank. The latter captured a feature short of the anti-tank ditch called 'The Pimple' and broached minefields and wire without much difficulty. The anti-tank ditch was on the reverse slope of a low ridge, and the artillery barrage was insufficient to subdue the enemy positions. The extra seventy-two field guns of divisional artillery might have reduced the casualties to come.

As soon as the leading Green Howard company got through the minefields and started to cross the ridge, devastating enemy fire, much of it from 47mm guns firing at short range, halted the attack, causing heavy casualties. The CO, who had won the Victoria Cross at Mareth, was now fatally wounded, some 300 yards short of the anti-tank ditch.

Exactly the same happened to 5th East Yorkshires on the left. The leading company suffered 70 per cent casualties and their CO, Lt-Col James, was wounded in the attack. Pte Eric Anderson won the division's third Victoria Cross. With 'A' Company under intense Spandau and mortar attack from a well-concealed enemy strong-point not more than 200 yards away, he, a stretcher-bearer, went out on four occasions to rescue wounded soldiers lying in the open in 'No Man's Land'. On the fourth occasion, while administering first aid, he was hit and mortally wounded.

The Highland Division was facing 200th Panzer Grenadier Regiment, backed by MkIV tanks of 15th Panzer Division with Italian infantry. It was also involved in a desperate struggle at Roumana. At 0900 hours Maj-Gen Nichols went forward to 'The Pimple' on the Green Howards' front to see the state of the battle. The medium machine guns of the 2nd Cheshire Regiment under Lt-Col S. Keeling, now in position on 'The Pimple', brought really effective fire on the enemy positions. At 1015 hours 6th Green Howards under Lt-Col D.J. Smith passed through the 7th, and, with the help of Maj Cameron's squadron of 3rd CLY (County of London Yeomanry), whose tanks infiltrated across the anti-tank ditch, the tide of battle turned.

At the battles of the Mareth line and Wadi Akarit the two Green Howard battalions suffered 500 casualties and won thirty awards for gallantry.

Pte Eric Anderson, VC, Wadi Akarit battle, Tunisia, 6 April 1943.

By 1100 hours, 4th Indian Division (including 4th Essex Battalion) rounded up hundreds of prisoners. Four hours later the Sherman tanks of 8 Armoured Brigade began moving through the breaches in the anti-tank ditch. The Eighth Army took more than 5,000 prisoners for the loss of 1,289 casualties, mostly from the Highland Division. During the night 6th Green Howards beat off a counter-attack and then the enemy withdrew. The Axis troops were now in full retreat from the coastal plain; Sfax was captured on 10 April and Sousse, sixty miles further north, on the 12th.

The division remained at Ouidane el Hachana in the 'No Man's Land' of Wadi Akarit and a week or so later concentrated south of Sousse. There Maj-Gen J.S. Nichols, the GOC who had led the division with such gallantry since early 1942, was relieved on 14 April by Maj-Gen S.C. Kirkman, CBE, MC, an artillery specialist.

'Montgomery meanwhile went crashing in for his last great battle [in North Africa] in the south of Wadi Akarit', wrote Alan Moorehead.

> This time he charged head-on with his Highland Division, the Indians and the Fiftieth. The Eighth Army was a wonderful machine when it was geared up to fight. It went forward with a terrible momentum and in a wonderfully adjusted rhythm – first the bombers, then the guns, then the infantry, then the tanks. Six gaps were blasted in the enemy line along the Wadi Akarit and then the First Armoured Division and the New Zealanders poured through for the kill. Once again the German line broke under the stroke of the piston. For 150 miles along the coast north of Akarit von Arnim had no defensive position. It was every man for himself now in the enemy camp.

There was a possibility that the division as part of X Corps might take part in a battle for Enfidaville, north of Sousse. On 19 April Maj-Gen Kirkman carried out two reconnaissances with his two Brigadiers, Senior and Cooke-Collis. For a week 151 Brigade had sent out patrols in the coastal area, and the gunners put in harassing fire on enemy transport using the coast road. The Cheshire Regiment gave machine-gun covering fire as the division prepared itself to support the New Zealanders in their attacks on the hills of Zaghouan and Takrouna.

To everyone's surprise Maj-Gen Kirkman was told late at night on the 19th that the Northumbrian Division was being withdrawn and relieved by 56th Division.

On the 24th the GOC and GSO1, Lt-Col R. Innes, flew by air to Cairo and the division started the long 2,000-mile journey back to Alexandria. A new brigade arrived, 168 Infantry Brigade from 56th Division, commanded by Brig K.C. Davidson, with 10th Royal Berkshires, CO Lt-Col I.R. Baird; 1st London Scottish, CO Lt-Col H.J. Wilson, and 1st London Irish Rifles, CO Lt-Col I.H. Good. The next campaign needed much planning and training.

For the division the long campaign in North Africa was over. They had lost well over 10,000 casualties and won three Victoria Crosses. Now for Operation 'Husky'.

CHAPTER 9

Operation Husky: The Assault on Sicily

By 11 May the division arrived at Alexandria without leaving a single vehicle behind, although many had to be towed. On arrival as many men as possible were given four days' leave to Cairo or Alexandria, some having had no leave for two years. Capt Ewart Clay, GSO3, and the GSO2, Maj M. Osborne DSO, MC, were mainly instrumental in the preplanning of Operation 'Husky'. This highly detailed assault plan took place in Cairo (Lt-Col Innes, GSO1, had fallen ill) and started on 25 April when Maj-Gen Kirkman and his staff arrived. The shipping allotted to 50th Division, part of Lt-Gen Miles Dempsey's XIII Corps, allowed for two brigade groups, 151 and 69, sailing with the D-Day convoys, and the third brigade group (168, which had not been in action before) arriving on D+3. Additional troops had been allocated to the division: 98th Field Regiment RA with self-propelled guns under Lt-Col C.G. Cubitt, DSO, and 44th RTR with its diesel Sherman tanks under Lt-Col E.D. Rash; 'A' Squadron of the famous Royal Dragoons Armoured Car Regiment and No. 34 Beach Brick under Col J.T. Gibson. The Beach Brick was composed of 1st Welch Regiment, and was responsible for all the initial vital work on the beaches – putting down roads, making exits from the beaches, marking assembly areas for troops, vehicles and stores, for reception, stacking and issuing all commodities as directed by the 'Q' staff. The Combined Training Centre at Kabrit was used for 'wet' exercises on the eastern shores of the Bitter Lake. The Mountain Training Centre near Tripoli in Syria was much used, since the terrain was known to be similar to Sicily. A major landing exercise took place in the Gulf of Akaba from 10 to 15 June, sailing from Suez. Most vehicles had to be waterproofed for a possible 'wet' beach landing. It was unpleasantly hot in Cairo but bearable at Alexandria, and the sea bathing helped relax the hard work of planning and training. But a two-day march by 69 Brigade from Kabrit to Suez showed that the state of many infantrymen's feet was not what it should be!

On 23 June Sir James Grigg, Secretary of State for War, spent a morning seeing units training. The next day Monty addressed all senior officers of XIII Corps and on the 25th he inspected all units of the division. For three and a half hours he drove through the training area. He had a great reception and he made his usual, rousing speech from the bonnet of his jeep. A final exercise was

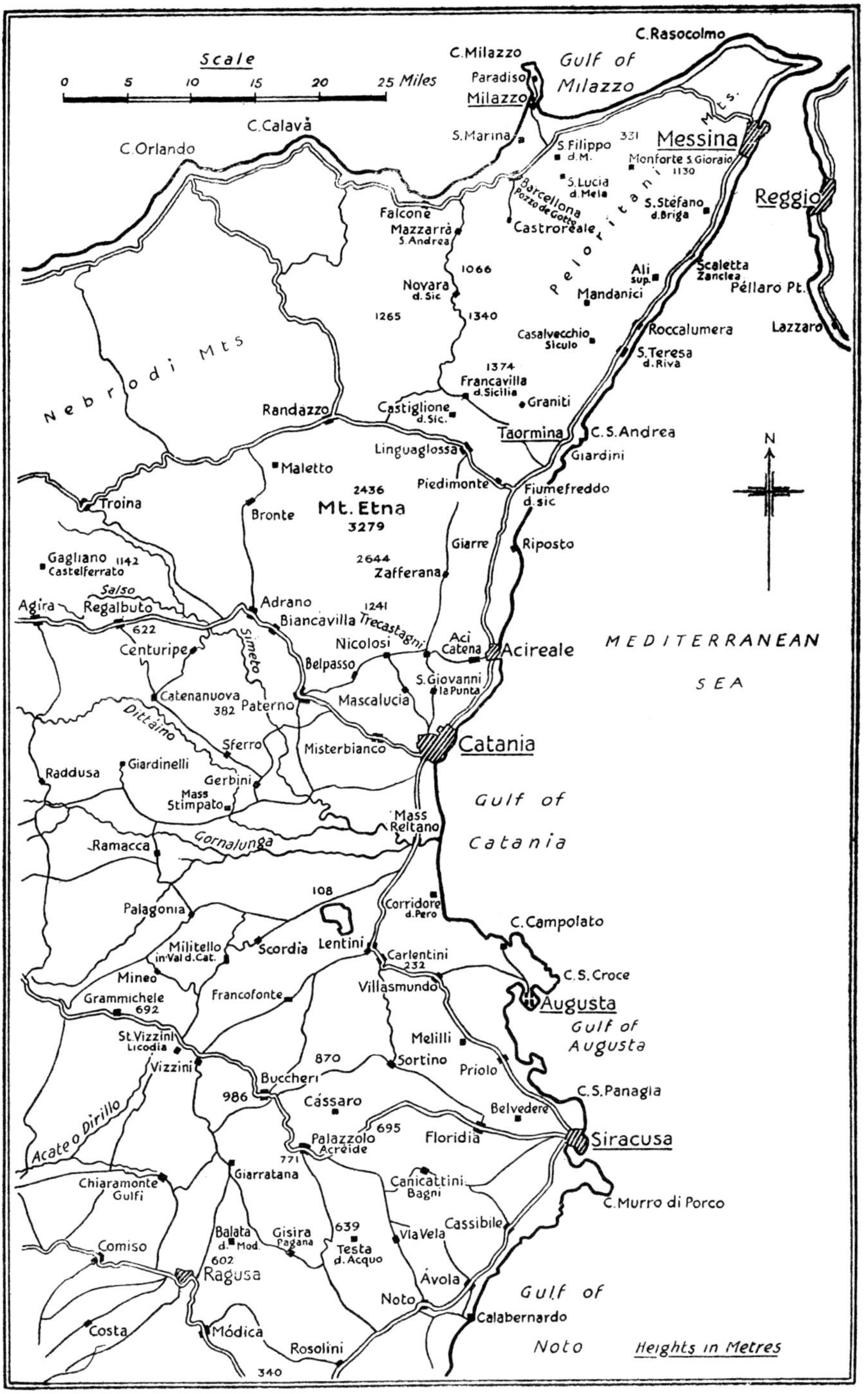

Operation Husky and the capture of Sicily.

held on land the next day. The loading of vehicles at Alexandria and Benghazi had by now been completed, although at the last moment, owing to a shortage of landing craft tanks (LCTs), some vehicles had to be driven 700 miles to Tripoli to be loaded. During the wait for embarkation at Port Said, Maj-Gen Kirkman visited each ship in turn and addressed all ranks on the assault ahead. The destination was still a secret to all but very senior staff, and Rhodes, Crete, Sicily and Sardinia were joint favourites, while Winston's favourite – the Balkans – was deemed to be a rank outsider! The D-Day assault personnel travelled in the *Winchester Castle*, *Orontes*, *Devonshire*, *Ruys* and *Christian Huygens*. The follow-up D+3 convoy sailed in the *Kosciusko*, *Takliwa*, *Karao*, *Oranda* and *City of Canterbury*. On 30 June and 1 July the personnel ships passed through the Suez Canal. XIII Corps HQ, 50th Division HQ and 69 and 151 Brigade HQs sailed in the *Bulolo*, on the principle of putting all one's eggs in one basket! Once the expedition had sailed, it was revealed that Husky meant the invasion of Sicily, with D-Day on 10 June 1943.

The Eighth Army was commanded, of course, by Gen Bernard Montgomery and consisted of XIII Corps under Lt-Gen Miles Dempsey and XXX Corps with a total of four infantry divisions (50th and 5th in XIII Corps), a minimal Sherman tank brigade, artillery and airborne support (particularly during and before the assault landings). Once a firm bridgehead had been established between Cape Murro di Porco and Pozzallo, the British objectives were to thrust northwards to Augusta and Catania to capture the vital Gerbini airfields. The US Seventh Army under the fiery, difficult Gen Patton would land on the western flank and lead north-west towards the capital, Palermo. Eventually it would be a race between the two armies to Messina in the north-east corner, only a mile or so from the Italian coast. XIII Corps would assault on a three-brigade front between Avola and Cassibile in the Gulf of Noto.

The plain of Catania measures twelve miles wide by eighteen miles in length, much of it marshy lowland through which many streams and the River Simeto flow into the sea. High summer humidity and temperatures and abounding mosquitoes made for an unpleasant battlefield! The 11,000-foot Mount Etna hampered road traffic and meant that control of the narrow coastal shelf and road was crucial. The Germans initially had two divisions on the island, the Hermann Goering and 15th Panzer Grenadier. Gen Alfreda Guzzoni's Sixth Army deployed six Italian coastal and five field divisions. A later reinforcement unit was the 29th Panzer Grenadier Regiment. In all there were 30,000 German and 200,000 Italian troops defending Sicily. Immediately opposing 50th Division were 374th and 437th Battalions of 146th Infantry Regiment of 206th Coastal Division, with 102 and 84 batteries in support. Not, in fact, high-grade troops! The start to Husky was inauspicious. Because of winds and inexperienced glider pilots, the American 82nd Airborne Division was scattered over an area of fifty miles, incurring heavy casualties. The British 1 Air Landing Brigade with more than 140 aircraft and gliders took off from airfields in Tunisia, and 47 out of 134 gliders were casualties with 500 men lost. 151 Brigade would assault first at H-hour, 0245 hours on 10 July, with 9th DLI landing on 'Jig Green' and 6th DLI on 'Jig Amber' beaches between Lido d'Avola and Marina d'Avola. Mainly because the landing craft assaults (LCAs) were dropped off by the Navy about twelve, instead of six or seven, miles offshore, almost everything went wrong. Capt Ewart Clay wrote, 'Most naval officers were uncertain as to their whereabouts, craft became scattered, flotillas were no longer together and some craft were quite out of touch with their neighbours.'

'B' Company 6th DLI landed one and half hours late, 3,000 yards away from its objective. It mopped up the weak beach defences, identified its position, marched to and occupied Avola railway station. There it met a company of King's Own Yorkshire Light Infantry of 5th Division (six miles adrift) and some American paratroopers (at least twelve miles adrift). 'A' Company landed 4,500 yards south of 'Jig Amber' at Calabernardo, identified by the naval officers as Marina d'Avola. 'C' Company landed south of Calabernardo, 5,000 yards off target. And so on. However, the 2 i/c, Maj Worrall, Maj Galloway and Lt French-Kihoe worked out where they were, despite increasing shell and machine-gun fire. Capt Walton, commanding 'A' Company, was killed as he stepped ashore. 9th DLI was marginally more fortunate, one and a half hours late and between 500 and 3,000 yards off target. The 8th DLI CO, Lt-Col R. Lidwell, asked the naval officer in charge of the flotilla to land his battalion – in broad daylight – at 'Jig Green' beach and found himself at 'How Amber', the left-hand beach of 5th Division, 3,000 yards away, which necessitated a three-mile march to Avola. The landing of 69 Brigade during the day was almost as haphazard. It was fortunate that there were no enemy coastal batteries deployed. Once ashore, 69 Brigade moved towards Floridia and, as transport was lacking,

Landing craft off Avola, where the DLI eventually landed.

marched and moved with the aid of mules and donkeys. For the next few days men had to march long distances, and the lack of drinking water, the prevention of sore feet and the heat were for a time the main problems. Divisional HQ was established near Cassibile. Gen Dempsey visited at 1300 hours. Farther north 5th Division occupied Syracuse. To the south XXX Corps had landed and captured its objectives. The American bridgehead at Gela was heavily counter-attacked but survived attacks by Tiger tanks.

The Luftwaffe, mainly *Messerschmitt* ME 109s, appeared in the afternoon and in the next few days bombed three of the division's motor transport (MT) ships, and 125 men of the Northumbrian Division lost their lives. Thus 234 vehicles, eight field guns and nine Sherman tanks were destroyed. By the end of the third day only fifteen RASC load-carrying vehicles were ashore. Monty ordered Gen Dempsey "to operate with great energy" for Syracuse and then Augusta. So Maj-Gen Kirkman passed on the message to his three brigadiers as, 'You're not going to sit down and rest. There's no one in front of you at all, the place is empty. You go on till you drop if necessary – occupying this ground which you'll have to fight for tomorrow. Get 'em all

DLI capture Gen Gotti-Porcinari, GOC Napoli Division, near Sortino, 15 July 1943.

on the move, go on, go on . . . Use your Bren gun carriers as tanks, get on, get on. I don't care how tired the men are – walk!' Nevertheless the German Battlegroup Schmalz and the Italian Napoli Division fought skilful delaying actions towards Lentini, leaving the approaches to Augusta undefended.

5th Division was allotted the good coastal road and 50th Division the minor inland road that runs through the hills from Floridia through Sortino. Both roads then join together at Lentini on the edge of the plain of Catania, and thence across the Leonardo river, along the top of a ridge until it drops to the Primosole bridge over the Simeto river. Then beyond, over flat country overlooked by Mount Etna, to Catania. 5th East Yorkshires were ambushed in a gorge south-east of Sortino and casualties were fairly heavy, but many Italian and some German prisoners were taken. By dawn on 13 July 6th DLI on the high ground beyond Sortino was attacked by the Italian Napoli Division supported by French R35 tanks. After the action more than 300 Italian soldiers surrendered, including the Napoli Division GOC, Gen Gotti-Porcinari, with great help from 44th RTR tanks and self-propelled artillery of 98th Field Regiment RA.

During the afternoon Palazzolo was reached and contact made with 51st Highland Division. Next Gens Montgomery and Dempsey ordered Kirkman to capture Carlentini and Lentini during the night of the 13/14th. No. 3 Commando would land from the sea to capture the bridge over the Leonardo river some 3,000 yards north of Lentini, at Malati, and 1 Parachute Brigade, backed by a glider force, would land on and around the Primosole bridge. The distances were from Solarino to Sortino, ten miles; Sortino to Lentini, ten miles; Lentini to the Primosole bridge, ten miles. Among the captured equipment from the wretched Napoli Division were fifteen lorries in working

DLI Bren-gun carriers cross Primosole bridge on the way to Catania, 5 August 1943.

order – very welcome. Nevertheless the objectives and timings were unlikely to be met. 6th Green Howards met stiff resistance three miles south of Carlentini. Unknown at the time, there were four German battalions of 115th Panzer Grenadier Regiment in and around Carlentini and Lentini and self-propelled guns and tanks around Mount Pancali. Moreover, the 904th Italian Fortress Battalion was sited north-west of Lentini, and a Mobile Column 'D' with 500 men and twelve tanks was between Lentini and the sea. By midnight on the 13th, 6th Green Howards had captured part of the approach to Mount Pancali but were held up by thirty machine-gun nests and the Group Schmalz. At dawn on the 14th, 7th Green Howards, supported by 98th and 124th Field Regiments and 2nd Cheshire MGs, put in a brilliant attack. There is a superb account of the action (related by Capt K.A. Nash, 7th Green Howards, in *Path of the 50th*). The County of London Yeomanry and 44th RTR tanks of 4 Armoured Brigade showed great dash, and by the afternoon Carlentini and Lentini had been secured and the bridge over the Leonardo river found intact. 9th DLI was greeted warmly by the inhabitants of both towns. In Operation 'Fustian' 1 Parachute Brigade sent 1,856 men in 125 planes from North Africa to drop and seize the Primosole bridge. Of these 14 planes were lost, 26 returned to base, and only 30 dropped in the correct DZ, 9 nearby and 48 between half a mile and twenty miles adrift. All three DLI battalions made forced marches of twenty-five miles to join the battle.

By dusk on the 14th, 6th DLI and a squadron of 44th RTR were only a mile south of the bridge. Unexpectedly Gen Kesselring, the GOC German forces in Italy, decided to throw Gen Richard Heidrich's 1st Parachute Division into the Catania plain and specifically defend the Primosole bridge. The determined nucleus of the British paratroops who had landed and seized the bridge removed all the demolition charges. As the day wore on they had to face a series of strong counter-attacks, and at 1930 hours lack of ammunition forced them to withdraw from the bridge – two hours before 9th DLI arrived on the scene. The airborne brigade casualties in the fight for the bridge were 117 with 27 killed in action. They also lost substantially from the widespread air drops. Brig Senior decided to launch his counter-attack on the bridge defenders, backed by both gunner regiments just after dawn on the 15th. There was a gap of six miles between 151 Brigade, intent on the bridge, and 69 Brigade around Lentini. Brig Davidson's green 168 Brigade had landed as planned on D+3 at Syracuse, with little transport, and moved to the north of Melilli. In a curious night action 124th Field Regiment RA east of Carlentini was attacked rather inefficiently by 4th Battalion *Contracarro Semoventi* of the 33rd Parma Regiment of the Livorno Division. By 0100 hours 200 prisoners, twelve little S47/32 tanks, fifty motor cycles, six lorries and much else were in the bag! The Primosole bridge was about 400 feet long, with a superstructure of iron girders eight feet above the deep, sluggish River Simeto. Neither bank commanded the other. On the northern, German side, were farms and barns and thick vineyards dotted with olive trees providing excellent cover. Two miles beyond the river is the dry Bottaceto Ditch with deep banks that made a natural tank obstacle. It was the southern defence of the Catania aerodrome, which included wired-in concrete pillboxes. The 9th DLI attack failed, despite platoons getting across the river. In hand-to-hand fighting the German paratroops who were concealed in the vineyards, supported by mortars, had the upper hand. Mines and vehicles and 88mm anti-tank guns firing over open sights stopped the Sherman tanks of 44th RTR.

Lt-Col John Frost, a paratroop CO, witnessed the attack.

> We had never taken part in such an operation and having seen this one were determined never to do so. It all went according to plan. There was a massive expenditure of ammunition on suspected enemy positions. Medium machine guns [of the Cheshire Regiment] kept up continuous pressure and tanks were interspersed with the infantry. There was a smokescreen to cover the last and most dangerous stretch. The infantry [8th DLI] plodded remorselessly on with bayonets fixed for the final assault across the river. The Germans held their fire until the Durhams were within some fifty yards, more or less point blank range, then mowed the leading platoons down. Then they engaged the follow-up platoons. They fired burst after burst of machine gun fire at the tanks which had the effect of forcing them to remain closed down and therefore unable to identify enemy targets. The enemy anti-tank fire appeared nevertheless to be ineffective but, without protection, the infantry attack just faded away and both Durhams and tanks came back.

There were 100 casualties that morning, with 34 killed, including 9 officers. The dead and wounded had to be left behind on the north bank. After the disaster the two sides (Lt-Col Ludwig Heilmann's 3rd Parachute Regiment, machine-gun battalion and signal company were veterans from Crete and Russia) remained facing one another, while the battered DLI regrouped and decided how and when the attack would be renewed. Lt-Col Clarke had not liked the hastily put-together plan, but Maj-Gen Kirkman, 50th Division GOC, had not only the Corps Commander, Lt-Gen Dempsey, but Montgomery himself urging him with utmost urgency to capture the Primosole bridge to allow the Eighth Army to break into the Plain of Catania (and perhaps beat Gen Patton's US Army into Messina!).

At about 1000 hours Gen Kirkman arrived at Brig Senior's command post and promptly ordered a fresh attack for that afternoon with even heavier artillery support. Later the two paratroop colonels Pearson and Frost attended a meeting between the infantry and tank brigadiers, which included Lt-Col R.P. Lidwell, CO 8th DLI, who was to lead the attack. Pearson told the conference, 'I suppose you want to see another battalion written off!' Pearson had found a ford about a mile down river, which he had used when the paratroops had withdrawn the previous night. Lt-Col Lidwell's various commanders approved the flanking plan. A huge barrage raked the entire enemy defences at midnight and Col Pearson led two companies of 8th DLI over the River Simeto, thirty yards wide, in single file without great difficulty, in four feet of water. Once across, the DLI moved to take the bridge defences in the rear through dense vineyards and achieved complete surprise. They took up positions along and beside the Catania road. The plan was for the other two 8th DLI companies to cross the bridge and link up with the first two, but all communications broke down. Wireless sets had been 'drowned' in the river crossing. Mortar-bomb flares had been separated from the mortars. The Bren-gun carrier with link radio received a direct hit. There was a vital period of four hours before at dawn Lt-Col Lidwell led the follow-up companies across the bridge. By this time, the 'Green Devils', as the German parachute troops were called, had predictably rallied and counter-attacked, and hand-to-hand fighting forced the little 8th DLI bridgehead back to just 100 yards north of the bridge.

Maj David Rissik wrote:

> Concealed Spandaus opened up at point blank range on the leading troops; but for the ditch, hardly a man in either company would have survived. As it was the whole of 'B' Company's leading platoon was written off. Both Companies rallied quickly, 'C' took to the fields on the right and began outflanking the enemy; 'B' got its Brens into action. A handful of men under Lt A. Jackman charged the leading German posts. He was badly wounded and most of his men killed or wounded, but the Germans withdrew. Then both sides set to with bayonets, grenades and automatics. CSM Brannigan rapidly killed several Paratroopers. British and Germans fired at trees by mistake thinking they were men. It was a grim game of hide and seek and within twenty minutes both sides had fought themselves to a standstill. The front of 'B' Company and the Germans facing them suffered almost 100 per cent casualties and only the dead and the wounded remained in the area of the fighting.

Rissik goes on to relate, 'The counter-attack came as soon as it was light, against 'A' Company among the grapevines. Heavily outnumbered, two platoons were over-run and after more fierce hand-to-hand fighting were forced back to the river – which some men swam – others withdrew to a farmhouse near the Catania road.'

Tank support was under threat from two 88mm anti-tank guns. The 2nd Cheshire Regiment fired 600 3-inch mortar bombs during the day. At 1330 hours Gens Montgomery and Dempsey visited Kirkman's HQ and confirmed that 50th Division had to enlarge the bridgehead during the night. It was decided that 6th DLI and 9th DLI would make a crossing by the same ford that 8th DLI had used. Once over and in position at the north end of the Primosole bridge, 6th DLI on the left side and 9th DLI on the right side would attack up Highway 114 for about 1,500 yards with 3rd CLY Shermans, which would follow and exploit. A tremendous barrage from six artillery regiments (95 25-pounders, 48 105mm howitzers and 126 medium guns) would support the attack. The third attack began at 0100 hours on 17 July after an easy river crossing. Despite the huge barrage, the defences caused heavy casualties to both 6th and 9th DLI. Nine CLY Shermans crossed the bridge, and close-quarter fighting went on all day. Dreadful carnage took place. The battlefield was strewn with the broken bodies of dead and dying men. The German 1st Parachute Division troops were dedicated veterans and fought like furies. A truce was arranged by medical orderlies on both sides to bring in the wounded. The Durhams managed to get two 6-pounder anti-tank guns in position at the northern end of the bridge, and several tank and infantry counter-attacks by the 'Green Devils' were beaten off. At about 0615 hours both 6th and 9th DLI were reported to be about 1,000 yards beyond the bridge. This time CLY Shermans crossed the bridge at dawn, and, since the British artillery had knocked out the enemy 88mm anti-tank guns, the tanks were more successful. Their CO, Lt-Col Willis, was sniped in his turret and mortally wounded. The CO of 44th RTR, Lt-Col Rash, was sniped and wounded, believed dead, but was taken prisoner. Movement began in the enemy lines, some white handkerchiefs appeared and some 155 German paratroops were captured. Enemy dead on the ground numbered about 300 from the three battalions of 3rd Parachute Regiment, reinforced by the German 904th Fortress Battalion. A company of London Scottish from 168 Brigade helped the tired DLI battalions to mop up. Maj Rudolph Bohmler, Lt-Col Heilman, Lt-Col Walther, Capt Paul Adolph, Maj Schmidt and Capt Eric Fassi and their units had fought with unbelievable bravery and tenacity. They had caused the Durhams about 500 casualties, 120 to 6th DLI, 100 to 9th DLI and more than 200 to 8th DLI. David Rissik, the DLI historian, wrote: 'The area around the bridge was a regular hell's kitchen: it was littered with smashed rifles and automatics, torn pieces of equipment, bloodstained clothing, overturned ammunition boxes and bodies of British and German dead. It was a scene of terrible destruction and telling evidence of a bitter struggle in which neither side had asked or given any quarter. There can have been few better German troops in Sicily than those who held the bridge.'

Back at Lentini 69 Brigade spent several days mopping up small Italian and German groups of survivors, and a squadron of Royal Dragoons armoured cars patrolled north-westwards into the Plain of Catania and encountered the enemy on the line of the River Gornalunga, south of, but parallel to, the Simeto. 168 Brigade started to take over from the Durhams and were ordered into their first battle. Covered by a barrage, Brig Davidson, with the London Scottish on the right and London Irish on the left, was ordered to advance on the night of 17/18 July to take the Bottaceto ditch defending Catania airfield. More or less everything went wrong. The German defenders used searchlights so that the surprise of a night attack was lost. The recce information was inaccurate; it promised negligible enemy strength. When the artillery barrage was fired the London Irish correctly followed up 100 yards behind, but the London Scottish unfortunately remained where they were, some quarter of a mile behind. Their CO by mistake brought British artillery fire down on his right-hand company. Enemy in the wood on the rear right flank opened up with Spandaus. Stragglers panicked and brought back rumours of heavy casualties and of whole companies being overrun. Sgt George Schmitz, 1st Parachute Pioneer Engineer Battalion, wrote, 'Heavy machine-gun and small arms fire greeted the brave attackers who again suffered high losses. The dead and wounded lay in rows before the German position and the cries of the wounded were heard for the rest of the night.' Maj-Gen Kirkman was forced to order the green 168 Brigade to withdraw 1,000 yards back from the Fosso Bottaceto. Group Schmalz and 4th Parachute Regiment turned Highway 114 into a death-trap for the Northumbrians' advance on Catania.

The enemy defenders held the Bottaceto anti-tank ditch with offensive intent. Any visible movement by the Northumbrian Division was greeted with shelling or mortaring. Long-range guns fired with uncanny accuracy on the Primosole bridge and eventually destroyed it. Fortunately the engineers had constructed three other bridges so that troops and transports could get safely across the Simeto. The front was held by two brigades, with the third moved back in reserve near the coast to rest away from battle. Unfortunately malaria was rife, which caused 430 sick.

The defenders, 1st and 3rd Battalions of 4th Parachute Brigade and the Hermann Goering with their 88mm guns, self-propelleds (SPs) and *Nebelwerfers* had realised that their retreat was inevitable. Lt D.J. Fenner, 6th DLI, described it.

> 4 August. Several very big explosions took place behind the German lines. The bomb dumps on Catania airfield were being destroyed, a clear indication that they would be pulling back. While the XIII Corps to which 50th Division belonged remained on the defensive, XXX Corps had been active inland and was turning the German flank. On 4 August we followed 8th DLI in pursuit. We were harassed by enemy 88mm gunfire and *Nebelwerfers*. We passed our dead anti-tank gunners killed on 16 July. None of our dead had been buried by the Germans. In 50th Division we were most careful to bury all of our own and the German dead. Catania was entered. The locals were busy looting the stores and shops. The advance beyond Catania was most unpleasant. The road was narrow and either walled or fenced. For some reason we seldom pushed off the road or moved at night. Leading companies were ambushed frequently. Losses among officers were severe. The platoon officer would be with the point section, the Company Commander with the lead platoon. The ambush would get the lot. Machine guns, mortars and 88mm guns were all used. The company establishment was five officers. We had lost five and I was the only one left of those who landed with the company on 10 July.

The CO, Lt-Col Bill Robinson of 9th DLI, and his 2i/c were killed by mortar fire.

All bridges on the main roads were blown, the verges mined and often the whole cliff face blown away. The sappers incurred heavy casualties, had little rest and were always in demand. Bulldozers were essential, and, since most roads were rendered unfit for motor transport, mules were often used to carry vital loads. Day by day, against brilliant defensive little actions, the advance continued, Acireale, Acis Antonio, Mangano river, Leonardello river, Macchia river, Riposto (on the 12th), Giarre and Mascarello ridge. 231 (Malta) Brigade joined the Northumbrians with 1st Dorsets, 1st Hampshires and 2nd

Devons. They had served throughout the siege of Malta and landed in Operation Husky on D-Day. 168 Brigade at the end of the Sicilian campaign rejoined 56th (London) Division. The Malta Brigade promptly occupied Piedimonte and patrolled towards Linguaglossa. 69 Brigade occupied Taormina without opposition and 7th Green Howards had a fight to take the medieval castle of Capo San Allessio on the 15th. 5th East Yorkshires took passage in a small naval force to bypass Cape d'Ali and Northumbrian patrols entered Messina at 1000 hours on 17 August. The enemy had gone but Gen Patton's troops reckoned they had won the race by ten hours.

During Husky the division had 462 killed in action, 1,132 wounded and 545 missing. The killed included 125 lost at sea during the D-Day landings. Almost 9,000 enemy prisoners, mainly Italians, passed through the Divisional cages. The Germans, not the Italians, fought a brilliant campaign. Out of their 60,000 strength, they evacuated 40,000 to fight again on the Italian mainland, plus 13,500 wounded. They lost about 5,000 killed, 2,869 missing and 14,410 wounded. Altogether the Axis Forces withdrew 100,000 troops, together with fifty tanks and 17,000 tons of supplies and equipment. But the Allies had made their first successful European campaign.

Lt D.J. Fenner, 6th DLI, continues his story:

> On 30 August the 8th Army Commander visited in turn the three DLI Battalions. Monty addressed us in the bed of a dried-up river. He congratulated us and said we had fought long and hard under his command since Alamein back in October. We could now have a rest. Meanwhile the Army would be going over to Italy soon. If Monty ran into trouble there he would send for us, because, he said, 'I like to have 50th Division with me wherever I go.'

No fewer than sixty-eight military decorations were awarded to the division for Husky: 36 to 151 Brigade, 10 to 168 Brigade, 7 to 69 Brigade, 10 to the Artillery, 4 to the Sappers and 1 to the Royal Army Medical Corps. They included three DSOs and two DCMs. And of course several hundred Northumbrians lie buried in Syracuse and Catania War Cemeteries, silent witness to the ferocious fighting. Lt D.J. Fenner, 6th DLI, again: 'We started training hard to prepare for the next campaign. Early in October we heard the fabulous news that the 50th Division was to return to the UK. One day later in the month [23rd from Augusta] the whole Durham brigade embarked on the Dutch ship SS *Sibojak* and sailed for home. It was the only "wet" ship in the convoy and we got used to Dutch gin.' Sailing via Algiers, the convoy split up north of Ireland and the ships arrived on 5 November 1943 at Glasgow, Liverpool and Bristol. There are two memorials to the Northumbrian Division in Sicily. The English church in Taormina has a tablet, and there is another on a grey stone cairn by the side of the Catania road just north of Primosole bridge. The latter is in memory of the Durhams who lost their lives in the week-long battle against the German Parachute Division.

CHAPTER 10

Countdown to Operation Overlord

Capt Ewart Clay described the homecoming:

> The ships sailed into the Mersey Estuary early in the morning of 5 November and were guided by tugs to their berths in Liverpool. Mist hung over the river, a thin, penetrating rain brought a glisten to the rooftops of the city. As the ships tied up, US military police with spotless white gaiters and helmets patrolled the otherwise deserted docks and a hidden loud-speaker blared stirring music to welcome home the soldiers. The silent docks, and beyond them, the hum and clang of traffic and trams in the city bespoke a public indifference to the event. It felt strange. This was the moment the 50th Division had imagined times without number in the burning desert, in the oilfields of Iraq, Cyprus, in Sicily and half a dozen other countries during nearly three years – the moment of arrival in England. And now it had come with rain and mist, with no applause and no relatives, with a battered, busy city spread around us . . .

Special trains took the troops to East Anglia, with Divisional HQ at Chadacre Park near Bury St Edmunds, the DLI 151 Brigade near Sudbury, 69 Brigade around Thetford and 231 (Malta) Brigade nearby. Leave was immediately granted. It was abundantly clear that the 'Second Front' was imminent and that Gen Montgomery had insisted on bringing back his three trusted 'Desert Legions' – the Desert Rats, 7th Armoured; 50th Tyne-Tees/Northumbrian and 51st Highland Divisions. There was little doubt that all three would again be in the spearhead of the planned invasion of France, possibly as part of the follow-up forces. The veterans of the Eighth Army were confident that they had had more than their fair share of fighting, while seven infantry and three armoured divisions had been training and exercising for several years in the UK. There was a clear distinction between the colonels, brigadiers and generals who saw 'leading the charge' as a great honour, while privates, troopers and the platoon and troop sergeants and young leaders who actually put their lives on the line were understandably not at all thrilled at the prospect of meeting the Panzer Grenadiers again. Montgomery rightly also insisted on a five-division D-Day assault landing instead of the three originally planned by the Chief of Staff, Supreme Allied Commander (COSSAC). Two American and one

Canadian, of course, but who would Monty choose for the two British D-Day assault troops? He chose his 'own' division, 3rd British, and it must have been a toss-up between 50th and 51st divisions – on whom he could rely with utmost confidence. However, the decision was made and 50th Division was tasked with penetrating the beach defences between the hamlets of La Rivière and Le Hamel and then securing a bridgehead, including the town of Bayeux to the west and Saint Leger, a hill on the Caen–Bayeux road, to the east. 47 Royal Marine Commando came under command to capture the small harbour of Port-en-Bessin, and a fourth infantry formation – 56 Brigade – also joined 50th Division for the D-Day landing assault. It consisted of 2nd Gloucesters, 2nd Essex and 2nd South Wales Borderers. Also 8 Armoured Brigade, with its regiments of Sherman tanks and no fewer than seven field, anti-tank and light anti-aircraft regiments, was under direct command. 50th Division, with 38,000 troops, was going to be the largest Allied formation for Operation 'Overlord'.

Shortly after Christmas there was a change of leadership. Maj-Gen Kirkman was promoted to command XIII Corps and left for the Italian front, being succeeded by Maj-Gen D.A.H. Graham, CBE, DSO, MC. Brig F.Y.C. Knox, DSO, replaced Brig Cooke-Collis, a highly experienced soldier, who went to 49th Polar Bear Division to command a brigade.

Almost half the division were newcomers with little or no fighting experience. Lt-Col George Fanshawe, CO 86th Hertfordshire Yeomanry Field Regiment RA, part of 50th Division, wrote:

> In late 1943 we were told that we were to join 50th (Tyne & Tees) Division just back from Africa. So we met these terrific war heroes, the more cowardly of whom only had one MC – most of them had three! I don't think we had a medal between us all, so we all felt about one inch high. They were terrific and as I subsequently found on D-Day, worth every medal they had or could ever earn. They said 'We know all about Desert Warfare, but nothing about invasions, you teach us.' Well we didn't either, but after that to work with them was the greatest period of the Herts Yeo's war life so far.

Of course the landings on Sicily were not only unopposed but were in the main a shambles!

Pte Peter Cuerdon, 1st Hampshires, 231 Brigade, recalls:

> I joined 50th Division at the start of 1944, one of those unfortunates who was put into a replacement holding battalion. When we were put into 50th Division, I was terrified – absolutely petrified on arriving at 1st Bn Hampshires, they were first-class fighting men who had been in Sicily and North Africa, coming back to England specifically for this invasion. A lot of them were very highly trained men who knew their job. I was absolutely scared stiff. We practised attacks, landings, taken down to Ipswich on training exercises, off the boats, on the boats, then night exercises week after week. We were fired on with live ammunition. I think Monty was keen on that sort of thing . . .

Normandy bocage, brilliant defensive battlefield country.

All over Britain exercises were held – Duck 1, 2 and 3, Beaver, Fabius, Tiger and many others. COSSAC and Supreme HQ Allied Expeditionary Force knew that the invasion would take place in Normandy, where the countryside is almost unique. The 'bocage' is green, rural with small fields, high, thick hedges built on banks, many copses, small hills, winding lanes and few major roads. It is brilliant defensive battlefield country, ideal for snipers, ambushes, mines, booby traps and dedicated 'bazooka' teams. The defenders can infiltrate easily and the attackers will have few artillery observation points. However, the bocage is also poor tank country, and the Allied Armies would have a huge superiority in armour that could not be fully deployed. So the Desert Rats trained with their Shermans in the East Anglian flatlands. 50th Division knew very little about the difficulties of fighting in the bocage and in any case its immediate priority was preparing for a seaborne 'wet' landing against coastal defences. But one bonus for 69 and 231 Brigades (who would lead the assault) was two weeks' training in cooperation with Hobart's 'Funnies'. Gen Percy Hobart had created the 79th Armoured Division with tank-borne monsters to overcome artificial and natural obstacles: crabs or flail tanks to thrash a corridor through minefields (much better than the Scorpions used in North Africa); Army Vehicle Royal Engineers (AVRE) Churchill tanks with Petard mortars to destroy blockhouses; crocodile flame-throwers to belch fire on enemy positions; Churchill tanks with scissors carrying bridging material; Churchills carrying huge fascines for dropping into anti-tank ditches or bomb/shell craters. One secret weapon used on all five beaches, with on the whole great success, was the duplex drive (DD) amphibious Sherman gun tank, which could swim – preferably in a mild sea – at 4 or 5 knots. 150 DD tanks were deployed on D-Day, and they cleared the beaches either ahead of, or by mistake just behind, the leading infantry on four out of the five beaches. Brutal modern machinery would lead the way in the assault to blast a way through the coastline defences. Then each assault brigade went for combined operational training at the Combined Training Centre at Inverary and finally to the Weymouth–New Forest area for collective training with the Navy and RAF. Every vehicle had to be waterproofed so that they would not drown in six feet of water. Four full-scale brigade exercises took place in Studland Bay in April and May onto and in landing craft infantry, loading vehicles to a strict plan, exercises with support craft and bombarding ships.

The two self-propelled artillery regiments perfected the difficult techniques of firing their 25-pounders from moving ships, the 'run-in shoot' to put a barrage onto the shore defenders. The final rehearsal exercises took place in fine weather and a calm sea on 5 and 6 May. To the management at a very high level it was known that the German 716th Division occupied a series of strong-points defending Gold Beach, the most westerly of the British and Canadian objectives. It was a low-category formation and included many foreigners captured by the Germans and forced to serve the Third Reich. It had no transport and could fight only one battle – the defence of the beaches. Nevertheless it occupied a series of strong-points at tactically important points, such as beach exits, villages and hamlets on the coast. The gaps between them varied from 500 yards upwards. Beaches were covered by fire from heavy machine-guns, mortars, anti-tank guns and field guns of various calibres. Minefields and wire fences ran between the strong-points and Field Marshal Rommel had had many months to make the 'obvious' beaches a death trap with steel tetrahedra, stakes with mines attached, ramps and every devilish kind of obstacle. Behind the 716th Division was 352nd Infantry Division near Bayeux and 91st Infantry Division near Carentan. Of five armoured divisions stationed in France, only 21st Panzer was sited close enough to be a rapid reaction force to the Allied invaders. In the Gold sector allocated to 50th Division were three fortified villages, each garrisoned by an enemy company – La Rivière on the left and Le Hamel and Arromanches on the right. Each village had high, strong sea walls with a straight, reasonably hard road along the coastline. The beach was mainly sandy with low sand dunes but with occasional tricky patches of peat or clay. Behind the villages were areas of boggy swamp land.

Monty was a superb general and his public relations activities usually endeared him to his military audiences. He always arrived in a jeep wearing his black beret with a tank and an infantry badge on it. His confidence, authority, magnetism and sheer personality came over to everyone. Lt-Col George Fanshawe, Herts Yeomanry, wrote, 'After his visit, if Monty had said "Jump" I would have cleared the moon.' Lt Geoffrey Picot, 2 i/c the 1st Hampshires mortar platoon, recalled in his book *Accidental Warrior* how, early in 1944 at Long Melford, Monty addressed 1st Hampshires, 1st

Dorsets and 2nd Devons, each about 850 strong, drawn up on three sides of a square, from the bonnet of a jeep. 'The Second Front has already started. The softening-up process is being carried out by Bomber Command and USAAF. I have chosen specially the famous 50th Division to lead the invasion assault because of their experience and prowess.' Picot noted that each regiment had more than its normal complement of thirty-eight officers, obviously anticipating casualties. But CSM George Warters, 7th Green Howards, remembered:

> We were in the south of England on manoeuvres when Monty gathered us all together and gave us a nice speech about how we were going to have the great honour of being among the first troops ashore on D-Day. We didn't take to it very kindly, after three years of fighting we reckoned we'd done our fair whack, we thought we were coming back to be given a break, but Monty's way was to keep you going and going and going . . .

King George VI, Gen Eisenhower, Prime Minister Winston Churchill, Field Marshal Smuts, even the Minister of Labour, Ernest Bevan, visited the Northumbrian Division in the first six months of 1944.

The divisional plan of attack from left (east) to right (west) was for 69 Brigade (led by 5th East Yorkshires and 6th Green Howards) to capture the coastal village of La Rivière, with the reserve battalion, 7th Green Howards, advancing through the bridgehead to capture the enemy battery at Ver-sur-Mer, a mile and a half inland. Their beach was coded King Beach, and support would come from 86th Hertfordshire Yeomanry self-propelled 25-pounders and 4/7th Dragoon Guards DD tanks.

On their right 231 Brigade (led by 1st Hampshires and 1st Dorsets) had as objectives Le Hamel, Asnelles-sur-Mer, Arromanches, Tracy-sur-Mer and Manvieux, supported by 2nd Devonshires following up to take Ryes and Longues. They would land on Jig Beach, supported by 147th Field Regiment self-propelled 25-pounders and the DD tanks of the Sherwood Rangers. 50th Division had two follow-up formations – 56 Brigade behind 231 Brigade and 151 DLI Brigade behind 69 Brigade. 47 Royal Marine Commando would be tasked with the capture of the small fishing port of Port-en-Bessin.

The overall objectives for 50th Division were to link up with the American forces landing at Omaha Beach to the west, to advance inland to capture Bayeux, to secure the line of the Bayeux–Caen road and to link with the Canadians (who would land on Juno) six miles east of Bayeux. This would require a bridgehead some 10–12 miles in width and seven miles deep.

The British landing plan for each brigade front called for four landing craft tanks (LCTs) each carrying four DD tanks to be ashore at H-5 minutes, followed at H-Hour by four LCTs carrying the specialised armour (flails, Crocodiles and Petards with sappers to begin work on the beach obstacles). Then at H+7 came eight landing craft assaults (LCAs) with the two leading infantry companies. At H+20 another eight LCAs with two more infantry companies. At H+25 came two LCAs with the Beach Group. At H+3 armoured bulldozers and more specialised armour. At H+60 nine LCTs with self-propelled guns. At H+90 ten LCTs with a full squadron of tanks. The tenth wave carried more field and anti-tank guns and twenty-one amphibious DUKWs loaded with stores and ammunition.

Before H-Hour the RAF would bomb, and the Royal Navy battleships, cruisers and destroyers would shell the coastal defences, and rocket-firing craft would fling Canadian Mattress salvoes of rockets ashore.

During the last week in May all invasion troops were sealed in their invasion camps. Divisional HQ moved from London, to Chadacre, then to the New Forest area, lastly to Force G's HQ ship in Southampton docks. By the evening of 3 June the entire division was afloat, partly in the west Solent, partly lying alongside at Southampton docks.

Maj-Gen D.A.H. Graham, the GOC, sent a special D-Day message: 'The time is at hand to strike – to break the Western Wall and into the Continent of Europe. To you, officers and men of the 50th (Northumbrian) Division, has been given the great honour of being in the vanguard of this mighty blow for freedom.'

D-Day was postponed a day by Gen Eisenhower because of bad weather in the Channel. At 0730 hours on 5 June the first part of the great seaborne force began to sail towards Normandy, led by trawlers sweeping mine-free passages for the ships behind.

No fewer than 5,333 ships and landing craft were at sea supported by 9,210 aircraft. Overhead flew the brave Airborne Divisions, one British, two American, hoping to seize key objectives behind the enemy lines.

Overlord – Winston Churchill's Second Front – had started. In a broadcast to the French people on 2 October 1940 he declared:

> Remember we shall never stop, never weary, never give in. Our whole people and Empire have vowed to cleanse Europe from the Nazi pestilence and saving the World from the new Dark Ages. Good night then; sleep to gather strength for the morning. For the morning will come.

It came on 6 June 1944.

Triumph on Gold Beach: The Hollis Victoria Cross

A 15-knot wind whipped up waves four feet high and drove white breakers against the shore. Admiral Sir Philip Vian, Commander Eastern Task Force, which convoyed in the seaborne armada, Operation 'Neptune', noted: 'the weather on 6 June is unexpectedly severe for the launching of an operation of this type.' Small craft turned back. Raft-like 'Rhino' ferries for carrying motor transport broke their tow-lines. Most of the DD tanks landed behind or with their infantry (far better than lying thirty feet submerged and drowned). Most of the unfortunate infantry in their LCAs and LCIs were weak and afflicted by sickness, and cold and wet from waves splashing over the plunging bows. Pte Bowen, 5th East Yorkshires, wrote:

Gold Beach, D-Day, 6 June 1944. Waterproofed Bren-gun carriers of 50th Division coming through the surf.

> A high percentage of people, not everybody, was seasick. Yes, I was sick. The naval ratings advised, 'Whatever you do, don't do without food. If you're going to be sick, let your stomach have something to be sick on.' It was even worse when we got in the assault landing craft. We got down the netting on the side of the ship. The ship was rolling and the landing craft were bouncing right up in the air and back again, probably twenty feet, but certainly six to twelve feet. Quite a few men got hurt, mis-timed the jump, fell quite heavily and never got to shore at all.

So strong was the wind that the tide was being driven in-shore half an hour ahead of its proper time. Field Marshal Rommel had sited most of his guns in their casements and pillboxes to enfilade the beaches as at high tide, and rarely could fire out to sea. Thus it was crucial to make a landing at lowtide and get armour ahead to bear the brunt of the enfilading guns and machine guns. Beach engineers of 280th Field Company on 69 Brigade front and 73rd Field Company on 231 Brigade front had the horrible job of clearing the hundreds of deadly obstacles on the beaches, many of them visible, many nearly invisible underwater. Six officers and men were decorated with four MCs and two MMs for their bravery on D-Day mine clearance. Lt Richard Peard won the MC and was wounded three times. On his LCT were twenty-seven sappers and an AVRE Churchill with Petard mortar. 'Our plan was to clear a small gap wide enough for the Sherman flail tank [in the right-hand LCT] to go up the beach to clear a single path through the land mines, then the Churchill to follow and blast the sea wall.'

Unfortunately an 88mm anti-tank gun destroyed the AVRE Churchill and its crew of five. The flail tank then 'posted' a shell at close range through the slit of the German pillbox, firing twice to destroy the 88.

> My Sappers' task was to fix plastic high explosive on the centre of the hedgehogs [beach obstacle mines], prime them up, then stand with right hand raised. When all were ready, I blew a loud blast on my special whistle. They fired up and retreated to the water's edge, laid flat on the sand. A loud bang and the first row were gone. The bulldozer [on the left hand LCT] cleared the debris, then more mine clearance for a completely clear path.

280th Field Company cleared a 250-yard gap from low water to high water. There were thirty-eight sapper casualties on King Beach on D-Day. The beaches were raked by machine-gun fire and shelled by mortars.

The 69 Brigade assault on King Beach was led by 6th Green Howards under Lt-Col Robin Hastings (who won the DSO that day) landing 1,000 yards east beyond the German strongpoint at La Rivière and 5 East Yorkshires under Lt-Col G.W. White, a quarter of a mile to the west. The LCAs started their run-in about seven miles off shore. Brig Knox in the frigate HMS *Kingsmill* noted: 'The landmarks on the coast soon became obliterated by vast clouds of dust and smoke rising from the coastal belt. The terrific pounding from cruisers, destroyers and aircraft rose to a crescendo immediately before H-Hour. Very little enemy battery fire was directed at the larger ships offshore.'

Capt Robert Kiln, forward observation officer with the Hertfordshire Yeomanry SP 25-pounder regiment, reported:

> To our front is the small town of La Rivière with a solid stone sea wall 1,000 yards or so long, with stone houses behind it and the rows of buildings rising 50 feet above the sea. We can make out the German pill boxes and gun emplacements facing westwards and covering the beaches west of the town. To the west and right ahead of us the beach starts with low dunes behind stretching in an arc of 2½ to 3 miles. We can see the high ground at Le Hamel and Arromanches away to our right. Firstly, there is the Mont Fleury lighthouse and the Mont Fleury gun emplacements. Behind the hump of ground near Ver-sur-Mer, then Meauvaines and on to Le Hamel. All exactly as expected!

Kiln saw a smoke-screen drift across the beach at 0730 as the first craft touched down. Two AVREs and two LCTs carrying Royal Marine Centaur SPs were destroyed. 'At 0740 the LCAs on shore and infantry going up the beach following the AVREs and the flail tanks; mixed with them are the Shermans of 4/7th Dragoons. What a superb sight as they swarm up the beach. At 0750, twenty minutes after the first touchdown, the 7th Green Howards land and move off the beach to Ver-sur-Mer. At 0800 the 5th East Yorks take the Mont Fleury lighthouse position. Wonderful.'

Sgt Max Hearst of 5th East Yorks wrote, 'When we hit the beach it was door down, out and run like hell. I was the seventh man on the right hand side and was carrying the Bren.' Maj Harrison led the charge up the beach but got shot in his heel. Capt 'Chalky' White brought his platoon up to the safety of the sea wall, 'who went over it with a pistol and down he went. There was this bloody great gun firing, the RSM got on the backs of a couple of blokes and lobbed three or four grenades through the gun aperture and went through.'

The East Yorks had many casualties from hand grenades as they sheltered under the sea wall. 'When we eventually got up onto the top we advanced on our first objective, a gun emplacement and a tower used for observation.' The right-hand company advanced inland for 1,000 yards across a minefield and took the battery of Mont Fleury, badly damaged by the earlier bombardment. The German CO committed suicide and thirty of his men were taken prisoner. The left-hand company suffered heavily on the beaches from 88mm fire and many Spandau machine-guns. Many craft were damaged by mines on the run-in and the infantry were thrown out and shot in the sea. But amphibious Shermans and AVREs worked round the back of La Rivière and started to clear the houses. By 0900 forty-two more prisoners had been taken, and many German defenders killed, and the village was captured after two hours of street fighting. The battalion, only three companies strong, then reached Saint-Gabriel. Two MCs and four MMs were won by the East Yorkshires on D-Day. On the right flank of

50th Division infantry near Saint-Gabriel, D-Day, 6 June 1944.

King Beach, 6th Green Howards fought their way ashore, despite being landed several hundred yards west of their correct beach.

Maj Jackson led his men up the deserted beach. 'After about 200 yards we must have reached a German fixed line. Suddenly they threw everything at us. The mortars took us first and I was hit badly in the leg. My radio operator and policeman were both killed outright. The radio was intact. I helped troop movements for a bit and the waves of infantry passed me.' Jackson could not move. The tide came in and reached his chest before he was rescued. Before 1000 hours the Green Howards captured the Meuvaines ridge a mile inland, and by 1500 hours were on the high ground dominating Villiers-le-Sec, a mile north-west of Creuilly. CSM Stanley Hollis won the Northumbrian Division's fourth Victoria Cross. On the beach he picked up a Bren gun and silenced heavy fire from a fortified house. The powerful Mont Fleury battery was surrounded by strong concrete pillboxes. With a Sten gun and grenades Hollis killed or wounded the garrison of 16 or 17.

Later in the day near Crepon a field gun protected by Spandau teams caused the Green Howards casualties. Armed with a PIAT, then with a Sten, Hollis stormed into the enemy position 'and shot four of them. It was just a case of who ducked first.' Even later on, at a crossroads Hollis and his company were fired on by two Germans manning a Spandau dug-in at the foot of a tree. He threw a grenade at them, which failed to go off, but they

CSM Stanley Elton Hollis, VC, Gold Beach, Normandy, 6 June 1944.

ducked, 'and I ran in and shot them both dead'. It was an amazingly brave and violent series of actions! Besides Hollis's Victoria Cross, Lt-Col Hastings was awarded the DSO, CSM Calvert the DCM, and others four MCs and eight MMs.

The reserve battalion 7th Green Howards, led by Lt-Col Richardson, landed three-quarters of an hour after H-Hour and after some difficulty finding a suitable route inland captured the Ver-sur-Mer battery position smashed up by the pre-invasion bombardment, with fifty prisoners taken. Then it moved on Crepon, followed by 5th East Yorkshires and by 1500 hours had seized the bridge over the River Seulles at Creuilly. Despite strong opposition south of Creuilly, 7th Green Howards were directed on Coulombs two miles south-east. Brig Knox, who won a bar to his DSO on D-Day, launched a brigade attack that evening on Brecy. 6th Green Howards, 5th East Yorkshires, 2nd Cheshire machine-gunners and the 86th Herts Yeomanry SPs all combined well, and Brecy was cleared. 69 Brigade had advanced seven miles inland and was firmly established in the area of Brecy–Coulombs, with HQ in Saint-Gabriel.

231 Brigade's plan was to land on a 900-yard beach immediately east of Le Hamel known as Jig Beach, and then establish itself on high ground to the south overlooking Arromanches. This town was selected for the site of the Mulberry port, prefabricated in England and towed over to be assembled into an anchorage the size of Dover harbour.

The brigade's task was to capture Ryes, Arromanches and Longues (site of a powerful battery), while 47 Royal Marine Commando would capture Port-en-Bessin. 1st Dorset Regiment under Lt-Col E. Norie landed on the left of 1st Hampshires and fortunately was out of range of the Le Hamel defences. Within an hour of landing, despite five of the Sherwood Rangers' DD tanks 'drowning', the armoured support of AVREs from 82nd Assault Squadron RE and the flails of the Westminster Dragoons all combined to make a successful landing. The treacherous clay patches were 'matted', the mines cleared, the pillboxes smashed and the bomb craters filled. Pte Wiltshire, a mortar man with the Dorsets, wrote, 'I jumped from the LCA into about seven foot of water and had to jettison the base plate of my mortar which weighed 50 pounds. After wading ashore I made a dash across the sand to reach the bank. We managed to assemble only one mortar out of six.' Wiltshire then found the barrel full of sand and water. 'After seeing my friends killed and injured around me I thought it would be my turn soon. I got off the beach after two hours. The bloodshed was terrible and the Germans were tough fighters.' Within an hour the sappers and flails had cleared three exits, and the Dorsets with great dash moved inland towards Ryes. In the afternoon they took part in a combined assault, helped by the Westminster Dragoons' flail tanks using their guns and the Sherwood Rangers' DD tanks, plus 90th Field Regiment's 25-pounders, against elements of 352nd German Infantry Division. They were followed by 2nd

Devonshires, who came through to occupy Ryes two miles inland and then moved south to tackle the battery of four 155mm guns at Longues. The Dorsets were awarded twelve decorations for their D-Day fighting. The CO got the DSO and others won a DCM, three MCs and seven MMs. The Devons earned a DSO for their CO, Lt-Col Nevill, two MCs and six MMs.

1st Hampshires were on the right of the 231 Brigade front, with the task of capturing Le Hamel, and then working along the coast to capture Asnelles-sur-Mer, Arromanches and the defences of Tracy-sur-Mer and Manvieux. At about 0730 hours they arrived and waded ashore to find their AVRE and flail armoured support already in action. The Sherwood Rangers' DD tanks had three 'drowned' with others destroyed by mines or 88mm anti-tank fire; only four reached their rendezvous. L/Cpl R. Eastwood was on LCT No 886. 'About 100 yards from the water line, the ramp went down into 8–10 feet of water, the leading AVRE disappeared and drowned under the waves. Then all hell broke loose.' The LCT was hit by heavy calibre shells, disabled, turned sideways on, 'and started hitting beach obstacles and defences, exploding mines and fused shells. Through my periscope I saw the Hampshires assault infantry being cut down on the beach and numerous tanks ablaze.' Capt Ben Taylor RE wrote, 'The infantry were taking heavy casualties on the beach and had only reached the dunes. Maj Elphinstone [CO 82nd Assault Squadron RE] had been killed. I spotted Lt-Col Nelson Smith of the Hampshires, who though wounded was trying to get his men off the beach. Some Sappers appeared and with their help we cleared mines, and repaired a damaged AVRE. The MG and small arms fire was slowing down and the Hampshires were now in Le Hamel four hours late.' The RAF bombers and the Navy bombardment had missed the main Le Hamel defences, and withering fire from pillboxes and 88mm guns sited further inland ranged onto the infantry on the beaches. Deep minefields covered by enemy fire blocked all the beach exits. At 0900 hours two Hampshire companies went through a gap to the east of Le Hamel, attacked Asnelles from the rear and, helped by AVREs, captured the village. L/Sgt Scaife of 82nd Assault Squadron RE fired two Flying Dustbin bombards into a large fortified sanatorium on the clifftop, destroyed it, and took twenty prisoners. Another Petard was fired into the back door of a concrete pillbox. Sgt Scaife spent a busy afternoon destroying several machine-gun nests along the coastal ledge of Le Hamel. He was awarded the DCM and was then commissioned in the field. Not until 1700 hours was Le Hamel firmly in the hands of the Hampshires, and Arromanches was captured by 1830 hours. Twelve decorations were awarded: a DSO to Maj D.J. Warren, MC, four MCs and seven MMs. The Hampshires lost half their officers. The CO died of wounds, as did the 2 i/c; a further sixty-four were killed in action and 118 wounded – a third of the battalion.

47 Marine Commando landed at 1000 hours behind 231 Brigade, but seventy men were lost when three LCAs were sunk in the run-in. Their first action on the way to Port-en-Bessin cost them forty casualties, but they captured Escures at last light on D-Day. They spent D+1 street fighting in

Durham Light Infantry with Sherman tank support advance through Douet, 11 June 1944.

the well-defended fishing port, and by 0400 hours on 8 June, helped by troops of 2nd Devonshires, finally captured Port-en-Bessin. They suffered altogether 200 casualties but took 300 prisoners and seriously damaged several hundred German defenders.

Both reserve brigades were ashore by 1100 hours, and 56 Brigade sent patrols of 2nd Essex into Bayeux. 151 DLI Brigade had landed in exactly the right place, unlike in Sicily! By nightfall all three battalions were established south-east of Sommervieu, and each sent a mobile company towards Bayeux. The 6th DLI column started from Ver-sur-Mer under Maj Thomlinson, and after having dispersed enemy near Villers-le-Sec, reached Esquay-sur-Seulles by 2000 hours and dug in for the night at Esquay.

The Northumbrian Division was once again firmly lodged in a successful, hard-fought European bridgehead.

CHAPTER 12

Bloody Chaos in the Bocage Battles

On 7 June 50th Division occupied Bayeux and pushed forward more than three miles towards Tilly-sur-Seulles, Sully and Longues. In the Second Army plan for Overlord the little town of Villers-Bocage twenty miles south of the beaches was a key objective, being a junction of five important roads. Operation 'Perch' was designed for 7th Armoured Division supported by 50th Division to capture Villers-Bocage. Capt Ewart Clay described the scene.

> Standing sentinel above this little Norman town were hill features which were to become bywords in the 50th Division's campaign – Tracy Bocage to the west, Point 213 on a ridge two thousand yards long to the north-east and points 140 and 158 to the east. This country was true bocage. It was closer than any country in which the Division had ever fought before – steep hills, deep valleys, small fields and tall hedges, ditches and narrow twisting lanes were its characteristics. It was difficult country for tanks and nerve-racking country for infantry and called for a battle technique of its own.

Initially a mobile column under 8th Armoured Brigade, 1st Dorsets (in vehicles), 147th SP Field Regiment, 61st Reconnaissance Regiment, plus 2nd Cheshires and RE, concentrated at Brecy. Their objectives were to move south into the heart of the bocage over the Caen–Bayeux railway, to Le Haut d'Audrieu, Point 103, Saint-Pierre and Tilly-sur-Seulles, then due south on a main road to Villers. By nightfall on the 8th, an advance of 6,000 yards had been made to the bridges between Tilly and Saint-Pierre. 8th DLI now joined the column. A hornet's nest had been stirred up. 130th Panzer *Lehr* and 12th SS *Hitlerjugend* divisions had arrived in strength as part of Rommel's counter-attack plans to contain the Overlord bridgeheads. Gen Bayerlein's superb Panzer *Lehr* Division had lost 130 trucks, 84 self-propelled guns and five tanks to Allied air attacks in its ninety-mile drive from Chartres. Each Panzer division (21st, 12th SS and Panzer *Lehr*) had about 3,000 vehicles, mostly AFVs. 8th DLI quickly captured St Pierre under a barrage but lost many casualties. The enemy were holding Buceels, Cristot and Tilly.

In the gardens and streets of Saint-Pierre fierce close quarter fighting broke out. As the Germans withdrew, the Durhams hastily dug in under a stream of mortar bombs (*Minnenwerfer*) and Spandau fire. With Shermans

A DLI Company searching the ruins of Douet for enemy snipers, 11 June 1944.

of 24th Lancers for company, the night of 9/10 June was deceptively quiet. At 0615 the predictable counter-attack came in, and 'C' Company was overrun and 'A' and 'D' attacked. Pte Protano and L/Sgt Wallbanks with Bren and Piat helped deter the Panzer Grenadiers. For thirty-six hours the battle waged and 8th DLI lost twelve officers and 200 men in the titanic struggle. For a time 8th DLI was surrounded, and the Panzer *Lehr* attacked with Tiger tanks. 1st Dorsets dug in around Point 103. By midnight on the 11th the Panzers gave up for the time being. On 12 June, 5th East Yorkshires relieved the Dorsets, and 8th DLI was withdrawn to Brigade reserve south of Bayeux. They earned eight MMs and an MC for the St Pierre battle and 1st Dorsets three MMs. The main attack by the Desert Rats started on the 10th, and three days later, having captured Villers-Bocage, they sustained a bloody nose and 4th County of London Yeomanry were overrun.

During this time 6th and 7th Green Howards had been in action against a fortified radar and wireless station near Saint-Leger, Duoy-Sainte-Marguerite and Brouay and had linked up with the Canadian bridgehead. 56 Brigade was now under the command of 7th Armoured Division. On the

'B' Company, 2nd Cheshires, support 69 Brigade on the outskirts of Audrieu, still occupied by German snipers, 13 June 1944.

12th, 50th Division was ordered to hold the line from Point 103 to La Belle Epine, a three-mile front. Capt Ewart Clay wrote:

> Along the beaches and on their fringes was strewn the wreckage of the German defences and our landing craft and tanks, rusting memorials to the first encounters of the Normandy campaign. On the roads between the beaches and the British front lines, there crawled and stopped and started again, endless streams of lorries, tanks, armoured cars and jeeps. The sea was rough, the sun shone. The little roads disintegrated into dust. Every journey a nightmare of traffic jams, dust, heat and engine fumes.

For the next month terrible attritional fighting took place along the three-mile front, mainly against the experienced Panzer *Lehr* formations. Gen Montgomery's plan to keep the maximum pressure on Rommel's army to allow the Americans to capture Cherbourg was much criticised. Operations

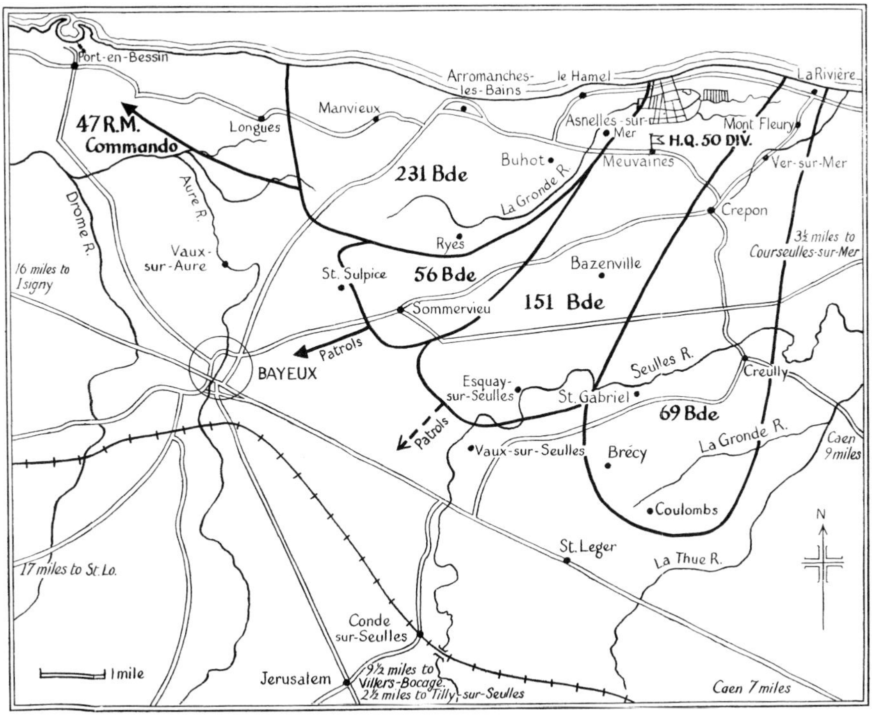

Operation Overlord, inland from Gold Beach.

'Epsom', 'Charnwood', 'Jupiter', 'Goodwood', 'Bluecoat', 'Totalise' and 'Tractable' – many of them directed to the capture of Caen – were successful in the sense that considerable casualties were suffered on both sides, for minimum territory gained. But, rather like Alamein, the 'crumbling' went on day by day. The Allies had total air superiority, tank numbers (if not quality), superb artillery power and coordination. Eventually the lethal Argentan–Falaise gap was closed. Meanwhile the 'Poor Bloody Infantry' (PBI) continued to suffer – 3rd British, 15th Scottish, 43rd Wessex, 49th Polar Bears, 51st Highland and particularly 50th Northumbrian divisions.

On 14 June there was a divisional attack by 151 Durham Brigade, to try to capture Lingèvres and Verrières; if this was successful, the plan was to move on to Hottot. 231 Brigade were tasked with the capture of La Senaudière, east of La Belle Épine. 69 Brigade was relieved by the Polar Bears Division and went back to the rest area near Condé-sur-Seulles. Bayeux, with its baths, wine bars and cafés, was much appreciated.

The RAF strafed the orchards and roads around Verrières, Lingèvres and Tilly, and 6th DLI set off across country at 1015. The previous day they had suffered 100 casualties advancing from Condé to the Hottot–Juvigny road. Capt Stephen Perry, FOO with 86th Field Regiment RA, wrote:

Sgt Trevor Ingram, 6 DLI 151 Brigade, wounded near Lingèvres, 14 June, has a cigarette at an RA post.

> By 0900 we are on the start line with 'A' Company, 6th DLI with the Company Commander, an enormous tough Spike Galloway, wearing the MC and Bar. The barrage starts and 120 guns pound the country in front of us unceasingly for half an hour but the infantry cannot keep up and the barrage rolls away. Now the fun starts, mortars, anti-tank guns, SP guns, Spandaus and rifles all open up on the infantry, advancing now over flat wheatfields. Galloway orders a halt. We bury our heads in the ground when the moaning minnies whine over. This really is a rough battle. Everything on earth seems to be landing in our fields. If we poke our noses above this corn the Spandaus in those farm buildings will knock us down like ninepines. We lie in the open for about half an hour while the Battalion CO [George Wood] sums up the situation. Then we get orders to advance. It seems suicide to stand up in the corn with a dozen Spandaus just in front ready to knock us down. The Spandaus open up and a dozen of our chaps go down. After 100 yards down again in the corn.

Galloway was wounded. The forward observative officer's wireless packed up and his carrier was shot up. Later,

> We are going into assault. The Durhams go like mad with the fixed bayonets into farm buildings. There are two 75s, three SP guns, a half track and seven Spandau positions dug into a sunken lane. Casualties are so heavy after the battle that two composite companies have to be formed from the whole battalion. But what magnificent troops these Durhams are. It was just sheer guts that got them into Verrières.

It took five hours of land fighting before the woods around the village were cleared. 6th DLI lost over 100 casualties on the 14th. 9th DLI on the right flank had an equally difficult time. The day before, a reconnaissance in force by 'B' Company had been disastrous, with all officers casualties. The main attack on the 14th was preceded by Typhoon fighter-bombers and a divisional artillery barrage. A large wood near Lingèvres lay astride the advance, crammed full of Panzer Grenadiers and Panther tanks. Although helped by 4/7th Dragoon Guards' Shermans, the bitter defence caused losses of twenty officers and 200 men – 9th DLI was torn apart. Its CO, Lt-Col Woods, was killed by a *Minnenwerfer* bomb. Many of the Dragoons' tanks were knocked out. But Lingèvres was captured by midday, and amazingly 'Sloppy' Harris with a 17-pounder Firefly knocked out five Panther tanks in and around the village. The enemy counter-attack came in at 1700 hours and the forward platoons were nearly surrounded. Typhoons with bombs and rockets helped ease the situation.

For its attack on the right, 231 Brigade was led by 1st Hampshires and 1st Dorsets, to advance from La Belle Epine to the crossroads and surrounding areas of the village of La Senaudière. The barrage came down on the Dorsets, inflicting heavy casualties. Lt Geoffrey Picot was in charge of the 3-inch mortar platoon of 1st Hampshires. His six weapons had a minimum range of 500 and a maximum of 3,000 yards. 'They were our own instant artillery, not particularly accurate, needing a large target such as a wood with a spread oval-shape of 50 yards wide, 100 yards in length. Our observation points needed to be very close to the front line and the wireless to work efficiently. Each mortar had a Bren-gun carrier with a crew, ammunition, the mortar, wireless and a line telephone set.' Picot's platoon sergeant was highly efficient; he organised guard duties, issued blankets and ordered digging of deep latrines and slit trenches for everyone in the platoon. The 'comp.' rations were adequate and breakfast was 'char', of course, with a complete hot meal, sausages and beans. Then stewed meat, carrots and potatoes for dinner, with rice or duff. Tea was biscuits, butter and jam. There was no bread but plenty of sweets, chocolate and ample tea. Picot's first battle was La Belle Épine and La Senaudière. 'One lesson of war. The enemy is not always in good shape. When you are unhappy, fearing an attack, perhaps so is he.' On the 14th the observation point's wireless did not work and five call messages could not be received. The Hampshires made several attacks that all failed.

The next day 69 Brigade moved from the Seulles sector to an assembly point north of Verrières for an attack on 16 June towards Hottot, a village on the Lingèvres–Tilly road. Again the Panzer *Lehr* caused casualties and few objectives were taken, but the line of the River Aure at Longraye was reached. Pte Tateson of 7th Green Howards wrote:

> Almost immediately we encountered strong opposition. There was an enemy 88mm gun firing directly down the road, which prevented vehicle movement. The two leading companies came under heavy fire and their commanders, Majs Bowley and Boyce were both killed . . . the sudden loss of these two officers had a terribly depressing effect on us all. We were in a very sombre mood. On coming under fire the men would go to ground in the standing crops. Our supporting tanks had no clear field of vision. On the morning of 18th morale was pretty low all round. The heavy casualties of the two previous days had a depressing effect on everyone. The dreaded moment comes, when after a few hours of rest, the word is given that we are to make another attack. Then the stomach sinks and a leaden feeling spreads throughout the body.

The Green Howards had lost fifteen officers and over 200 men. Lt-Col Richardson said that both officers and men were very tired and suffering from lack of sleep. The Panzer *Lehr* grenadiers launched heavy counter-attacks on the afternoon of 18 June against 5th East Yorkshires and 7th Green Howards, forcing them to withdraw westwards. Sgt Max Hearst with the East Yorkshires recalled:

> We took over from the Hampshires. As we marched in, everybody was in the open when mortar bombs began to drop on us. Blokes were hit by the dozen – mainly Hampshires. Sgt-Maj Bert Greener was hit. We'd started to dig in. There were casualties laid everywhere, blokes were pinned under fallen trees, others had been impaled and were screaming – it was bloody chaos.

Ptes Mountford and Tateson with 7th Green Howards were some of the dozens captured on the way to Cristot. 'We became hopelessly pinned down in a shallow ditch alongside a hedge which we had scrambled through, with what was left of two rifle companies. All the same nobody surrendered until our colonel did. After being disarmed we were marched past a line of Panzer tanks.' Tateson wrote: 'The psychological effect of being taken prisoner is an almost complete numbing of the senses. We were lined up with our hands on our heads by men with Schmeisser automatics.' Eventually Tilly – or rather the ruins of Tilly – was captured by 69 Brigade led by 6th DLI and 2nd Essex (from 56 Brigade). By last light on 18 June both battalions had seized segments of Tilly. Three field regiments laid down a barrage at the rate of 100 yards every five minutes, closely supported by tanks. A DLI officer noted:

> Tanks crashed through hedges, shooting into hedge junctions and giving magnificent support. The fire brought down on the enemy was simply terrific and he was well and truly blasted out of his positions. The forward companies had a magnificent day. They kept pace with the barrage. Battalion reached its objective

1 Dorsets, 231 Brigade, mine clearing in Tilly-sur-Seulles, 19 June 1944.

> by 1700 hours and dug-in, tanks and M-10 tank destroyers stayed with us on the ground, lying in wait for suspected enemy tanks. This was by far the most successful attack the battalion carried out during six days of heavy and continuous fighting. The perfect cooperation of artillery, tanks and infantry really showed what could be done.

And casualties for once had not been heavy.

But Hottot, a mile or so south-west of Tilly, was another matter. In pouring rain 231 Brigade attacked Hottot in the afternoon of 19 June. Lt Blackmore was with 1st Hampshires: 'No sign of the rain stopping after ten hours. Everyone is tired and wet. We have moved nearly a mile from La Senaudière, with Hottot another thousand yards ahead. We pushed forward under a heavy barrage, with our Brens fighting a staccato duel against the faster b-r-r-r-p of Jerry's Spandaus.' A sunken lane was well pinpointed by the enemy mortars. 'The place was decidedly too hot for comfort, so we climbed up the bank and dashed across the next field through a hail of mortar bombs and bullets, luckily without any casualties.' The Hampshires reached the village, but a counter-attack by Panther tanks drove them out. Later that day 2nd Devons forced their way back into the ruined village and were forced out again during the night. For nearly three weeks the exhausted Northumbrians and the equally exhausted Panzer *Lehr* accepted stalemate. Patrols on both sides probed. Everybody lived in slit trenches and kept clear of houses, which were frequently booby-trapped and were often

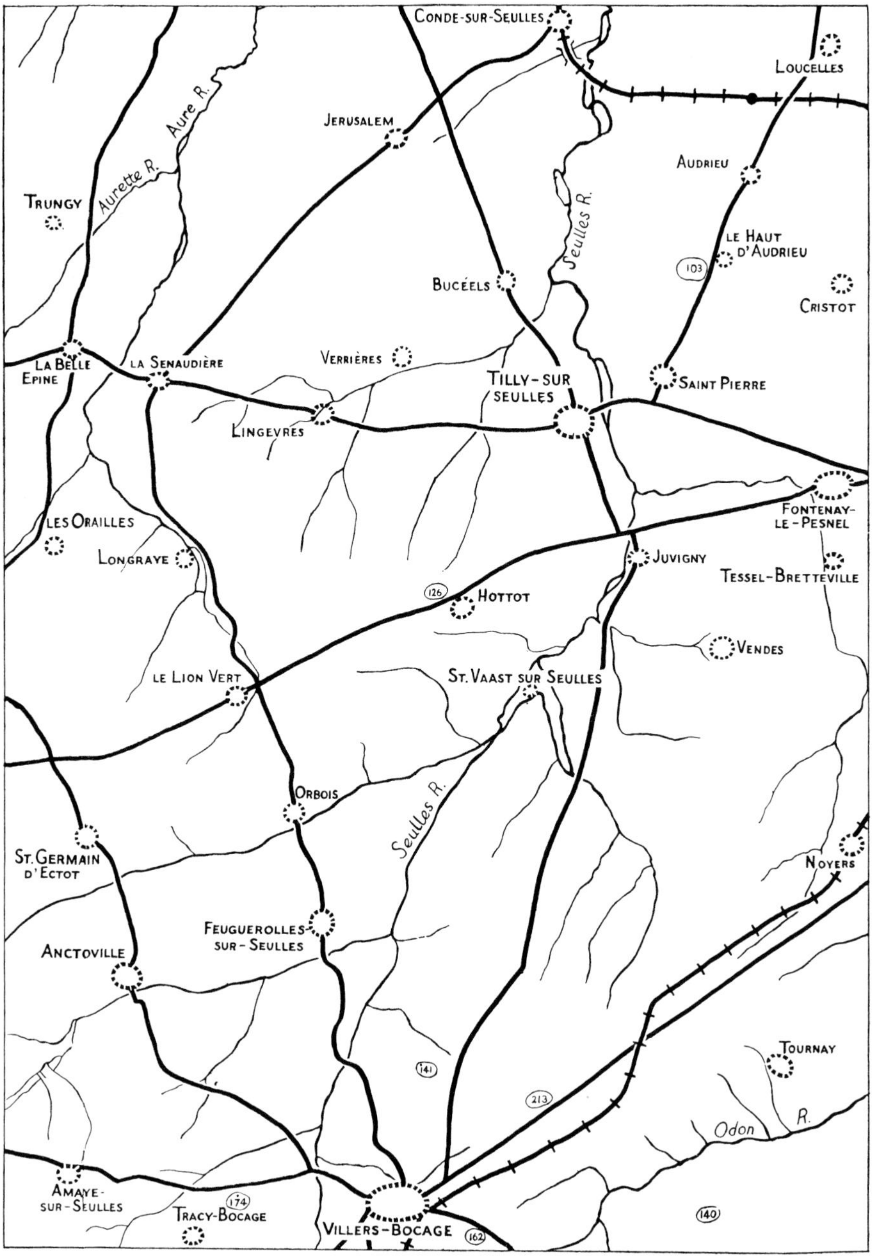

Ferocious bocage battles in Cristot, Tilly, Andrieu and Hottot.

enemy-registered mortar targets. Carrier platoons were dismounted and used as extra infantry. There was no major German tank activity, so anti-tank platoons had little to do. But battalion mortars put down harassing fire on most days on map targets. Bulldozers were used to clear the rotting carcasses of long-dead cows caught in the cross-fire. It was still a sniper's paradise in the bocage countryside. The division was disposed – 231 Brigade north of Hottot, 151 Brigade around Tilly and 69 Brigade south of La Belle Épine and La Senaudière.

Lt Geoffrey Picot disagreed with his fiery, abrasive CO, Lt-Col Howie. In the bocage country the small fields with high banks, many woods and copses meant that forward visibility was very limited, often down to fifty yards. Moreover there was no high ground for observation points to spot targets. The CO wanted mortar sergeants to be in the forefront of every rifle company and to be equipped with a wireless set each (which the enemy might easily spot). With tanks and artillery wireless networks in use, in wooded country the Hampshires' poor-quality wireless sets had a maximum range of 1,000 yards. Picot said that best results were by fire plans on map reference targets nominated by company or platoon commanders. Howie was a fierce, storming and confident commander and told his officers, 'This battalion *will* capture Hottot. We will hold it at all costs.' On 8 July 56 Brigade tried, advanced, was pinned down and counter-attacked. 2nd Essex bore the brunt of an attack by thirty Panzer *Lehr* Mk IV tanks. Three days later 231 Brigade tried again with the Sherwood Rangers' Sherman support, with 2nd Devons on the left and the Hampshires on the right. In addition, the huge barrage moving fifty yards every two minutes preceded flails, AVREs, mortars and Cheshire medium machine guns. A bitter battle was fought throughout the day. Initially the Devons made progress and six enemy tanks were knocked out, but the Panzer *Lehr* not only stopped them but forced the Devons back. It was a disaster. RAF Typhoons rocketed the Hampshires. The first and second attacks failed. The German shellfire was deadly and two company commanders were wounded. Lt Picot had two mortar sergeants wounded and two carriers written off.

Lt Blackmore described the action.

> We began the attack on Hottot at 0700 hours starting off with a hand-to-hand party [slang for fight] in the orchard. Then Jerry gave our 7 Platoon everything he had at point blank range. Pte Robins did a good job single-handed, charging with a Bren into a heavily defended post and silencing it. The enemy now began to surrender. Fourteen of them came out, several boys of about eighteen but fierce fighters for all that. I counted seven enemy dead in the orchard and several badly wounded. Then 'A' Company reached 'Orange', its first objective, under moderately heavy mortar fire. After we consolidated, all hell was let loose on us by mortars and 88mm shells for two or three hours, causing further casualties. We reached the outskirts of Hottot at about 1530 hours. Here we dug in. There were woods to our left and right and houses about 500 yards in front. Then at 1600 hours our Typhoons came over.

Gen Montgomery and Maj-Gen Graham, GOC 50th Division, with the officer group awarded decorations for the D-Day assault, 18 July 1944.

One rocket landed in the Hampshires' position. 'Then a Panther tank opened up on our right flank and moved towards us. A Typhoon spotted it and attacked. There was an ear splitting explosion and the Panther rocked sideways, halted abruptly while red and orange flames rapidly engulfed it and set fire to its ammo.' The Hampshires hung on grimly until nightfall. The CO, Lt-Col Howie, directed their final assault. 'He fought the enemy with a furious passion. His ambition was to die for King and Country and he did and won a posthumous DSO,' wrote Lt Picot. The Hampshires that day had 120 casualties, including 43 killed in action. The enemy launched several counter-attacks from the woods south of the Château de Cordillon that fell mainly on 1st Dorsets. However, quite a few Germans were taken prisoner.

A week later on 18 July, the Panzer *Lehr* abandoned Hottot, ruined beyond belief, heavily mined and booby-trapped, of course. 50th Division came out of the line on 22 July. By the end of July Gen Montgomery must have viewed the appalling casualties in his army with dismay.

Since D-Day 50th Division had had 69 officers and 604 ORs killed, 211 officers and 2,861 ORs wounded, 26 officers and 705 ORs missing or captured – a total of 4,476 casualties. 3rd British Division had suffered 7,100 casualties, including 904 killed in action, and 15th Scottish 5,354 casualties. The Wessex Wyverns and the Polar Bears had similar figures. Soon 59th Staffordshire Infantry Division was broken up and its survivors,

Gen Montgomery and Maj-Gen Graham, with NCO and other ranks awarded decorations for D-Day landing bravery, 18 July 1944.

plus heavy and light anti-aircraft gunners, sent as reinforcements to other infantry divisions. The Northumbrians had taken about 3,000 German prisoners, many from the Panzer *Lehr* Division.

Burying dead soldiers, the Padre of the Hampshires said:

> If the Christian religion means anything at all, it means that this is not the end of this soldier. We believe in the Christian religion; if we did not, we could not be giving him a burial such as this, and the Christian religion means that his soul and spirit live on; only his body stays in the earth. We cannot feel sorry for him, because he has gone to a better place than this. We can feel sorry for his family and the friends he has left behind, but for him, no.

Lt Geoffrey Picot reflected

> that many veterans were running out of courage. Most men have a finite amount of this commodity and it can get used up. The Germans had no such problem. All deserters were shot. Thus everybody stayed in the firing line. The average infantryman has fought in six major attacks without being hit, he knows he won't last another six. There is a feeling that sooner or later death catches up with you, but casualty and death are not synonymous. Three or four or five people are wounded and survive without permanent injury for everyone that is killed. Not nice to think that the best that can happen is to be wounded – get a 'Blighty'.

Operation Bluecoat and the Final Battles in Normandy

In the Arromanches rest camp there were tents over everyone's heads not groundsheets, canvas beds, latrines with seats to sit on, water on tap nearby, showers, hot baths, film shows, a NAAFI canteen, a library, horses for riding, swimming, games of various kinds. The sound of gunfire and of moaning Minnies had vanished. Of course regimental adjutants, RSMs and CSMs earned their pay by ordering smart parades. Pte Albert Carman joined 6th DLI from a Bayeux reinforcement holding unit. 'I'd read about 50th Division when they were fighting in North Africa when I was only 15 or 16. I never thought I'd be part of them. They were great lads, a lot of them were veterans. I felt quite honoured to be with such experienced people.' Every infantry battalion was constantly absorbing reinforcements, retraining them, fitting them in and encouraging them. Many of the veterans – not all – took the young rookies under their wing. The Hampshires welcomed thirty young Welshmen into their ranks!

50th Division had, in the battle for Tilly, helped destroy the Panzer *Lehr* Division. By 25 June it had lost 5,400 men and 160 officers and only 66 out of 190 tanks were fit for action. Gen Sepp Dietrich was able to keep his defensive line from breaking only by using sappers, signalmen, transport drivers and crews of knocked-out tanks and guns. He protested to Rommel, 'I am being bled white and am getting nowhere.' After the loss of Tilly-sur-Seulles, Dietrich warned the German Seventh Army HQ, 'If replacements do not come soon, the front cannot be held in the event of attack.' During the armoured battle of Goodwood, 18–22 July, Rommel was badly wounded at Sainte Foy and never came back to the front. In the same week the long-delayed plot to assassinate Hitler took place but miscarried. It was also the time when Gen Montgomery lost patience with two of his Desert Legions and fired their GOCs and a Corps Commander, Lt-Gen Bucknall. This happened during Operation 'Bluecoat', which started at the end of July. 50th Division was now part of XXX Corps under Lt-Gen Brian Horrocks, who had fought with Monty in the BEF and at Alamein. Horrocks's view of the Northumbrians was positive, 'good at patrolling, doggedness in battle and had a healthy contempt for enemy tanks'. The object of Bluecoat was for VIII Corps and XXX Corps, starting from Caumont, to seize Hills 361

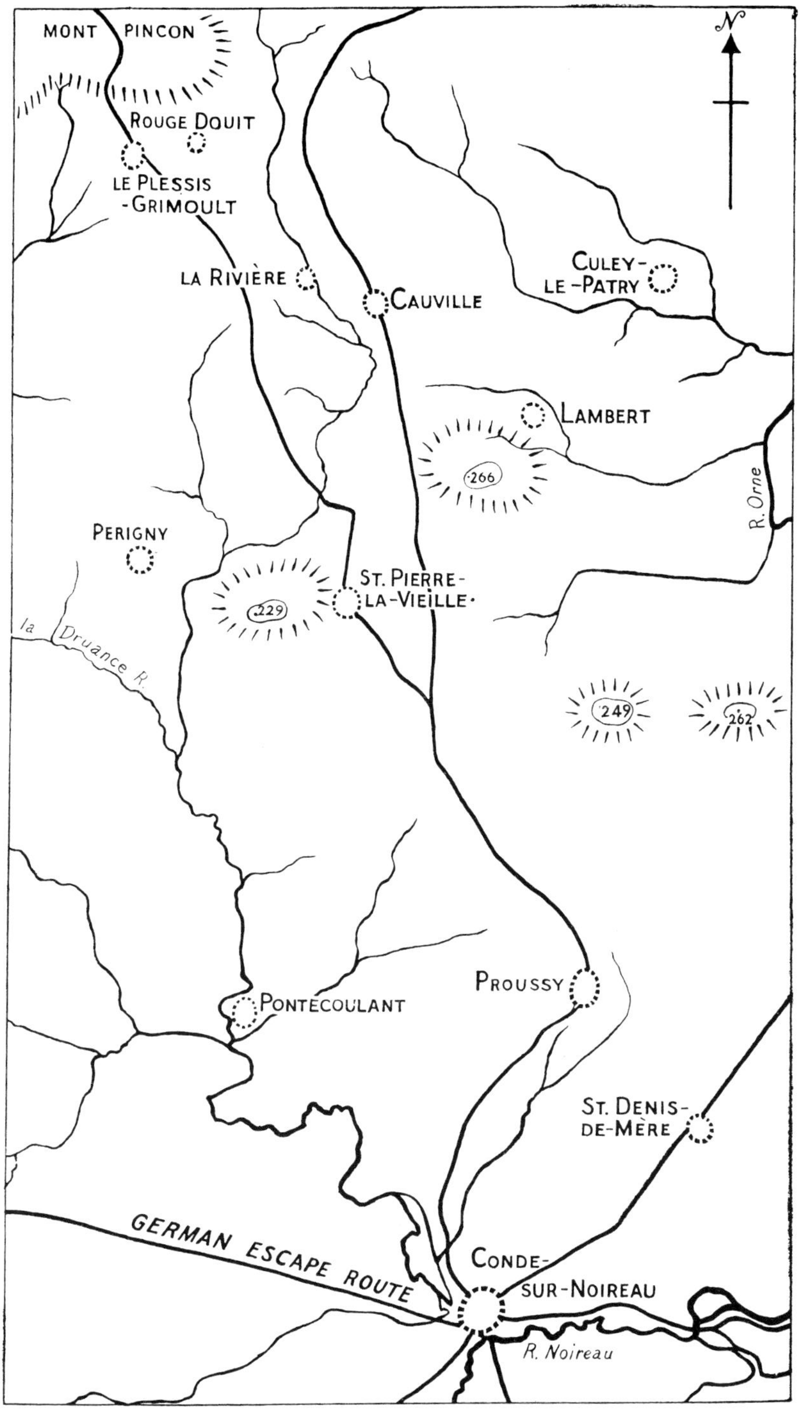

Operation Bluecoat and the final battles in Normandy.

and 309 (the western half of Mont Pinçon Ridge) and exploit towards Vire. Montgomery and Dempsey wanted to protect the American flank of Operation 'Cobra' as Patton was bursting through into Brittany. The German armoured divisions had to halt the three British armoured divisions in Bluecoat or Field Marshal von Kluge's army would be cut in half. 50th Divisions role was initially to capture the Amaye-sur-Seulles feature (three miles east of Caumont), then Saint-Pierre-la-Vielle and Villers-Bocage, and eventually to drive south to Condé-sur-Noireau. Between 30 July and 1 August, 56 and 231 Brigades fought their way onto the high ground of Anctoville and Feuguerolles-sur-Seulles, north-west of Villers-Bocage. The new CO of 1st Hampshires was Lt-Col Tony Turner, described by Lt Picot 'as a large man who wore a pullover with badges of rank, an MC, puffed a pipe and appeared to be slightly retiring'. His first action was the capture of the village of Anctoville. Picot had tested the working range of his radio sets. He sent his three mortar sergeants in different directions. They could hear and send at 800 and 600 yards. None worked at 1,000 yards. On 2 August 69 Brigade captured the Amaye feature and then 5th East Yorkshires took the village of Tracy-Bocage. Its CO, Lt-Col James, famous for his DSO earned at Mareth, was killed by a shell. Two days later a patrol from 1st Dorsets found Villers-Bocage empty. It had been smashed up by Lancaster bombing raids after the Desert Rat disaster. Sgt Moss and Cpl Boydell surveyed the scene of carnage. British and German tanks and vehicles, burned out and probably booby-trapped, littered the streets of the once pretty little Norman town. On 5 August the division was relieved and pulled out from the front line for three days, during which 13/18th Hussars and the Wessex Wyverns captured the vital Mont Pinçon, ten miles south of Villers-Bocage. From the top, Lt-Gen Horrocks could see for many miles in all directions and XXX Corps gunner observation officers – dozens of them – could now see actual, live targets rather than relying on map references. Towards the end of Bluecoat, 11th Armoured Division east of Vire had intercepted and destroyed the battlegroups of three Panzer divisions trying to reinforce the German 7th Army. Adolf Hitler personally ordered desperate counter-attacks to cut off Patton's troops marauding in Brittany. Avranches was attacked by the Luftwaffe and Mortain (south of Vire) recaptured. 50th Division came out of reserve to follow and mop up behind 7th Armoured in an advance south-east from Le Plessis Grimoult to Saint-Pierre-la-Vieille, Proussy, and into the key town of Condé-sur-Noireau to cut the main road, the enemy's northern line of withdrawal.

The divisional plan was for 151 DLI Brigade on 9 August to start from Le Plessis Grimault and advance four miles south to St Pierre-la-Vieille. Halfway there and 69 Brigade would then take the village and leapfrog again with the DLI. 9th DLI moved into Le Plessis Grimault, captured by the Wessex Wyverns, to be a firm base for 6th DLI and 8th DLI with tank support to start the advance south. The German rearguards fought with their usual skill and tenacity. Lt-Col Bob Lidwell, the CO of 8th

DLI, who had commanded since Mareth, was badly wounded. 'C' Company lost all its officers and many NCOs, so Capt Maier took command of a composite B–C Company. So with 8th DLI on the right, 6th DLI, supported by 13/18th Hussar tanks, fought its way in the face of artillery, mortar and Spandau fire to objectives two and a half miles north of Saint-Pierre. 8th DLI reckoned it was one of its most successful actions and captured 120 prisoners. Maj Ian English and CSM Iveson were outstanding that day.

69 Brigade took over the advance at 1400 hours, and 6th and 7th Green Howards made slow progress for another mile. Two hills, Point 229 on the west and Point 266 on the east, overlook Saint-Pierre. Then the road runs over higher ground to the north of Proussy and down into the valley at Condé. Lt-Col Robin Hastings, CO of 6th Green Howards, noted: 'The Germans came mainly from 12th SS *Hitlerjugend* and 130th Panzer *Lehr* Divisions, mainly young men who were prepared to die rather than surrender.' The plan for 10 August was for 5th East Yorkshires to continue the attack and capture Saint-Pierre and Point 229. Thick early morning mist helped the attackers, and thirty prisoners were taken, but both sides lost heavily and eventually the East Yorkshires were halted short of both objectives. The same thing happened next day on the 11th, when all three battalions of 231 Brigade tried and failed in the hot sunshine – but not altogether. The Hampshires were directed on Point 229 and Saint-Pierre, with 2nd Devons on the left. There were 600 German defenders in the village and dug in on the two hills. The Hampshires lost fourteen killed in action and fifty wounded. In the evening 1st Dorsets attacked and managed to bypass Saint-Pierre and regain the road to Condé. Meanwhile 9th DLI, under Lt-Col (later Field Marshal) John Mogg, was ordered to capture Points 249 and 262 to the south-east of Saint-Pierre, and by late afternoon he had succeeded. The DLI brigade was then pulled out of the line until 18 August. The Devons and Dorsets pushed further on the 12th and were two miles south of St Pierre before they encountered a ferocious counter-attack from a battalion of infantry backed by self-propelled guns, tanks and 125mm guns. Capt Ewart Clay described the battle:

> Just before last light the enemy attacked from west and south with Bn HQ as a target. HQ company held a 'thin red line' on a good reverse position and fought a spirited action for 2½ hours with cooks, batmen, orderly room staff joining in. A fierce fire fight ensued at ranges between 30 and 50 yards. A Dorset carrier was set on fire. The blaze silhouetted the enemy, many of whom were killed. 90th Field Regiment RA put down artillery fire which caused the enemy heavy casualties.

During the night of 12/13 August 7th Green Howards finally threw the German defenders out of Saint-Pierre. On 16 August Condé was taken. The Canadians entered Falaise and the Poles reached Trun. On the 19th the trap was closed; within the pocket formed by the towns of Falaise, Condé,

Flers and Argentan some 100,000 German troops were trapped. Adolf Hitler said, 'August 15th was the worst day of my life'; of the five German Corps Commanders still in the pocket, four got away to safety and twelve out of fifteen divisional commanders as well! They left 50,000 prisoners and another 10,000 dead. Nearly all their tanks and assault guns – about 500 – were captured or destroyed. 50th Division had done well. It had created a salient 12–15 miles in depth and 1–2 miles wide. Lt-Gen Brian Horrocks sent a message to the GOC, 'I cannot give you higher praise than by saying that the most experienced battle-fighting Division in the British Army has once more lived up to its high reputation. Well done 50th Division.'

Maj I.R. English, in his history of 8th DLI, wrote:

> The route of the Durham brigade took them through the area of the Falaise–Argentan pocket and each man was able to see for himself the havoc which the Allies had inflicted on the fleeing enemy. Both sides and often the middle of the road were jammed with wrecked lorries, guns, horses and tanks. Here and there a truck or gun limber, set on fire and smouldering. Abandoned staff cars and many vehicles were packed with loot, field glasses, typewriters, pistols and small arms by the hundred, cases of wine and boxes of ladies' clothing. It was a sight few who saw it will ever forget.

It was a battlefield that decided the fate of France.

CHAPTER 14

Break-out from Normandy: Singing *Tipperary*

Lt Geoffrey Picot, 1st Hampshires, believed 'the war would be over in a few weeks. Some of us thought we had already won it.' Picot and the Hampshire officers believed that 'the German soldier was always a hard worker. He dug deeper and more often than our chaps did. His defence works bore evidence of much hard work, the obstructions were numerous and substantial.' 231 Brigade spent a peaceful four days at rest in Flers. 50th Division was tasked with protecting the flank of 11th Armoured and mopping up behind and moved from Argentan on 22 August towards the Seine. 9th DLI was in Chambois, with 8th DLI sweeping the Forêt de Gouffern. The next day in Bourth Lt-Col Hugh Oldman, the new 8th DLI CO, addressed the villagers in French. A local band of four cornets played the Marseillaise and the Durham officers sang the National Anthem – unaccompanied!

After Normandy the GOC issued new tactics. Each battalion would travel behind an armoured force who would keep moving ahead, moving by bounds, waiting until the tanks had a lead of ten or twelve miles, then travelling that distance in one spell, then harbour up. The tactical duty was to mop up everything the armour left behind or bypassed and form a firm base behind them. The infantry battalions had about 130 vehicles, which, spaced forty yards apart, took up three miles of road. The riflemen were bundled into three-ton TCVs, lorries, Bren-gun carriers, jeeps, every possible vehicle. The section of Bren-gun carriers led, then the vanguard rifle company, Battalion HQ, then the three other rifle companies. The supporting arms were divided among the rifle companies and placed under their command. Strict orders were to travel at 12 m.p.h. 50th Division's route was L'Aigle, Verneuil, Saint-André and Pacy-sur-Eure. On 29 August it crossed the River Seine through the Wessex Wyvern bridgehead at Vernon, on the 30th it progressed via Crèvecoeur-le-Grand to Amiens. 9th DLI had two brisk mopping-up tasks at Beauvais and 8th DLI in Picquigny.

Isolated pockets of enemy sometimes fought, sometimes surrendered, sometimes hundreds at a time. Occasionally a bridge would have to be fought for or a wood cleared, which might cost casualties. Maj Mellor, 'B' Company 2nd Cheshires, with Cpl Evans and Pte Cotterill, found himself in a jeep in Fouilloy, near Beauvais. With the aid of three FFI (Free French Forces of the

1st Hampshires cross the River Seine at Vernon, 28 August 1944.

Interior) the three of them carried out a small war and ended up with 500 prisoners. Maj Martin, 'A' Company, took fifty-three prisoners near Doullens. The Cheshires were offered plums in Tournai, beer in Renaix, matches in Ninove and in other places tomatoes, cakes, nuts, flowers and fruit. The girls demanded kisses from 'Tommy'. At Le Bas, Sgt Lamb discovered the Cheshire side-drums hidden there in the 1940 retreat to Dunkirk. 61st Reconaissance Regiment sent its carrier troop under a sergeant to guard a bridge at Oudenarde on 4 September. An enemy column of 250 infantry, a Mark IV Special tank and three half-tracks approached the bridge. At seventy yards' range the carrier troop's anti-tank gun opened up and with four rounds destroyed all four enemy armoured vehicles. The action went on for seven hours. Sixty wounded enemy were collected. The remainder retired and were ambushed by a troop of 'C' Squadron. 6th DLI garrisoned Amiens after its daring capture by 11th Armoured, and the

Hampshires drove thirty-five miles to Arras to hold the town against counter-attack.

Lt Geoffrey Picot recalled the atmosphere:

> Old men wept for joy. Old men who had fought their war and won it a quarter of a century before and had lived through the shame and horror that had come to them. Outside one house a bearded man in shabby clothes stood rigidly to attention and at the salute as we passed by – as a military duty. On all faces were such expressions of thankfulness, joy as I had not seen anywhere before. I was confident that they would remember Britain with gratitude for the rest of their lives. For us also it was unforgettable. All the troops were deeply moved.

On 2 September 231 Brigade followed the Guards Armoured to Brussels, via Arras and Douai. Lt Picot 'didn't like the cobbled roads in Belgium; the carrier drivers and motorcycles skid.' He noted, 'the French sang the *Marseillaise*, the Belgians, *Tipperary*. The French shouted, "we are free" and the Belgians "welcome to our liberators".' They harboured at Enghien, via Ath. On the way two enemy tanks knocked out carriers and lorries and took petrol but left the food rations. 'In the evening in the plain ahead of us, I saw a large city of white gleaming buildings, Brussels.' 231 Brigade took part on 4–6 September in the ceremonial liberation forces parades. It was led by Maj-Gen Adair, GOC Guards Armoured Division, with the Household Cavalry armoured cars, Lt-Gen Horrocks, HQ staff, the 1st Belgian Brigade, units of Guards Armoured and a company of 1st Hampshires. Their mortar section was in the suburb of Duilbeck, some of them in a brewery. Hundreds of troops were teaching the Belgians to dance the Hokey-Cokey. They thought *Tipperary* was the British National Anthem. The champagne the liberators drank was marked '*pour le Wehrmacht*'. Rumours abounded. The war was over. Hitler had gone to Spain. Most of the Hampshires believed the war was over. 'It's on the wireless, isn't it.' The *Daily Mirror* and the *News Chronicle* implied the end of the war was imminent. Meanwhile 11th Armoured fought a smart little two-day battle to capture Antwerp and 231 Brigade was sent there to garrison the city, while 151 Durham Brigade garrisoned Brussels. Casualties for the month of August in 50th Division were 64 officers and 1,162 other ranks, mostly incurred in Bluecoat and the advance towards Condé-sur-Noireau.

CHAPTER 15

The Battle of the Gheel Bridgehead

On 7 September once more the real war started up again and the three brigades gathered from Antwerp and Brussels as the Germans cobbled together battlegroups to defend the Albert and Meuse–Escaut Canals. Montgomery knew that the Ruhr was vulnerable but had not the strength to take advantage. Antwerp port was not open and so there were acute logistical problems. His VIII Corps with two infantry divisions and the tank brigades was still grounded on the River Seine. Crerar's six Canadian divisions were still fighting bitter battles to capture or neutralise Hitler's fortresses guarding the Scheldt and thus denying access to Antwerp docks. XII Corps on the western flank was trying to contain the German 15th Army. So Gen Dempsey ordered Horrocks's XXX Corps to continue the advance from Belgium into Holland, with Guards Armoured moving on the axis Louvain–Diest–Eindhoven–Nijmegen and 11th Armoured moving out of Antwerp through Tilburg to s'Hertogenbosch. 50th Division was now ordered to force crossings over the Albert Canal, the last important water barrier before the Dutch frontier. The Germans had mustered about ten battalions to defend the crossings over the Albert Canal between Antwerp and Hasselt. Some of these were Luftwaffe Flak units, *Fleiger Ersatz* regiments, various Grenadier regiments and a considerable number of determined and experienced paratroops. The Guards Armoured Division's bridgehead at Beeringen was heavily counter-attacked by German paratroops. 11th Armoured was also switched to the Beeringen bridgehead. On the morning of 8 September 69 Brigade crossed the canal between Steelen and Herenthals, south-west of Gheel. The road bridge, of course, had been blown. The canal was about thirty yards wide with a very high, steep nearside bank. Lt-Col Exham's 6th Green Howards would cross first, with 7th Green Howards following. H-Hour was fixed for 0130 hours on 8 September. There were only two assault boats and twelve reconnaissance boats. Heavy rain fell (which was good), but the moon came out at midnight (which was bad).

Rather surprisingly the dawn found both battalions safely across; the sleepy defenders in Het Punt hamlet woke up and opened fire with mortars and machine guns. At dawn on the 9th 5th East Yorkshires arrived and went across the canal unopposed that evening. The enemy in Het Punt were now

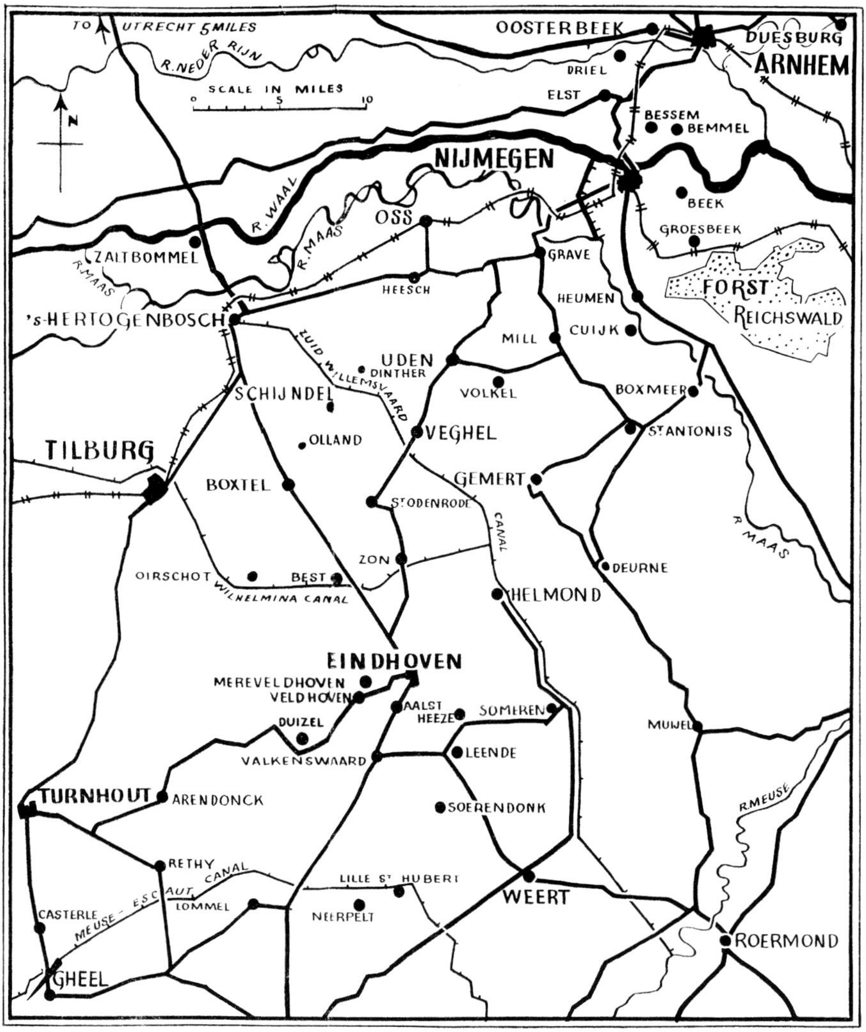

Final battles in Holland, winter 1944. Gheel and Best were particularly brutal.

rudely assaulted by Piat, 2-inch mortar, Bren and rifle fire. Lt Smith with ten men captured two officers and twenty other ranks and rescued some Green Howards who had been taken prisoner. Brig Knox's 69 Brigade had performed a difficult task; now Brig Gordon's 151 DLI brigade was tasked with enlarging the bridgehead and capturing Gheel. Near Steelen, 8th DLI crossed the canal late on the 8th; its 'A' company suffered heavily and its OC Maj Beattie was mortally wounded. The 2nd Cheshires deployed their MMGs and 3-inch mortars to great effect. 8th DLI, once across, was counter-attacked and lost twenty-nine casualties. During the night sappers built a new Class 9 folding bridge (suitable for carrying light vehicles), which allowed some of 61st Reconnaissance Regiment armoured cars to get across. Sapper Ron Sheather helped build the folding boat bridge over the Albert Canal.

> We made a recce to see where to build this bridge, about 100 yards to the left of the blown road bridge. There was a high flood bank to peep over to see the other side and estimate the width for the amount of materials needed. Next afternoon the bridge arrived. We began to unload it. The DLIs arrived with their assault boats for the crossing. The machine guns and mortars were ready to move. When it was dark we started to build it then the shelling started. But lucky for us they concentrated on where the old bridge had been blown. We finished the bridge and got the Recce cars and ambulances across before a shell hit the bridge. We got the damaged part out and rowed another raft out to replace it. Soon the ambulances were coming back [full] and a lot of prisoners walking back under escort.

As 7th DLI prepared to cross, shellfire destroyed the bridge. By 1100 hours it had been repaired and 6th DLI carriers and anti-tank guns crossed and helped take the village of Doornboom, 1,500 yards north of the Albert Canal. Lt-Col Green was now ordered to attack Gheel itself, about two miles ahead, behind a barrage and helped by tank support. 'A' company was partly over-run but was reorganised by Maj George Wood; 'B' Company was infiltrated and mortared before Maj Atkinson got things under control. Maj Ken Wood with 'D' Company and their big friends pressed on behind the barrage and reached Gheel.

Capt Winston Field, 6th DLI, was ordered to collect as many men as possible from 'A' Echelon and take them urgently to Gheel to reinforce 'C' Company, which was in danger of being overrun. Afterwards he wrote:

> If we were thankful to reach Gheel, Maj Ken Wood of 'D' Company was even more glad to see us. His men had been fighting against heavy odds in the fields in front of the town, across dykes, into the town and then from house to house inside the town and now they were being heavily counter-attacked by the enemy who were numerous enough to cut off odd parties and sections in the street fighting. We loaded the wounded into three carriers and sent 40 prisoners off with them right away – just in time – and that left one platoon, Company HQ and my extra men.

Many enemy dead littered the battlefield, and 6th DLI took 165 prisoners plus much equipment – at a cost! The CO was wounded and Maj George Wood took command. 9th DLI arrived in Steelen and took Winkelom, a village a mile south-east of Gheel. 8th DLI moved beyond Doornboom towards Gheel to support 9th DLI. 'A' Company was nearly overrun by enemy tanks. Their OC, Capt Ridealgh, was killed, and Sgt Self took command. 8th DLI reached Stokt by nightfall, helped by Sherwood Rangers' Shermans.

The regiments of young Luftwaffe ground troops and elements of 2nd Parachute Division (who had just arrived in lorries from Germany) were determined to retake Gheel and destroy the 50th Division bridgehead. Capt Ewart Clay wrote:

> During the period 8–12 September 151 DLI Brigade made and held a bridgehead on the right flank of the original one [which included Gheel, Winkelom, Stokt, Doornboom and Willaars, a triangle with each side of about 3,000 yards]. They did so in the face of the most determined opposition and at the cost of bitter fighting, which led to severe casualties for the Germans. The two German Air Force regiments always had a reputation for good fighting qualities and at Gheel they maintained their traditions until the Durham Light Infantry wore them down and finally disposed of them as fighting units.

Then the Germans brought up the 2nd Parachute Division to try to contain the bridgehead (a repeat of the savage battle at the Primosole bridge in Sicily – same opponents, same results). Early on the evening of 10 September the first enemy tanks appeared against 8th DLI and 9th DLI. One counter-attack came at dusk against 8th DLI, with 200 men and ten tanks determined to reach and smash the Sappers' bridge at Steelen. 'The night was one of confusion. The attack was a full-scale one on the brigade positions. Each battalion stood to all night and there was a good deal of mortaring and shelling. But neither side was willing to move while it was still dark. So the position remained confused and uncertain throughout the brigade area for the rest of the night,' wrote David Rissik, the DLI historian. Besides the divisional gunners, who were kept busy firing defensive fire tasks most of the time, the Sherwood Rangers (who lost many tanks to Panthers), the 2nd Cheshires' medium machine guns and mortars and the anti-tank battery of the Northumberland Hussars all played their part in the four-day battle. At one stage, 6th DLI in Gheel was completely cut off. It was probably the most awful battle the DLI had been involved in since D-Day in June.

On the evening of the 12th the DLI Brigade withdrew over the canal to Pael, three miles west of the Beeringen bridgehead, and 15th Scottish took over responsibility for the Gheel bridgehead. During September 50th Division incurred 918 casualties, mostly in the Gheel bridgehead, and took 2,300 prisoners. Shortly afterwards the shattered German forces pulled back from Gheel and retired over the Escaut Canal.

CHAPTER 16

Operation Market Garden and the End of the 50th

Between the two major canals – the Albert and the Meuse–Escaut – on the sandy heaths, small streams and swamps, the German battlegroups established themselves in strongly built villages, difficult to bypass, which controlled the few respectable roads. As at Gheel, the defenders mostly from parachute regiments and Luftwaffe units fought with great courage and skill. They were only dislodged when Allied bombers and massed artillery demolished the key defences and the PBI in house-to-house fighting winkled the defenders out. In addition to the two canals there were three major water obstacles between the Escaut and the eastern bank of the Rhine – the rivers Maas and Grave, the Waal at Nijmegen and the lower Rhine at Arnhem. For some time Montgomery had been seeking an opportunity to employ the Allied Airborne Army – the British 1st Airborne, the American 82nd and 101st Airborne Divisions. Gen Eisenhower had proposed in early September that the airborne divisions should be dropped in front of the First US Army to make a gap through the Siegfried line. Gen Omar Bradley was in no way enthusiastic, so Eisenhower then ordered Lt-Gen Brereton to operate in support of the Northern Group of Armies (that is, Montgomery's 21st Army Group) up to and including the crossing of the Rhine. Hence, the complex and extremely risky Operation 'Market Garden' planned for Sunday, 17 September.

The airborne troops would drop and would then seize the vital towns and crossing points at Eindhoven, Veghel, Grave, Nijmegen and Arnhem. XXX Corps, composed of Guards Armoured, 43rd Wessex Wyverns and 50th Northumbrian, would advance – effectively centred on one road from the Meuse–Escaut Canal to link up with the three airborne drops. VIII Corps on the right flank was not ready to attack and XII Corps on the left flank faced difficult, marshy country. 50th Division's tasks were to follow the Guards and the Wessex Wyverns as Corps reserve and eventually secure a crossing over the River Ijssel at Duesburg, twelve miles north-east of Arnhem, and then to secure the high ground of Arnhem. Lt-Gen Horrocks, GOC XXX Corps, gave all the senior officers an up-beat, optimistic speech about the forthcoming operation. At 1330 hours on 17 September 50th Division saw most of the gigantic air Armada pass overhead. No fewer than

1,240 fighters, 1,000 bombers and 1,500 aircraft (tugs and glider troop carriers, 500 to each airborne division) were flying in support of Market Garden. The division's field artillery and mortars of the Cheshire Regiment joined in the opening barrage. The ground attack started at 1435 hours, and, despite 'Division Walther' of five battalions defending the white concrete road to Eindhoven, the Irish Guards' Shermans reached Valkenswaard five miles south of Eindhoven by dusk. The 1st Dorsets and 2nd Devons were now called up to clear woods on the left of the Guards' advance. 'We went over the Escaut bridge to relieve the Irish Guards,' wrote Lt Picot, 1st Hampshires.

> The only operational maps were German with much more detail. We came across a German patrol of 12 men with bazookas stalking Sherman tanks. There was a lot of 'guns over the Rhine' optimism. But it was 65 miles from the Canal to Arnhem. There was a huge barrage in a semi-circle ahead of the advancing tanks. We saw men on parachutes dropping and Typhoon aircraft firing their rockets, and the Guards armour going over the main bridge 700 yards to our right, three vehicles abreast.

Early on the 18th the Dorsets took over Valkenswaard. Their CO became town governor and established liaison with PAN, the Dutch resistance. 9th DLI had to repel a counter-attack on the Escaut bridgehead. On the 19th the Guards advanced north through the bridgeheads at Zon, Vehgel and Grave and into Nijmegen. There it took two days of severe fighting before the town and its great bridge was cleared. On the 22nd 69 Brigade was in trouble when two battalions of Hermann Goering Parachute training troops and a regiment of tanks cut the main Corps centre-line near Uden, eight miles south of the bridge at Grave. The East Yorkshires in the north were separated from the Green Howards. Fortunately the divisional artillery and the 101st US Airborne troops fended off the German attackers, who next day repeated their incursion to Veghel. This time the artillery and Guards Armoured stood firm.

Sgt Max Hearst, 5th East Yorkshires wrote:

> We crossed the bridge and took over from the Yanks, our forward platoons were engaging Jerry. When we approached the bridge there was a lot of dead American Paras laid out [in Nijmegen]. Here we met the German storm-troopers, the death or glory boys, they were firing at our lads. One or two of our boys – good marksmen – were picking off these Germans. We dug in both sides and held the position for a number of days. Frogmen came up the river to blow the bridge but they were spotted in time and shot in the water.

Rations were short because of the road congestion. 69 Brigade was thus forced to eat captured German rations. There was an uproar – the jam tasted like rubber, the margarine was rancid and the regimental medical officers confirmed that the meat was bad! 151 DLI and 231 Brigades were ordered to move north and east of Eindhoven to guard the right flank;

Eindhoven had been badly damaged by allied bombers. The two brigades moved through Lieshout, Stiphout, Veghel to Boekel. On the Sunday 20 per cent of the troops could attend their padres' religious services – occasionally under fire. On the 26th the villages of Mill, St Hubert and St Agatha near the German border were occupied. On the same day a determined counter-attack by German forces, again at Veghel, was thrown back after two days' confused fighting. It was no wonder that the attempts to relieve the brave, beleaguered British Airborne in Arnhem were eventually doomed.

The exhausted survivors of 1st Airborne Division were arriving in Nijmegen on the afternoon of 26 September. It became even more important to retain the area on the north side of the River Waal as German infantry and tanks engaged at Arnhem were now freed for action against the Nijmegen bridgehead. The recapture of the bridge was the enemy's immediate objective. The whole of 50th Division was now tasked with guarding the bridge and bridgehead. The battleground between the Rivers Maas, Waal and Neder Rijn became known as 'the Island', an area of flat, rich pastures, mingled with orchards of apple and pear and criss-crossed by numerous canals and ditches. It was also overlooked by the high ground beyond Arnhem. The low-lying ground meant that it was difficult to dig a trench deeper than two feet without striking water. From 25 September for more than a week battles raged for possession of the little villages of Bemmel, Baal and Haalderen, and the woods between them. First of all 5th East Yorkshires captured Bemmel on the 25th, and the two Green Howards battalions tried on the 26th and 27th to take Haalderen, a village with factories whose tall chimneys made excellent observation points for the enemy. Panzer tanks and 88mm anti-tank guns dominated all the approaches. On the 28th the Luftwaffe in aggressive attacks tore a forty-foot gap in the Nijmegen railway bridge and frogmen damaged the main road bridge. The first serious German counter-attack came on 30 September on the East Yorkshires, with seventy tanks and the equivalent of an infantry divison. The rest of 69 Brigade and 5th Guards Brigade were holding the line, and another attack was put in on the Wessex Wyverns across the Neder Rijn. The intensity of the attack and defence can be judged by the fact that 124th Field Regiment RA fired a total of 12,500 25-pound shells during the action and 'B' Company of 2nd Cheshires 95,000 rounds of medium-machine-gun fire. Twelve enemy tanks infiltrated the 7th Green Howards' position, which they held with great difficulty from 0700 to 2300 hours, when the East Yorks relieved them. Squadrons of 13/18th Hussar tanks supported 69 Brigade most effectively. The GOC ordered 151 Durham and 231 Brigades up to relieve 69 Brigade.

On 4 October 8th DLI attacked towards Haalderen and 9th DLI towards Baal with the familiar barrage and close support from rocket-firing Typhoons. 8th DLI succeeded and took sixty prisoners, but 9th DLI encountered heavy Spandau fire and 'A' Company lost all its officers except Capt Thomson. By 1600 hours 100 prisoners had been captured, as well as many anti-tank guns, mortars and bazookas. 6th DLI moved forward to tackle a factory near Bemmel and for several days carried out fighting patrols. On 7 October the brigade moved back into Nijmegen for a few days rest. Lt-Col Hammer, CO of 6th DLI, commanded a bridge defence force of AA, anti-tank gunners, searchlights, DUKWs for river patrols, a field security section, a Dutch Civil Police section and four explosives experts. 231 Brigade was also tasked with straightening the line of Haalderen and Baal and clearing woods. During 4–5 October Lt Picot, 1st Hampshires, wrote, 'It was the first set-piece attack since St Pierre-La-Vielle in Normandy, with shelling and mortaring heavy on both sides. Although the attack was successful, the Hampshires had 22 men killed in action.'

For nearly two months static warfare was the regime on the Island. The forward troops rotated regularly. 1st Hampshires stayed in Bemmel for two weeks. Lt Geoffrey Picot found the ideal observation point for his mortar platoon in a ruined two-storey cottage in front of the infantry forward positions. He whispered instructions into his wireless set and brought down fire on all likely targets. Alexander Clifford, the *Daily Mail* journalist, visited and wrote an article giving reasons why and how the German army had recovered and was offering full resistance to the Allies and had again complete control of their formations. The great bridge at Nijmegen was under constant shellfire and journeys over it were made at full speed. A smokescreen was maintained over the river east of the bridge and at night searchlights shone across the water as daring underwater attacks were made by German frogmen. Divisional HQ was at Slijk-Ewick, and behind the lines sport of all kinds took place and the DLI regimental band from Brancepeth produced music for concerts, church parades and dances with the friendly Dutch families.

The 5th East Yorkshires were in Elst near a big jam factory. Leave was quite frequent to Brussels, Antwerp and Eindhoven. There were hot baths, visits to the theatre, cinema and ENSA variety shows. There was wonderful hospitality from the Dutch, and many lasting friendships were made. The casualties in the battles on the island in early October had been severe: almost 900 including 12 officers and 111 ORs killed in action, 30 officers and 611 ORs wounded and another 114 missing.

Early in November Field Marshal Montgomery made a speech to the division's officers in a cinema in Bourg Leopold. 50th Division – most of it anyway – would return to England as a training division for reinforcements. Python was a new scheme whereby veterans who had served for 3½ years or more overseas would be repatriated to England. Alternatively LILOP (Leave in Lieu of Python) would ensure generous leave instead. 59th Staffordshire Division had already been broken up, and now it was to be 50th Division's turn. There was a strong demand for reinforcements for other units. Since D-Day 50th Division had suffered total casualties of 488 officers and 6,932 ORs, but had also assimilated 358 officers and 8,019 ORs. Many of these reinforcements were soon posted to other formations. For instance, 1st

Hampshires sent 12 officers and 100 men back to the UK as instructors. Their normal fighting strength was 500–600. Since D-Day they had had 231 killed in action and 1,050 wounded. Field Marshal Montgomery stressed that it was unthinkable that a division with so fine a record should lose its identify, hence it would become a training divison. One exception was 9th DLI, which now joined the Desert Rats infantry brigade and fought with them to the end until the Berlin victory parades in May–June 1945.

In the corridors of power the Prime Minster fought to save 50th Division. It was too late. On 29 November the Division was relieved on the Island and moved back to concentrate in Belgium, and then the skeleton division returned to Yorkshire to train men of other arms as infantrymen.

After Operation Husky Montgomery wrote to Maj-Gen Kirkman, the GOC, 'One somehow never imagines that 50th Division can do otherwise than well and in this short campaign it has lived up to its best traditions.' He also wrote a splendid accolade to the stout-hearted Durham Light Infantry.

> Of all the infantry regiments in the British Army, the DLI was the one most closely associated with myself during the war. The DLI Brigade fought under my command from Alamein to Germany . . . It is a magnificent regiment. Steady as a rock in battle and absolutely reliable on all occasions. The fighting men of Durham are splendid soldiers; they excel in the hard-fought battle and they always stick it out to the end; they have gained their objectives and held their positions even when all their officers have been killed and conditions were almost unendurable.

Order of Battle, 50th (Northumbrian) Division

COMMANDS AND STAFF, 22 MAY 1944

GOC	Maj-Gen D.A.H. Graham, CBE, DSO, MC
ADC	Lt B. Henderson
GSO1	Lt-Col R.L.G. Charles
GSO2	Maj J.M. Dickenson
GSO3 (O)	Capt N.H. Golding
GSO3 (L)	Capt G. Mansell
GSO3 (CW)	Capt G.R. Aspin
GSO3 (L)	Capt R.J. Somerville
Intelligence Officer	Capt P.D. Crichton-Stuart
AA and QMG	Lt-Col T.J. Black
DAAG	Maj W.H.L. Urton, MBE
DAQMG	Maj I. McLeod
Staff Capt 'Q'	Capt J.G. Wood
ADMS	Col J. Melvin OBE, MC
DADMS	Maj R.L. MacPherson
ADOS	Lt-Col R.C. Gibb, OBE
Orderly Officer	Capt H.L. Thomson
APM	Maj C.F. Dunn
SCF	Revd J.W. Warner (CF, 3rd Class)
Camp Commandant	Capt A.A. Standley
Provost Company	Capt W.E. Hunter
Catering Adviser	Capt R.H. Nott
Liaison Officer	Lt J.C.B. Mant
Liaison Officer	Lt H.N. Meek
Liaison Officer	Lt A.R.B. Ellis
D/E Platoon	Lt R.S. Ball
FSS	Lt Hockliffe
Postal	S/Lt F. Calip
Field Cashier	Capt S.W. Beattie
Education Officer	Capt R.D.N. Tamblyn
Transport Officer	Lt D.C. Russell

56TH INFANTRY BRIGADE

Commander	Brig E.C. Pepper, OBE
Brigade Major	Maj L.B.B. Beuttler
GSO3	Capt J.C.R. Riley
Staff Capt	Capt A.G.L. King
Intelligence Officer	Capt R.T. Gilchrist

2ND BN THE ESSEX REGIMENT

Commanding Officer	Lt-Col J.F. Higson, MC
Second in Command	Maj C.G. Elliott
Adjutant	Capt J. Townrow

2ND BN THE GLOUCESTERSHIRE REGIMENT

Commanding Officer	Lt-Col D.W. Biddle
Second in Command	Maj J.O. Hopper
Adjutant	Capt R.C. Nash

2ND BN THE SOUTH WALES BORDERERS

Commanding Officer	Lt-Col R.W. Craddock, MBE
Second in Command	Maj F.F.S. Barlow
Adjutant	Capt K.V Coles

69TH INFANTRY BRIGADE

Commander	Brig F.Y.C. Knox, DSO
Brigade Major	Maj C.P.N. Parker
GSO3	Capt C.W. Mallinson
Staff Captain	Capt N.H. Nicholson
Intelligence Officer	Capt J.M.B. Isaac

5TH BN THE EAST YORKSHIRE REGIMENT

Commanding Officer	Lt-Col G.W. White, MBE
Second in Command	Maj J.H.F. Dixon
Adjutant	Capt T.G. Fenwick

6TH BN THE GREEN HOWARDS

Commanding Officer	Lt-Col R.H.W.S. Hastings, MC
Second in Command	Maj C.M. Hull
Adjutant	Capt G.S. Piper

7TH BN THE GREEN HOWARDS

Commanding Officer	Lt-Col P.H. Richardson
Second in Command	Maj H.A.R.D. Oldman, MC
Adjutant	Capt F.W.M. Underhay

151st INFANTRY BRIGADE

Commander	Brig R.H. Senior, DSO, TD
Brigade Major	Maj The Viscount Long
GSO3	Capt J.W. Thompson
Staff Captain	Capt R.R. Coddin
Intelligence Officer	Capt W.W. Teggin

6TH BN THE DURHAM LIGHT REGIMENT

Commanding Officer	Lt-Col A.E. Green
Second in Command	Maj G.L. Wood, MC
Adjutant	Capt R.S. Loveridge, MC

8TH BN THE DURHAM LIGHT REGIMENT

Commanding Officer	Lt-Col R.P. Lidwell, DSO
Second in Command	Maj A.H. Dunn
Adjutant	Capt J.C. Walker

9TH BN THE DURHAM LIGHT REGIMENT

Commanding Officer	Lt-Col H.R. Woods, DSO
Second in Command	Maj H.J. Mogg
Adjutant	Capt R.C. Rickett

231ST INFANTRY BRIGADE

Commander	Brig Sir A.B.G. Stanier, Bt, DSO, MC
Brigade Major	Maj I.A. Robertson
GSO3	Capt D. Montgomery
Staff Captain	Capt H.M. Johnson
Intelligence Officer	Capt K.S. Hollebone

1ST BN THE HAMPSHIRE REGIMENT

Commanding Officer	Lt-Col H.D. Smith, MC
Second in Command	Maj A.C.W. Martin, DSO
Adjutant	Capt F.H. Waters

1ST BN THE DORSETSHIRE REGIMENT

Commanding Officer	Lt-Col E.H.M. Norie, OBE
Second in Command	Maj A.E.C. Bredin
Adjutant	Capt L. Browne, MC

2ND BN THE DEVONSHIRE REGIMENT

Commanding Officer	Lt-Col C.A.R. Nevill, OBE
Second in Command	Maj G.B. Brown
Adjutant	Capt T.A. Holdsworth

61st RECONNAISSANCE REGIMENT
Commanding Officer Lt-Col Sir W.M. Mount, Bt, TD
Second in Command Maj P.H.A. Brownrigg
Adjutant Capt E.E. Mocatta

2ND BN THE CHESHIRE REGIMENT
Commanding Officer Lt-Col S.V. Keeling, DSO
Second in Command Maj H.R. Moon
Adjutant Capt L.J. Cutler

ROYAL ARTILLERY
Commander Brig C.H. Norton, DSO, OBE
Brigade Major Maj H.A.C. Dundas
Staff Captain Capt E.N. Briscomb
Intelligence Officer Capt N.S. Harrison

74TH FIELD REGIMENT
Commanding Officer Lt-Col H.W.W. Harris, DSO
Second in Command Maj E.N. Dawson
Adjutant Capt R.B. Hutt

86TH FIELD REGIMENT
Commanding Officer Lt-Col G.D. Fanshawe, OBE
Second in Command Maj J.B.M. Smith
Adjutant Capt P.R. Thornton

90TH FIELD REGIMENT
Commanding Officer Lt-Col I.G.S. Hardie
Second in Command Maj L.E. Murphy
Adjutant Capt M.E. Shepheard

124TH FIELD REGIMENT
Commanding Officer Lt-Col P.H. Gough
Second in Command Maj E.H. Colville
Adjutant Capt L.G. Heptinstall

147TH FIELD REGIMENT
Commanding Officer Lt-Col R.A. Phayre
Second in Command Maj C.V. Broke
Adjutant Capt P.W. Gee

102ND ANTI-TANK REGIMENT
Commanding Officer Lt-Col A.K. Matthews
Second in Command Maj D.J. Cowen
Adjutant Capt G.S. Spence

25TH LIGHT ANTI-AIRCRAFT REGIMENT
Commanding Officer Lt-Col G.G.O. Lyons, MBE
Second in Command Maj C.D.B. Campling
Adjutant Capt J.D. Johnson

ROYAL ENGINEERS
CRE Lt-Col R.L. Willott, DSO
Adjutant Capt P.G. Bishop
Intelligence Officer Lt R.L. Bolt

233RD FIELD COMPANY
Officer Commanding Maj J.R. Cave Browne
Second in Command Capt A.D. Campbell

295TH FIELD COMPANY
Officer Commanding Maj C.W. Wood
Second in Command Capt R.E. Sperling

505TH FIELD COMPANY
Officer Commanding Maj C.A.O.B. Compton, MC
Second in Command Capt W.L. Kent

15TH BRIDGING PLATOON
Officer Commanding Maj G. Sumner

ROYAL CORPS OF SIGNALS
Commanding Officer Lt-Col G.B. Sevenson
Second in Command Maj G. St L. King
Adjutant Capt J.E. Sergeant

ROYAL ARMY SERVICE CORPS
CRASC Lt-Col G.W. Fenton, MBE
Second in Command Maj D. Dalton, MBE
Adjutant Capt L. Panton

346 COMPANY
Officer Commanding Maj A.B. Belcher
Second in Command Capt J.B. Adams

508 COMPANY
Officer Commanding Maj V.H.J. Carpenter
Second in Command Capt J.E. Osborne

522 COMPANY
Officer Commanding Maj H.S. Butterworth, MC

524 COMPANY
Officer Commanding Maj L. Carrick
Second in Command Capt J.V. Marlow

ROYAL ARMY MEDICAL CORPS
149TH FIELD AMBULANCE
Commanding Officer Lt-Col S.R. Trick
Second in Command Maj O.G. Prosser

186TH FIELD AMBULANCE
Commanding Officer Lt-Col C.W. Arnot, OBE, MC
Second in Command Maj W.A.S. Gale

200TH FIELD AMBULANCE
Commanding Officer Lt-Col W.A. Robinson, OBE
Second in Command Maj M.N.S. Duncan

22ND FIELD HYGIENE SECTION
Officer Commanding Maj R.W. Elliott

47TH FIELD DRESSING STATION
Officer Commanding Maj J.M.C. Almond

The D-Day Tyne-Tees Miscellany

1. Maj George L. Wood, 6th Battalion Durham Light Infantry
2. Capt Donald Warrener, 7th Battalion Green Howards
3. Lt H.M. Irwin, RNVR, in charge of G2951 Flotilla on a LCA (HR)
4. Maj R.J.L. Jackson, 6th Battalion Green Howards
5. Lt Chris Bartley, RAMC
6. Company Sgt-Maj H.W. Bowers, 1st Battalion Hampshires
7. Pte Francis Williams, MM, 6th Battalion Green Howards
8. Pte Dennis Bowen, 5th Battalion East Yorkshires

1

Maj George L. Wood, 6th Battalion Durham Light Infantry

The men are in good spirits. They know now that the real party is on. They are fit and well, and have had little work to do in the past three days. To keep ourselves amused we have had ENSA concerts, cinema shows and, best of all, we ran our own unit sports which we thoroughly enjoyed and which did more to foster good comradeship than anything which I had seen for some time past.

We have had a visit from Anthony Eden. A most pleasant and cheerful man and a great personality. Shook hands with him. He was most interested in our past history, especially as he has a family connection with this Battalion. He walked round our camp. Very interesting to note how easily he conversed with the men. They all seemed to enjoy his conversation and are all smiles.

Our Brigade Commander talked to the men this morning. As he spoke, confident in manner, direct gaze, a little touch of humour and lastly, 'Good luck and God speed to every one of you', one could read in the faces of the men their admiration for him. Their complete trust in his leadership. Their growing confidence in this so-called Second Front. They know it will be successful. Monty said so. Their only doubt: 'I wonder how I shall come through all this?'

We marched out of our camp this morning [3 June] and embussed beside the gates. There is a small boy standing just outside the gate. He attracts the attention of all eyes. On his jersey he is wearing our Regimental and Divisional signs. On his chest is pinned the ribbon of the Africa Star with Eighth Army clasp. I find myself thinking whether any of our men felt as proud of their Africa Stars as this little boy so obviously does. If so, they certainly don't show it. But then they always hide their true feelings. It is not always easy to know what the men are thinking. However, they are all cheerful this morning. Smiling and whistling, waving and calling to the girls as they pass them en route for the docks. People gaze from their windows, stand on the pavement and wave. Somehow one has the feeling that they know 'this is it'. Some are very cheerful and shout 'Good luck, get it over quickly'. Others look sad, some silently weeping. Perhaps they have a husband, son or sweetheart whom they know will be on this move also.

My thoughts are very mixed. What a grand set of men. Hope we don't lose too many of the old faces this time. Already they've seen so much and done so much. They know what it's all about, what to expect, they've done it before. No false illusions. War is not a pleasant pastime, besides we cannot possibly hope for such an easy landing as we had in Sicily. The English countryside is at its best. So lovely. How long will it be before we see it again? I believe this thought is in everyone's mind. I wonder what my wife is doing at this moment? It's such a nice day, I expect she is taking the baby for a walk. Lord, how heavy and irksome this equipment feels. Christmas-tree order the troops call it. However we can't do without any of it, it's all essential. I suppose we will sail tonight. I have never been sea-sick before. Hope we have a smooth crossing.

2

Capt Donald Warrener, 7th Battalion Green Howards

Reveille 0325 on *Empire Lance.* Formed up in boat loads on 'C' deck listening to commentary on loud hailer from bridge and orders of the day from Gens Eisenhower and Montgomery. Lowered in our landing craft at 0500.

Awesome and inspiring sight of Allied fleet shooting with everything they had at the coastal defences, an umbrella of steel following the massive air bombardment by the Allies. The beach littered with casualties and beached landing craft from first wave, and a pall of dust and smoke making identification of targets difficult.

Our first objective, a heavy battery, surrendered after a few moments of gunfire. I led the battalion for the rest of the day.

Skirmishing in area of Crépon . . . light resistance and surrender after a brief firefight. We were ordered to make good a bridge north of Creuilly, but there was no opposition. The enemy had withdrawn.

Shot at in Creuilly by Winnipeg Rifles entering from the east who mistook us for enemy. We made friends and waited for the rest of the battalion to come up.

Sent off in lead, south. Skirmish around Fresné-le-Crotteur, where we were shelled by a supporting cruiser. Frantic signals stopped it after three salvos. By now we were so far forward we were being mistaken for the enemy!

On to south of Coulombs, a few hundred yards short of the Caen–Bayeux road and our D-Day objective. At 2200 hours we were ordered to dig in north of Coulombs for the night. It had been a very long day.

3

Lt H.M. Irwin, RNVR, in charge of G2591 Flotilla on an LCA (HR)

Our tiny open-decked boat with its crew of four butted into the Channel with sturdy purpose. It was dark, we were soaking wet and we hadn't eaten for 24 hours. There was a heavy swell and rough seas. In June 1944 the White Ensign was flying bravely from many a strange vessel that went on to perform sterling deeds, but the Landing Craft Assault Hedgerow was the smallest of its breed. It bristled with armaments including a Lewis gun. Our task was to get up to the enemy-held beach, then, irrespective of opposition, we would pull a switch and launch a barrage of spigot bombs on to the beach defences and detonate any mines, clear away entanglements and leave a safe gap through which troops, tanks and guns could be rushed ashore on Gold Beach, D-Day. Through that gap later that day the famed 50th Division, men of the East Yorks, Durham Light Infantry and the Green Howards would pour. Flak lit up the night sky. An aircraft was hit and slowly dropped to earth, a blazing ball of fire. Dawn came and my little fleet passed through the ranks of cruisers and battleships busy firing their guns at distant targets. Their crews lined the rails of their ships to cheer them [the flotilla] on. At D minus 1 minute I made my run in. My crew shut themselves in the engine room. I pulled down the cockpit and navigated through slits in the armour plate. The tide was rising. Just after 7 a.m. my friend Bruce Ashton in the adjacent boat was rammed by a following landing craft and went down. He and the entire crew were drowned. Then it was time. I pulled a switch. My spigot bombs lifted into the air and fell on the beach ahead exploding satisfactorily. I immediately pulled aside to make way for the following LCTs. I watched as one tank drove ashore and moved upwards, its mine-exploding flails whirring. Two mines exploded. Suddenly a tank exploded in smoke and flames as it took a direct hit from a German 88mm gun fired from an emplacement. There were no survivors. A second tank also took a direct hit. Then a third tank moved in and silenced the gun emplacement. Bullets were spattering our craft from a machine-gun post to the east of our landfall. Twenty minutes had elapsed since the first of the assault troops of the 5th Battalion East Yorks Regiment had landed and rushed – many of them to their death – up the beaches. They were met by machine-gun fire and shells and I watched, shocked as one man fell and then stumbled into cover never to move again. I was only 150 yards away from the infantry assault.

4

Maj R.J.L. Jackson, 6th Battalion Green Howards

Maj R.J.L. Jackson, 6th Battalion Green Howards, was one of the Beachmasters, the traffic controllers directing everyone, irrespective of rank, to their correct positions on arrival on Jig or King sections of Gold Beach.

The beach on arrival was apparently still deserted. The water was about a foot deep. One sergeant jumped too soon into the sea when the LCI hit a false bottom. He fell into eight foot of water, and with his heavy equipment sank like a stone and drowned. I advanced up the beach flanked by a radio operator and a Regimental Military Policeman with a Sten gun. After about 200 yards we reached a German fixed line of fire. Suddenly they threw everything at us. The mortars took us first. I was hit badly in the leg. My radio operator and the MP were killed outright by the same explosion. The radio was intact and for a while I helped troop movements. Two waves of infantry passed me by. After a time the field of fire receded. The tide came in, icy cold. Badly wounded, it seemed absurd to die in inches of water. An RMP sergeant from my home town saved me and carried me to a sand dune where I lay all day.

5

Lt Chris Bartley, RAMC

Chris Bartley was a young commissioned RAMC doctor attached to 1st Hampshires.

> We trained on the Isle of Wight with amphibious three-ton trucks (DUKWS). We learnt how to load them with stretchers bearing wounded and how to unload them efficiently. The vehicles could be driven down a beach into the sea and then swum out to mount the bow ramp, let down into the water, of a landing craft anchored off shore. It was an ingenious but hazardous procedure. However once safely aboard and unloaded the casualties could be simultaneously treated while in the process of being transported to base hospital.

Bartley's RAMC team travelled from Southampton Water in an American LST, a 'roll-on, roll-off' ferry with a lift to the upper deck.

> Deep at the rear of the cavernous LST was our theatre tent neatly concertina'd back against the rear wall, containing our main medical and surgical equipment. Including the American naval crew there were three hundred men – all from the 50th Division – due to land by Rhino float on to JIG Gold beach next to the village of Le Hamel at H+2 hours. Just before landing a naval chaplain celebrated Holy Communion on the foredeck. Dressed in a fluttering white surplice over his uniform he stood in front of two hundred armed men with landing craft heading for the shore line behind him as a back drop. The words, sometimes blown away by the wind so as to be inaudible, of the hallowed prayers of repentance, forgiveness, humble access and consecration were recited. Then the elements of bread and wine were shared out. I knew personally that I had made my peace with God at least for that day. I felt now that nothing really mattered. What had to be, just had to be and that was that.

And later:

> Now the casualties of war predominated, but for the most part had already been operated on at the beach dressing stations. Some of the worse cases went straight to the hospital ship anchored a mile or so out. Our work was mostly administering morphine, keeping drips going, renewing dressings and continuing the administration of sulphonamide and penicillin. This magic new drug, scarce in civilian practice, was now freely available to any who were wounded. Our own troops naturally tended to attract most of our attention, particularly those from the Hampshire Regiment who had been caught by a flame thrower and concealed machine gun as they were clearing Arromanches of enemy troops. The awful psychological shock of seeing their comrades die was as painful as their own burns and wounds. But all were astounded at the organisation and unbelievably gratified by the speed with which their needs had been attended to, and that they were safe.

6

Company Sgt-Maj H.W. Bowers, 1st Battalion Hampshires

My main concern when we landed was to get a nice pair of German boots because my own were killing me. The assault craft landed and we made a dash up the beach. Terrific fire was coming from our right flank, from a pillbox which we didn't know was there. We decided to attack it. At that moment a wireless message came through to the Company Commander to return and take over the remnants of the Battalion. He went off with a runner, leaving me and the wireless operator, who at that moment got killed, leaving me alone and not feeling too happy. It was impossible for me to attack the pillbox on my own and I tried to return to my original position. On the way I found the Commanding Officer badly wounded. He said, 'Hello Bowers, you still alive', I said 'Yes just about!' and explained the position to him. 'OK, you carry on.' I thought, Christ, he must think I can take on the whole German army!

Bowers edged through the wire and picked up a couple of naval commandos

who in their humorous way asked if they could come along for a bit of fun. We crawled through minefields, across a couple of fields, eliminating the Germans that were in the slit trenches there and eventually reached the sanatorium building, the end of which was the pill box. I put them into a firing position and crawled into the sanatorium and so on to the top of the pill box. The Germans immediately put out a white flag. I thought, to hell with you after all this trouble and slipped in a 36 Mills grenade. After the explosion they came out running with their hands up shouting 'Russkis'.

CSM Bowers was quite sure he would acquire some nice soft boots that they were wearing!

7

Pte Francis Williams, MM, 6th Battalion Green Howards

We moved forward all day losing men to snipers and booby traps. By then we had lost most of our NCOs and our three platoon commanders had all been killed or wounded. I would say that owing to the loss of officers and NCOs there were several of our lads that should have received decorations but didn't. One in particular was Pte Bernard Charles Elmer who was known as 'Before Christ' because of his initials. Charlie and I were both No 1 Bren-gunners and we were on our own going along a track with a thick hedge on one side and open ground on the other. We heard an artillery piece being fired and also the rattle of a couple of Spandaus. Not far away was the beginning of a wood. BC would work his way behind the enemy position. As soon as I saw him come into the open ground I was to open up and fire as fast as I could through the hedge.

Later,

> I fired three magazines into the enemy position. Charlie ran at them firing from the hip and they gave up very quickly. I scrambled through the hedge and joined up with Charlie. There were 5 or 6 dead, some wounded and eight prisoners, who we made to run back down the track towards the beach with their hands on their heads.

8

Pte Dennis Bowen, 5th Battalion East Yorkshires

Pte Dennis Bowen, 5th Battalion East Yorkshires, was aged 18 when 50th Division assaulted Gold Beach.

> We started heading in towards the beach. The naval barrage had started by then. It seemed as if every ship in the Channel were firing. The landing craft was flat bottomed and it was lifting up in the air and banging down. Everybody was spewing over everybody else. The run-in took about an hour. As we got close to the beach, the ramp went down. I was near the front and ran off down the ramp, like a little gang-plank, and started to scoot-up the beach. I looked back and saw the LCA was going backwards. On the little piece of beach there was a road built on top of the sea wall and we all ran up and got close up underneath the edge of that. There were lots of explosions on the beach and quite a few casualties, though it was difficult to say how many men were dead, how many were wounded and how many were just there because they thought the best thing to do was just to get down into the sand. There was a tank burning which they exploded – just a continual roar of sound. There was no individual sound of bang-bang-bang, it was a roar whether it was us firing at Jerry, or Jerry firing at us, I don't know. There was lots of smoke and dust and it was hot even though the sun hadn't come up properly, because we had loads and loads of equipment. Everything was stuffed in your pockets in addition to what we'd got in our battle order and anybody who could have grabbed extra rations had done so. So everybody was covered in sweat and of course steel helmets always make you sweat. Of the thirty men in our platoon, perhaps twenty-five had got up and under this wall. I was exhausted, hot, tired, worried, eager for it all to be over, but I don't think I was frightened. Your heart is pounding like mad of course and you're hoping and hoping that you won't get hurt, but I wasn't frightened.
>
> The tide started to come in so it was imperative that we got off the beach, and some laddie, a private soldier, jumped up on top of the wall with his Sten gun and said, 'Look, come on you lot, get over this wall, get over it.' So we got up, over onto the road and ran like mad across this marsh, wet land on the other side. As I ran across I heard rounds flying off the tarmacadam and I presume Jerry had a fixed line on it. It wasn't our stuff. Jerry must have had a fixed line on it. It was stuff coming in from Jerry. I could hear ricochets coming off the road and whining across the beach and a lot of men were going down. I could hear Sgt Mayhew shouting, 'Keep going, keep going.' We got right across the marsh into some houses on the other side and dug-in in the gardens. The civilians in the house, French, only spoke French and we only spoke English.

PART 2
15TH SCOTTISH DIVISION

CHAPTER 1

The Scottish Lion

15th Scottish Division was formed in the First World War and fought in many battles on the Western Front. These included Loos (September 1915), the Somme (August 1916), Arras (April 1917), Ypres (1917 and March 1918) and on the Marne–Buzancy (July 1918), where the French 17th Division erected a monument in homage to the Scottish Division. A Territorial Army formation, it was reborn on 2 September 1939 at the instigation of the Secretary of State for War, Mr Hore Belisha. Its 'parent' was 52nd Lowland Division, which initially provided three infantry brigade majors, the Divisional Commander, Maj-Gen R. Le Fanu, and the CRA, Brig John Scott. Divisional HQ, and that of 46 (Highland Light Infantry) Brigade, was in Glasgow. 45 Infantry Brigade was in and around Hamilton and in Ayrshire. 44 Lowland Brigade was in the Lothians and the Border Counties. In the first winter the Divisional Concert Party, the 'Tam O' Shanters', was formed, recruited from artists serving in the division. After the Norwegian debacle followed by Hitler's invasion of the Low Countries, the division moved by rail and road across the Border and was stationed in England for the next four years. Brig 'Tiny' Barber took command of 46 Brigade in the autumn of 1941, and served, and later led, 15th Division until its disbandment in 1946. But once the threat of invasion had receded after the aerial Battle of Britain, the division suffered a near-mortal blow, when it was downgraded to 'Lower Establishment'. Units were bled white to provide drafts of officers and men for the overseas campaigns in North Africa and the Far East. Retrenchment took place in Northumberland. 45 Brigade left and was replaced by 6 Guards Tank Brigade. In April 1943 the division became part of I Corps and was upgraded to 'Higher Establishment'. Soon the final shape started to take place. 227 Infantry Brigade, an all-Highland formation, joined with 10th Highland Light Infantry, 2nd Gordons and 2nd Argylls. Transfer to VIII Corps, which had two armoured divisions, Guards and 11th Black Bull, ensured a vital role as a 'break-out' corps in the imminent invasion of Europe. The new GOC was Maj-Gen G.H.A. MacMillan, and training and exercises were stepped up in intensity: Cheviot, Brasso, Blackcock, Glaxo, Peter, Heretic, Oyster 1, Clansman, Tally-Ho, Eagle, Thrust, Scot and Tatler. All these exercises took place in Yorkshire.

15th Scottish Division senior officers at Exercise Peter, York, December 1943.

Clearance of minefields and assault of river crossings were key features. VIPs visited, including the King and Queen with Princess Elizabeth, then Winston Churchill, Lt-Gen Sir Richard O'Connor (the Corps Commander) and in particular Gen Sir Bernard Montgomery, Commander of the British 21st Army Group (radiating total confidence).

Early in 1944 'Monty' was the most famous commander in the British Army. His triumphs in North Africa – Wadi Halfa, Alamein, Tripoli, Medenine, Mareth line, Tunis – Sicily and southern Italy had transformed morale. He had brought back to the UK his three Desert Legions – the Desert Rats (7th Armoured), 50th Tyne-Tees Northumbrian and 51st Highland Divisions. But waiting in the wings, with years of training and exercises, were the 'virgin' untested divisions: 3rd British, 43rd Wessex Wyverns, 49th Polar Bears, 52nd Lowland, 53rd Welsh, 59th Staffords, 11th and Guards Armoured, and, of course, 15th Scottish. Robert Woollcombe, a young officer in 6th Battalion King's Own Scottish Borderers (44 Lowland Brigade), describes Monty's visit:

> The Brigade were drawn up [in a Yorkshire town] in three sides of a square. The Royals – First of Foot [8th Royal Scots] forming the right flank battalion, the Fusiliers [6th Royal Scots Fusiliers] the centre battalion, with the massed pipes and drums in the rear of them [they had just played the familiar lilt of 'Pibroch of Donhuil Dhu' (The Gathering of the Clans)], and we the left-hand battalion. In the centre of the square stood a jeep and upon its bonnet, on a stand, was a microphone. After the inspection, ranks were to be broken and all were to gather round this vehicle and listen to the address . . . it was a crisp, sunny March afternoon with a hint of spring behind it. The assembled ranks in bonnets, Tam O' Shanters with their gleaming cap-badges, and clean, sharply pressed and sun-splashed battledresses, waited.

Brig Douglas Money called the 3,000 troops of the Lowland Brigade to attention, then the Slope Arms and finally General Salute, Present Arms. The pipes and drums broke into the first four bars of 'Scotland the Brave'.

Woollcombe described Montgomery: 'To every hundred pairs of eyes, there were his to pierce back – they were the most arresting feature of him, the eyes. They dominated. Piercing grey eyes with a touch of blue . . . leaving an impression of shrewd, cold clarity . . . with the eyes and the lean, beaky face and that tense spare figure, he seemed to be willing some part of himself into these, his unknown soldiers.'

The drowsy gay grief of the 'Skye Boat Song' in slow march time from the massed pipe bands of the three battalions and the slow, punctuating roll of the drums. Montgomery was in the midst of a Grand Military Tour of all of his invasion troops and his message was probably the same to all of them.

> In 1940 I was pushed back into the sea [at Dunkirk] . . . Didn't like it . . . But a lot has happened since then, Alamein, Tripoli, Tunis . . . Enemy pushed back into the sea . . . Four hundred miles up Italy . . . Some people say the Italian Campaign slow – four hundred miles in four months fast enough for him! . . . RAF now blasting West Wall to pieces . . . Then we go over to mop up what's left . . . Simple – quite simple . . . All that's needed is confidence . . . Must have our confidence . . . Must have confidence in us . . . confidence . . . Quite simple . . .

Woollcombe described Monty's inspection:

> Col Ben [Shillington] escorted him through the battalion. His slow approach down the lane. The highly polished thick-soled brown shoes; the buff-coloured canvas trousers: battledress blouse with a startling number of medal ribbons. The face, bronzed and lined and older than you had imagined. The deep lines formed on either side of a fiercely willed mouth. The thin stern lips and scanty greying hair at the temples. The beret with its two badges [infantry and tanks].

This was the general who was destined to order 15th Scottish to make dangerous assault crossings over four major water obstacles, across the River Seine, the Escaut Canal, the mighty Rhine and Elbe rivers on the way to the Baltic. Little did they know at the time, those 3,000 young soldiers (average age 25), that they would be in action for 325 days and their division would suffer nearly 12,000 casualties in the process.

The next month, April, the division moved south to the Worthing area in Sussex and the tanks of Guards Armoured Division harboured in and around Brighton. A strange, tense but happy two months followed. Exercises, of course – Tatler 2 and others on the Sussex Downs – long route marches carrying FMO (Full Marching Order, greatcoat, blanket and rifle or Brens or 2-inch mortars), 25-pounder live firing exercise (Steyning was once an unplanned target), combined operations with Sherman or Churchill tanks, Tactical Exercises Without Troops (TEWTs), lectures in Worthing pier pavilion, the film of Alamein, *Desert Victory*, in the Odeon, night patrols on the golf courses and PT every day (Monty had a fetish about PT and sacked portly officers on sight). But country pubs were crammed full every night.

2nd Argylls frequented the Ship and the Fountain. Waterproofing of all vehicles was carried out. The armoured cars, Bren-gun carriers and trucks had their engines sealed and exhausts pointing like chimneys to the sky. The 15th Scottish Reconnaissance Regiment was stationed at Angmering-on-Sea, and, while representatives of Humber Ltd supervised the waterproofing of the armoured cars, the regiment marched by squadrons eighty miles over the Sussex Downs, finishing with a forced march back from Amberley. Weapons were fired on Kithurst and Seaford ranges, and WASP flame-throwing carriers were also tested. And cricketers had a brief and glorious season.

The Highland Games were held at the Greyhound Stadium in Brighton (won by the Lowland Brigade, the dancing by the Recce Regiment and the throwing of the hammer by a sapper). All-ranks dances were held in the local village halls. Gaps were cleared in the minefields on the Sussex beaches for sea bathing. It was a unique time, perhaps similar to the eve of Waterloo, except that 15th Scottish was infinitely better trained and almost certainly a happier formation than Wellington's army of 1815.

Lt-Gen H.G. Martin's superb, detailed history of the division published in 1948 gives a pen portrait of some of the division's leaders. Maj-Gen MacMillan was a distinguished front-line regimental officer, a good 'trainer, leader and driver of men', and had fought in North Africa and Sicily. Brig Douglas Money, OC 44 Lowland Brigade, had been wounded in 1940 with the BEF, as a battalion commander. He was proud of his Lowlanders (8th Royal Scots, CO Lt-Col R. Delacombe; 6th Royal Scots Fusiliers, CO Lt-Col C.R. Buchanan; 6th KOSB, CO Lt-Col J.G. Shillington) and was convinced they would compare very favourably with the two Highland brigades. Brig 'Tiny' Barber, OC 46th Highland Brigade, was a Cameron Highlander, immensely tall, with a dry sense of humour (9th Cameronians/Scottish Rifles, CO Lt-Col R.M. Villiers; 2nd Glasgow Highlanders, CO Lt-Col P.V. Campbell and 7th Seaforth Highlanders, CO Lt-Col E.H.G. Grant). Brig Ronnie Mackintosh-Walker, OC 227 Highland Brigade, had been captured at Saint-Valery in 1940 when the Highland Division had been surrounded and over-run. Fortunately he escaped and now commanded 10th Highland Light Infantry, CO Lt-Col J.D.S. Young; 2nd Gordon Highlanders, CO Lt-Col E.C. Colville; 2nd Argyll and Sutherland Highlanders, CO Lt-Col J.W. Tweedie.

The Commander Royal Artillery (CRA) was Brig 'Bosun' Hilton, an RFC flyer of the First World War who commanded three regiments, each of twenty-four 25-pounder guns: 131st Field Regiment, CO Lt-Col J.M. Hailey; 181st Field Regiment, CO Lt-Col A.C.E. Devereux; 190th Field Regiment, CO Lt-Col R.J. Streatfield. Also under command were 97th Anti-Tank Regiment, CO Lt-Col K.L. Beddington, and 119th Light AA Regiment, CO Lt-Col J.F. Young. The Commander Royal Engineers (CRE) was Col R.K. Millar, a Scottish rugger international in his youth.

The Reconnaissance Regiment was commanded by Lt-Col J.A. Grant-Peterkin, the Royal Signals by Lt-Col F.C. Seeley, the RASC by Lt-Col K.M. Whitworth, the ADMS (Medical, Field Ambulance and Field Dressing

Services), OC Lt-Col D.L. Kerr. Before the North-West Europe campaign was over they would have treated and cared for 8,160 casualties wounded in action. The OC 1st Battalion Middlesex Regiment of medium-machine guns and 3-inch mortars was Lt-Col J.P. Hall. At Divisional HQ the GSO1 was Lt-Col Desmond Tyler and the AQ was Lt-Col Kingsford-Lethbridge.

Under the Canloan scheme, every division in the British Army was loaned some of 623 brave Canadian officers, of whom 75 per cent became casualties, many were decorated and 128 were killed in action. They came to 15th Scottish from the Highland Regiments of Canada. Eight were posted to the Argyll and Sutherland Highlanders and similar numbers to the other battalions.

The GOC made a final inspection on 31 May. VIII Corps would not land on D-Day but on D+7.

Robert Woollcombe described the last 'Beating of Retreat' before the division set sail for Normandy.

> These rare displays of the entire Divisional pipes and drums expressed the corporate spirit of the 15th Scottish Division. Represented here were the intermingled tartans of almost every infantry regiment of Scotland. Even the Divisional Artillery contributed a band to that moving maze, marching and counter-marching, of kilts and sporrans and the trews of the drummers. The great cry of the pipes ascending, weaving its spell. Upwards of a hundred pipers and over fifty drums. In front a solid row of pipe-majors.

The KOSB drum-major was superb: 'The great wide-flung circle of pipers was formed, changing on the beat of ten big drums and all the tenors, from quick march to reel, from reel to strathspey and our drum-major, supreme in the centre, arm upheld, like God.'

And so, two days after D-Day, 15th Scottish went to war, advanced parties and transport via Tilbury, the marching troops to cross the Channel to Normandy by LCI from Southampton and Newhaven. Maj J.F. Marnan, Divisional Staff Officer GSO3, described the arrival off Courseulles.

> Three hundred yards away, a cruiser was firing inland over the beaches. Less than a mile away was the coast of France, white surf and yellow sand against a green countryside. It was a brilliant morning [13 June]. In every direction, even astern and out to sea, ships at anchor were dotted across the dancing water in a close pattern. Like skaters in an old Flemish painting or the elegant crowd in a piazza, by Guardi. Close at hand small craft fussed about. A huge Rhino ferry – a raft powered by four outboard engines – manoeuvred miraculously. Further down the coast two battleships, grey shimmering pyramids in the early sun, gave focal height to the pattern. There was joy in the air. A great achievement lay spread out in the sunlight before our eyes.

The division landed on the eastern beaches between Gold and Sword. But unseasonal fierce storms between 19 and 22 June sank or smashed hundreds of landing craft and rafts, even small ships, and delayed Gen Montgomery's plans to take the vital objective of Caen.

CHAPTER 2

Operation Epsom: The Odon Battle

Gen Montgomery's plan for Operation 'Epsom' was ambitious and would involve most of the British 2nd Army. VIII Corps under Gen O'Connor would make the main thrust midway between Caen and Tilly-sur-Seulles. 15th Scottish Division would pass through Canadian units to seize one or more bridgeheads over the little River Odon and create a firm basis for 11th Armoured Division to attack the south-east, seize the vital commanding Hill 112 and advance to the River Orne running south from Caen. 43rd Wessex Division would support 15th Scottish and consolidate behind.

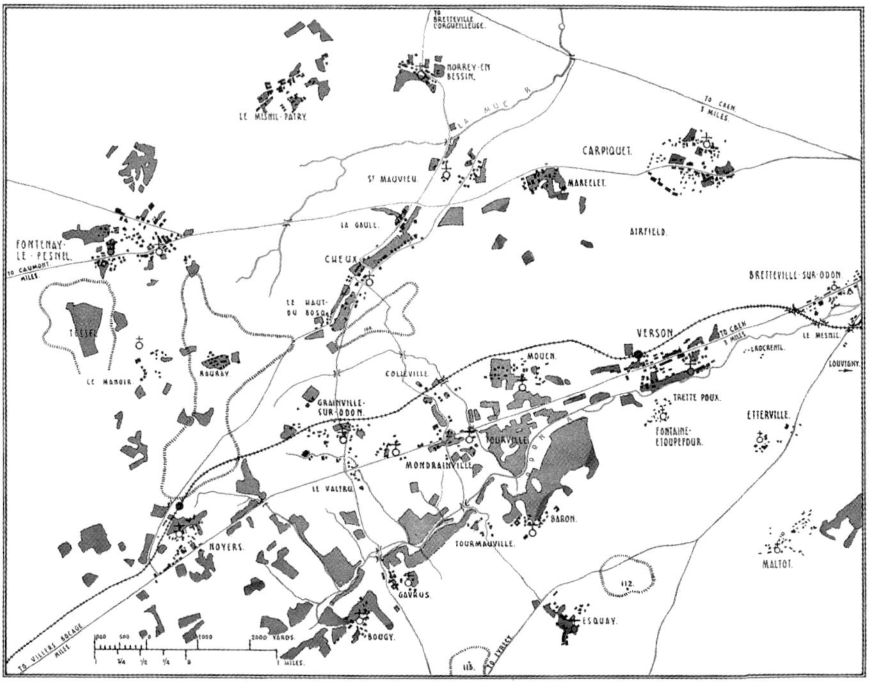

Operation Epsom – the first great battle in Normandy.

XXX Corps, led by 49th Polar Bear Division on the right flank, would seize the important Rauray ridge and thus protect 15th Scottish's right flank. Finally Canadian I Corps on the left flank would seize the crucial Carpiquet airfield, three miles west of Caen. The RAF would give maximum support, as would the Royal Navy's battleships firing 15-inch broadsides.

As with all of Montgomery's battle plans, the Royal Artillery barrages would be a key factor. 181st Field Regiment RA worked very closely with 44 Brigade, 190th Field with 46 Brigade and 131st with 227 Brigade. In fact, a total of 900 guns fired barrages almost continuously for the next seven days from 0700 hours on 26 June.

Divisional HQ was at Saint-Gabriel-Brécy (east of Bayeux) and the GOC, Maj-Gen MacMillan, outlined his plan of attack and objectives. Two brigades would lead, 46 on the right (south) to take Cheux, and 44 on the left (east) would seize Saint-Mauvieu. Then later 227 Brigade would move through on a two-battalion front, the HLI to capture Grainville-sur-Odon, 2nd Gordons directed through Colleville to Tourville as their final objective. 2nd Argylls then had the key role to seize two bridges, one at Gavrus and another at Tourmauville.

Planning was meticulous. Excellent air photographs were studied and Intelligence Sections built cloth models to scale. But the British Army had no experience of fighting in the close Normandy bocage, all woods, orchards, small fields with high hedges on high banks, winding roads and many small hills and ridges, interspersed with streams. It was brilliant defensive country, with tanks always a close-quarter risk, gunnery observation points were almost non-existent (church towers were popular before their destruction) and there were minefields and booby-traps everywhere.

The dozen or so little villages and hamlets were quickly destroyed by artillery gunfire (the RAF was often grounded by bad weather). A destroyed hamlet is ideal for enemy snipers and bazooka men. Quite soon the British Army would encounter the ferocious *Minnenwerfer*, the mobile multi-barrelled mortars nicknamed 'Moaning Minnies' because of their banshee noise in the air as the mortar bombs arrived.

The main objective, the little River Odon, ran through wooded, steep banks and made an effective anti-tank obstacle. The river ran across the existing battleground from south-west to north-east and lay only five miles behind the German Forward Defence Localities (FDLs). Field Marshal Erwin Rommel's defensive ring from east to west was 12th SS, 21st Panzer, 1st SS, 10th SS, 2nd SS, 2nd Panzer, 9th SS and Panzer *Lehr*. Gen Paul Hausser commanded II SS Panzer Corps and reported to Col Gen Friedrich Dollmann, commander of the Seventh German Army. Spurred on by Rommel and with the Führer masterminding every battle, German counter-attacks were frequent, ferocious but often in 'penny pockets' as reserves were flung in to block Montgomery's 2nd Army.

Tank support for the division came from 7th Royal Tank Regiment Churchill I tanks with 46 Brigade, 9th RTR with 44 Brigade plus various

'Funnies', flail tanks to clear minefields, AVRE Petards to smash pillboxes and also scissor-bridges for stream crossing. Immediately in front were 12th SS Panzer Division – the Hitler Youth. 'Their chief desire', said Robert Woollcombe's KOSB company commander, 'is to die for their Führer – and they will shortly be given every opportunity to do so'. 3rd Canadian Division forward troops were ensconced in Bretteville, and in Le Mesnil-Patry and, a mile to the east, Norrey-en-Bessin. They had dug in since their arrival on D+1 and were helpful with practical advice to the Scottish reconnaissance parties. Their little villages were now but rubble and stones, swept by enemy mortars and Spandau fire. The Canadians also lifted their own defensive minefields to let armour and infantry through.

Lt T.J. Stokes was a young troop-leader with 177 Battery, 181st Field Regiment RA, a towed 25-pounder artillery regiment supporting 44 Brigade. He had a difficult crossing in the liberty ship *Fort Biloxi*, as they arrived at the start of the ferocious five-day storms; not only was unloading impossible but a large Rhino with forty vehicles, four guns and four ammunition limbers was swept away and sunk. Eventually they landed near Saint-Côme de Frésne and joined the regiment dug in at Brouay. One of Stoke's first tasks was to supervise a telephone line between his guns and the forward observation point with the Royal Scots at Le Haut du Bosq in case wireless communication failed.

> It is impossible to imagine the destruction which met our eyes – every house in ruins, trees and telephone poles strewn across the roads, the orchards on the roadsides had been blasted, a convoy of 3 or 4 25-pounder guns and quads had been burnt out. Bren-carriers lay derelict, one Panther tank had been killed, its long barrel resting on the road, another Panther half blocked the road further on. On the way up we had seen several Shermans, German tanks and armoured cars knocked out and derelict in the orchards and lanes. No wonder the tanks had found this belt of woods so difficult to penetrate.

Near the Battalion HQ of 8th Royal Scots, mortar bombs, shelling and machine-gun fire forced the 'line' party to seek cover. 'The hedgerows were honeycombed with German dugouts, strongly roofed. Slit trenches and well constructed weapon pits were cunningly hidden in the thick hedge bottoms and at the edges of woods, as well as anti-tank gunpits covering the exits from woods, orchards and narrow roads. Impossible to winkle out the Hun from these beautifully dug trenches. Shelling and bombing would have little effect except from direct hits.'

It was either rainy on 26 June or it drizzled, low cloud and mist reduced visibility and the RAF support from British airfields was called off. The barrage dropped on the opening line, as planned, while the advance battalions closed up, then it moved up 100 yards every three minutes. Within 400 yards of the start-line a minefield caused casualties and held up the RTR Churchills, Funnies and carriers. The No. 38 wireless set for infantry/tank communications failed miserably. There were snipers hiding in the high unharvested cornfields, and

Minnenwerfers and Spandaus caused more casualties. On the right flank, 46 Brigade 'lost' its barrage but reached its objectives, the Glasgow Highlanders reached ruined Cheux and the Cameronians mopped up Le Haut du Bosq. Losses were very heavy – the former lost 12 officers and almost 200 men and the latter 6 officers and 120 men.

On 26 June Lt MacLellan joined 2nd Glasgow Highlanders (who had the right to wear the Black Watch tartan) at the start of Epsom.

> We were well trained, confident, in fine physical condition and knew our battle drill. We knew how to cope with a set piece attack, i.e. a head-on collision with the enemy well dug into defensive positions, we knew advance-to-contact encounters, how to clear houses, street fight, clear bunkers, move through barbed wire, attack pillboxes, climb cliffs and do reconnaissance and fighting patrols. We knew signalling, how to read maps, the formations to use in moving over various types of terrain, how to drive all vehicles then in use, how to handle and correct misfirings of all weapons issued to us at the time, how to lay weapons on fixed lines, how to call for and lay down artillery fire and call in air support. We knew how to dig-in, defend and fight off counter-attacks. We were well trained to meet the enemy. We did not yet know how to read a battle, nor how we would react under fire.

The Canloan officers were as well trained (perhaps better trained) as any of the young British infantry leaders. The CO was friendly, but the OC 'D' Company and the sergeant temporarily i/c 17 Platoon were distinctly unfriendly. Capt Sandy Millar, 2 i/c 'B' Company, another Canloan officer, was not friendly either!

About 1400 hours, bypassing Cheux, 7th Seaforth tried and failed to capture the 'ring contour 100' a mile south-east of Cheux. They suffered fifty casualties, including four officers. By the end of the first day the Brigade had lost nearly 500 officers and men in its first day of battle, but had achieved almost all its objectives. On the left (eastern) flank 44 Lowland Brigade started off at 0730 hours. Lt Robert Woollcombe remembered 'A' Company 6th KOSB assembled near Bretteville–L'Orgueilleuse, where 'houses and cottages stood crazily pitted, or gaping under shattered roofs with slate, plaster and rubble spilled around'. Marching ahead on foot, they passed a huge sixty-ton German Panther (or Tiger) tank miraculously overturned and in a nearby open field charred hulls of brewed-up British Shermans, and a sad, lonely calvary, thence the devastated little church of Norrey-en-Bassin; 'arising out of distant trees like fate, we could see the spire of Saint-Mauvieu church tower'.

Brig Douglas Money's 'O' Group was told that officers and NCOs would not wear their badges of rank into battle. The risk from snipers was too great. (The author, in 11th Armoured Division a mile or so away, in a smart RHA regiment wore highly polished 'pips' of rank, visible to snipers a mile away.) Other preparations for the first battle were green camouflage cream smeared on faces and hands, cleaned, oiled weapons, magazines loaded, bayonets fixed. Mid-day rations (slabs of bully beef and cheese and biscuits) were packed into haversacks, boiled sweets and chocolate stowed in a battledress pocket, cigarette tins in another.

Lt Woollcombe was impressed by the barrage ahead.

> Concealed guns opened from fields, hedges and farms in every direction. During pauses between salvoes more guns could be heard, filling and reverberating the very atmosphere with sustained, muffled hammering. It was like rolls of thunder, never slackening. The thunder angry, violent and death-dealing. Hurling itself over strong points, enemy gun areas, forming-up places, tank laagers, above all concentrated into the creeping mass of shells that raked ahead . . . every single gun at maximum effort to kill: to help us.

Just like the sustained immense barrages of the First World War, the battles of Normandy produced the same result. Despite the sound and fury, enemy machine-gunners, mortar crews, 88mm anti-tank crews and snipers, the tough brutal adolescents of the 12th SS Panzer *Hitlerjugend* survived to inflict terrible casualties in the 'Scottish Corridor'. In 44 Lowland Brigade, the Royal Scots and Royal Scots Fusiliers headed for the hamlets of La Gaule and Saint-Mauvieu respectively. The Fusiliers' starting position was a sunken road, too close to the opening barrage, and they immediately lost casualties to 'friendly fire'.

Enemy observation points near Carpiquet aerodrome just to the east put down their counter-barrage on them, causing more casualties. Crossing the dry little River Muc, the Fusiliers fought their way into Saint-Mauvieu through apple orchards. All day long close-quarter fighting went on in and around the little village. Elements of 21st Panzer Division and 12th SS Division counter-attacked in the afternoon from Marcelet to the east.

181st Field Regiment 25-pounders were in action all day and the medium machine guns of the Middlesex Regiment helped break up the enemy attacks. Lt T.J. Stokes, 181st Field Regiment RA, met his forward observation officer, Capt G.D. Munro, at the Royal Scots Battalion HQ about 1700 hours, near Cheux. He observed

> the battalion commander Lt-Col Delacombe DSO a few yards along the hedge, getting reports from his two forward companies. Casualties were mounting up from the mortaring and machine gunning. Would they be able to withstand the battering much longer? The CO was calm. He still had two companies forward, holding out, not necessary to ask for reserves. It was nerve-racking, the hideous din, the waiting, the smoke and the mist which hid even the next hedgerow from view. But the Churchills and Shermans just to our right flank were a great source of comfort and strength.

Brig Money then sent up the KOSB (less one company already helping the Royal Scots). At 1800 hours in torrential rain 6th KOSB reoccupied Saint-Mauvieu and beat off another counter-attack early the next morning. Some

– not many – *Hitlerjugend* were captured, often helmetless, sullen, even arrogant, sometimes bewildered youths, in grimy camouflage smocks and trousers, their hands held up in a resigned, tired way above their blond heads. Their snipers, often tied to tree trunks or branches, were shot routinely. Most of the *Hitlerjugend* prisoners also expected to be shot.

Much credit was due to the Churchill support of 7th and 9th RTR and Crocodile flame-throwers (who helped the Fusiliers into Saint-Mauvieu) and the AVRE Petards too. Woollcombe encountered a battered group of twenty-eight Royal Scots Fusiliers in the village, the sole survivors of one whole company that had started their war that morning.

When the GOC sent 227 Highland Brigade into action at 1800 hours, the Gordons on the left flank directed to Tourville, 10th HLI on the right flank objective, Grainville-sur-Odon, the whole Epsom timetable was behind schedule. From Cheux, amid a colossal log jam of traffic, in heavy rain and approaching darkness, 10th HLI met dug-in German tanks short of their start line, and so they themselves dug in for the night. The Gordons with 'C' Squadron of 9th RTR Churchills reached Colleville, together with some 17-pounder anti-tank guns of 97th Anti-Tank regiment. A large force of German Panther tanks with supporting infantry smashed up eight Churchills and surrounded 2nd Gordons. During Epsom they lost 189 missing or captured, most of them in Colleville. Five officers were casualties that evening. Lt-Col Colville's battalion only just survived. The anti-tank gunners probably saved them, inflicting heavy losses on the powerful Panthers around Colleville and Le Haut du Bosc. 46 Brigade was relieved at 0500 hours on the 27th, and withdrew to north of Cheux. But the Seaforths were left to put in a successful attack on the 'ring contour 100', an important ridge south of Cheux and Le Haut du Bosc, before they were relieved. 44 Brigade were also relieved by a 43rd Wessex Wyvern formation. However, 227 Highland Brigade bore the brunt of the battle on the 27th. 10th HLI was pinned down all day around Le Haut du Bosc under *Minnenwerfer* fire and suffered badly. Capt Scott's anti-tank platoon knocked out four enemy tanks near Battalion HQ.

Probably the most remarkable (successful) action in Epsom was performed by 2nd Argylls on the 27th. Their objective had always been the bridges over the River Odon at Mondrainville. Starting from ruined Cheux, Lt-Col J. Tweedie's battalion advanced four miles through deep Indian country. They cleared out the enemy holding Colleville level-crossing, through thick woods and then with house-to-house fighting in Colleville itself and in Mondrainville village half a mile south-west, and then 'C' Company under Maj H.M. Fyfe went across country by leaps and bounds to capture the vital bridge, intact and unmined. By 1900 hours the whole battalion formed a small bridgehead, until the 23rd Hussars' Shermans and 8th Rifle Brigade carriers charged across and up the equally vital Hill 112. Lt Edwards, a Canloan officer from the Black Watch of Canada, and Sgt Brand, who knocked out a Tiger, were also heroes that day. Maj Fyfe deserved his MC, and 2nd Argylls were christened 'the Crossing Sweepers'. By the night of the 27th 44 Brigade and 7th RTR were reorganising around Le Mesnil-Patry. 46 Brigade had the Glasgow Highlanders in Colleville, the Cameronians outside Grainville and the Seaforths reorganising near Cheux. 227 Brigade had the HLI south-west of Cheux, the Gordons near Mondrainville–Tourville and the triumphant Argylls in their lonely bridgehead across the River Odon.

Maj-Gen Macmillan's next objectives for 28 June – D+3 of Epsom – were to strengthen the left-flank corridor through Colleville and Mondrainville, south to the River Odon and across to Tourmaville. Equal priority was given to the right-flank corridor to secure the bridges over the Odon and the village of Gavrus at the foot of Hill 113. This, with their usual dash, the Argylls proceeded to do. Canloan Lt Morris and Lt Evans led platoon patrols one mile west along the banks of the River Odon through dense woods and captured the two bridges undamaged and undefended. The whole battalion duly followed on a nightmare trek across country and rather surprisingly found Gavrus itself deserted. The left-flank corridor consolidation started at 0530 hours when the Cameronians renewed their attack on Grainville-sur-Odon. Backed by divisional artillery and the faithful 9th RTR, they took the village (at the second attempt) and destroyed three Panther tanks. The Cameronians consolidated and held the village until 1 July, under constant harassing fire. Early on the 28th, 11th Armoured Division was holding bridgeheads across the Odon and its armour was battling with Panzers on the summit of Hill 112. By coincidence the German generals Rommel and von Rundstedt were on their way to Berchtesgaden for a conference with their Führer. Gen Dollman, GOC 7th German Army, died that day of a heart attack. Hitler was about to court-martial him for the fall of Cherbourg to the Americans. His forces in Epsom were under immense pressure, as was he. Nevertheless elements of six German Panzer divisions were committed to battle during the day, including 1st and 2nd SS Divisions. ULTRA information from Bletchley Park indicated that a major armoured counter-attack was coming in on Gen O'Connor's western flank, mainly on 49th Polar Bears Division. The Seaforths were ordered by Brig Barber to take Le Valtru, a straggling hamlet with an important crossroads south of Grainville-sur-Odon. Their attack started at dawn, crossed 'ring contour 100', then went south-west for Colleville, with the Glasgow Highlanders there on their left flank. Le Valtru was taken with tank and artillery support, but with heavy casualties to the Seaforths. The GOC next ordered up 44 Brigade from reserve, the KOSB to relieve the HLI with the Royal Scots on their right, and by 2100 hours were within half a mile of the Cameronians in Grainville.

29 June was a crucial day. Gen Paul Hausser GOC II SS Panzer Corps, launched his two SS Panzer divisions on the western flank aiming for Rauray and Cheux, with a subsidiary thrust on the eastern flank. It was a fine day for flying and the RAF had a field day. Hausser reported, 'The

Epsom Battle: 8 Royal Scots move forward between Rauray and Le Haut du Bosq, 28 June 1944.

offensive cannot begin until the afternoon. Our concentrations are under continual artillery and air bombardment. The enemy is causing heavy losses by fighter-bomber attacks.' Nevertheless the threats were sufficiently dangerous for 11th Armoured Division tanks on top of Hill 112 to be ordered down and back, south of the Odon.

That evening 10th HLI was ordered to clear the area east of Colleville along the railway to Mouen, a scattered village among woods. Helped by 4th King's Shropshire Light Infantry of 11th Armoured, it fought a fierce and costly battle that cost it twenty-one killed in action and many wounded. It had encountered Hausser's forces on the eastern flank.

On the night of the 28th the 'Scottish Corridor' was only 2,500 yards wide and open to attacks from three sides. The main enemy attacks continued heavily on the western flanks towards Cheux and Le Haut du Bosq, and Brig Money's 4 Brigade came in for some rough handling. The Royal Scots took, lost and retook the area round Grainville Château against troops of 9th SS Panzer Division. As 6th RSF was relieving the Royal Scots in the evening, a ferocious armour and infantry attack came in with flame-throwers and Panthers in hull-down positions. Enemy tanks almost overran the Scots, who suffered heavily. Lt-Gen O'Connor sent in Shermans of 4th Armoured Brigade and anti-tank SPs of 91st Anti-Tank Regiment to stabilise the very dangerous situation. 6th KOSB then came up to take over the 44 Brigade front.

The triangle held by 46 Brigade, Le Valtru, Grainville and Mondrainville, garrisoned respectively by Seaforths, Cameronians and Glasgow Highlanders, also came under ferocious enemy counter-attacks.

Two platoons of the Seaforths were overrun and some of their 6-pounder anti-tank guns knocked out, but they were saved by artillery defensive fire targets, even though four enemy Panther tanks charged down the hill, over the crossroads and down the main street of Le Valtru. Every anti-tank weapon was fired at them until all four tanks were 'brewed up'. The Seaforths had ten officer casualties in the bitter fighting to hold Le Valtru. The Cameronians in Grainville were caught unawares, with hand-to-hand fighting, every building afire and wireless links knocked out. In the chaos the Cameronians had heavy casualties, despite 9th RTR and artillery support. The Glasgow Highlanders in Mondrainville were also attacked by tanks and infantry, and in severe fighting suffered heavily, although greatly helped by 7th RTR. Cpl Robert Bateson, Glasgow Highlanders, who was in an orchard for four days under constant mortar fire, wrote:

> We were having difficulty getting supplies in and wounded out. It was really sad to see some of your best pals being slaughtered by shrapnel and gun fire. I never expected to get back home. One poor chap got out of his trench and, with teeth clenched and bayonet fixed, charged towards the enemy. He got riddled with bullets, like thousands more in those days. I many times missed death by inches.

At midnight Brig Barber could report that his triangular sector was still firmly held.

Meanwhile the Argylls in their Gavrus bridgehead were rudely disturbed by 9th SS Panzer Division, which for five hours viciously counter-attacked from the direction of Bougy to the south-west. Infantry came first, again supported by tanks, plus a lot of well-directed mortar and shell fire. Two Tigers rolled down Gavrus main street and were knocked out, whilst another three prowled down the Bougy–Gavrus road. But Majors Fyfe and McElwee organised their defence brilliantly and the 25-pounders of 131st Field fired almost non-stop to deter the enemy SS.

The Divisional CRA, Brig R. Hilton, had been badly wounded on the 27th, so Brig Lyndon Bolton arrived in the nick of time to supervise the artillery support for the division. The Germans kept up the pressure on all the brigade fronts by heavy mortar fire during the night. Even in daytime it was very difficult to pinpoint the mobile multi-barrelled *Minnenwerfers*. They bombed the HLI in Colleville, including its CO and 2 i/c. The 29th was spent in reorganisation and defensive fighting. 43rd Wessex and 11th Armoured Division infantry relieved the eastern sector of the 'Scottish Corridor', leaving Le Haut du Bosq, Cheux, Grainville, Le Valtru and Gavrus to be held by the Scottish units. By early morning on the 30th the 11th Armoured tanks had all moved south of the River Odon. 46 Brigade was relieved by 53rd Welsh and withdrew north to Le Mesnil Patry. 44

Brigade had a peaceful day and only the Argylls in Gavrus were under great pressure. The bombardment caused heavy casualties to men and vehicles, and by 1900 hours Brig Mackintosh-Walker ordered the Argylls to withdraw across both bridges via Le Valtru to Colleville, then Cheux, with pipers to cheer them on the long march to Bretteville-L'Orgueilleuse. In the Gavrus bridgehead they had suffered 33 killed in action and 156 wounded or missing. Lt-Col Tweedie was awarded the DSO, Maj McElwee the MC.

On 1 July the KOSB was still holding the area round Grainville Château. 9th SS Panzer Division and 2nd SS Panzer Division launched heavy attacks against the junction of the boundaries of VIII and XXX Corps. German Mk IVs and Panthers picked off the KOSB anti-tank guns early in the morning, and by mid-day Capt Rollo's 'C' Company was almost surrounded and down to platoon strength. 'The chaos of battle enveloped us. Noise raged, indescribable. It beat on our senses. It dulled us. It bludgeoned us. Never again did the enemy attain quite the intensity of shelling they put down against us here,' wrote Lt Robert Woollcombe. Despite magnificent support from 181st Field Regiment 25-pounders, 'As attack after attack was mounted, the deadly 25-pounder gun-howitzers poured out their deluges.' Woollcombe described the battle: 'But 'C' Company had been overrun. Tiger tanks had ground into their positions and crouched on their great bellies stood machine-gunning our men in their trenches.' In the evening the Royal Scots Fusiliers with tank support carried out a sweep and the SS Panzer troops withdrew. The KOSB suffered 150 casualties on that day before being withdrawn to Secqueville-en-Bessin to rest. 227 Brigade withdrew to Norrey-en-Bassin.

Epsom lasted five days. 15th Scottish Division had been torn apart. 130 officers were casualties (31 killed in action), 257 ORs were killed, 1,547 wounded and 786 missing. Five battalions suffered over 300 casualties each; 44 Brigade had 700, 46 Brigade 900 and 227 Brigade 900 casualties.

Accolades arrived from the GOC, Corps, Army and Army Group commanders. Monty wrote, 'Scotland can well be proud of the 15th Scottish Division, and the whole division can be proud of itself.' And Frank Gillard on the BBC war news on 1 July praised 'a famous Scottish Infantry Division, most of whom have never been under fire before, but nevertheless they stood up to the ordeal with amazing coolness and courage'.

Today the Divisional Memorial made of Caen stone stands at the tip of where the Scottish Corridor reached, facing across the valley of the River Odon to Hill 113.

CHAPTER 3

Operations Jupiter and Greenline: July 1944

15th Scottish Reconnaissance Regiment had arrived in Normandy with its 270 vehicles (28 armoured cars, 24 light recce cars, 69 carriers, 55 motor cycles, armoured half tracks, jeeps and trucks) just in time to join in at the end of Operation Epsom. The First World War type of battleground that was Epsom was unsuited to thin-skinned, fast-moving Humber armoured cars. The regiment, of course, knew this and had trained to be a Jack of many trades – the division's odd-job man. Roles were now as infantrymen, traffic policemen, messengers, chauffeurs, ambulance men, but also as anti-tank gunners.

For a few days out of the line, those immediate reserves 'Left Out of Battle' rejoined the colours, plus hundreds of reinforcements. 2nd Argylls, for instance, received and welcomed many men from the King's Regiment and from the Oxford and Buckinghamshire Light Infantry, and soon turned them into Highlanders! The business of integrating large numbers of newcomers had to be done, not in weeks or months, but in days. Baths were most welcome, and NAAFI, cinema shows, football, even basketball did a lot for morale – as did hot food, beer, cider and some pretty rough calvados!

Alan Warburton noted, 'We were put in a transit camp. I went with a party of other Seaforth Highlanders to join the 7th Battalion, which had just been severely mauled at Caen [*sic*] and had lost many men [310 casualties]. We were the first reinforcements and I joined Battalion HQ which was in an apple orchard.'

Operation 'Jupiter' was the battle plan for 43rd Wessex Wyverns on 10 July, to attack south-east from the Baron, Mouen, Verson area to occupy Hill 112, Maltot (a large village beyond and to the east) and Eterville to the north-east. 44 Brigade HQ was moved to Tourville, the Royal Scots Fusiliers into Baron, the Royal Scots in Tourmauville to relieve 43rd Division units. The KOSB were in reserve in Mondrainville. The weather now in midsummer was fine and hot and all movements raised dust. Dust brought mortar bombs guided by the many German observation points on Hill 112. The CRA and CO of 119th LAA Regiment (Lt-Col Young) now devised a crafty counter-mortar scheme, based on 1st Middlesex Machine-Gun Regiment's wireless network. Radar sets, listening posts and

A piper leads 7th Battalion Seaforth Highlanders into action.

communications sent back immediate information on suspected enemy mortar fire sites. This brought down instant retaliation from medium field artillery, 4.2-inch mortars at brigade level, and by 3-inch mortars and medium machine guns. It was a sledgehammer to crack a (dangerous) mobile nut. The *Minnenwerfers* could unleash their deadly, noisy salvoes and be on the move in a few minutes.

46 Brigade provided left-flank protection to 43rd Division's attack. They moved from Mouen, and the Cameronians were tasked with relieving 4th Dorsets after they had taken Eterville. It took four hours for the relief; meanwhile the enemy mortared heavily and elements of 9th and 10th SS Panzer Divisions counter-attacked vigorously. In the dark they infiltrated the village, taking prisoners and causing heavy losses. The CO, 2 i/c and three company commanders became casualties, so Maj J.C. Davies, 2 i/c the Glasgow highlanders, came up and took command. When Maj Lambie brought up 'C' Company of the Glasgow Highlanders in support, they too lost many men to mortar fire. On the next day determined counter-attacks were made by 200 enemy infantry and tanks, but hand-to-hand bayonet fighting left more than 100 SS dead. When the remainder of the Glasgow Highlanders moved up to support their 'C' Company, they suffered too, and

lost eighty-five casualties that day. Lt Roger MacLellan with 'D' Company Glasgow Highlanders was tasked with relieving a company of Seaforths across a main road near Eterville. 'At one mobile dressing station a Medical Officer covered in sweat and blood was working like a Trojan to save the lives or relieve the suffering of severely wounded and mangled British soldiers.' The Canloan officer was horrified to see the RAMC orderly heave a dead body out of one door and lift a new stretcher case in through another. On the handover, the Seaforth captain asked, 'Please bury my dead.' 'There were indeed many dead – enemy as well as friendly. As the battle see-sawed back and forth, the Germans and the Seaforths took turns keeping the other prisoner.' The following day, after another German counter-attack, he counted more than 125 dead German infantry in front. On the night of 11 July 46 Brigade was relieved by a Canadian formation, and on the next night 44 Brigade was also taken out of the line. 15th Reconnaissance Regiment sent its 'A' Squadron to assist the Cameronians. Trooper J. Connor in a Bren carrier gave this account: 'The situation was extremely tricky, as the whole troop was perched on the top of a hill, from which we could see the opposite bank of the river. The Brens in the carriers and the Besas in the armoured cars were firing at enemy snipers who would pop up, fire and dive back into the corn. I saw two Jerries rise at once and had a go at them.' A smokescreen on the right flank cleared and five German tanks immediately knocked out two leading armoured cars. 15th Recce had twenty casualties in its first battle.

So Jupiter ended, and three days later Operation 'Greenline' started. On the night of 15 July, XII Corps, led by 15th Scottish, would be directed on Bougy (south-west of Gavrus), Evrecy and Maizet in a drive towards the River Orne. 53rd Welsh Division in its first major action was given the targets of Cahier and Ferme de Mondeville. Traffic control in June and early July had for a variety of reasons been a bit of a shambles. The few metalled roads, often under fire, had to bear an immense number of vehicles and tanks, usually head to tail. 15th Scottish Recce Regiment was tasked with traffic control of Greenline with five routes called Hereford, Dundee, Quarry 2, Coal 1 and Coal 2.

The Glasgow Highlanders, lent to 227 Brigade, started with only three companies (because of recent heavy losses), tasked with the capture of Esquay (east of Gavrus) and the important Le Bon Repos crossroads. Their objective was to protect the left flank of the main divisional attack. They had Churchill tank support, AVRE Petards, a squadron of flame-throwers and a company of Middlesex medium machine guns. From Miebord towards the saddle between Esquay and Baron, the column was heavily mortared, causing some confusion. But the Glasgow Highlanders, helped by Crocodile flame-throwers, burned or shot the German defenders dug in between Le Bon Repos and Croix des Filandriers. With the Churchill support Esquay was cleared by 2300 hours. The CO allotted each company defensive areas around Esquay. Lt Roger MacLellan of 17 Platoon 'D' Company reported:

10th Highland Light Infantry with tank support between Hill 112 and Hill 113, Operation Greenline, 15 July 1944.

'Not only did the enemy reinfiltrate the village, but they launched several tank and infantry attacks. We could see them forming up in dead ground. Both "A" and "D" companies were in the middle of grain fields so target recognition was difficult. Both Company Commanders acted as Forward Observation Officers for our artillery and they called down salvo after salvo on the enemy with amazing accuracy.' MacLellan saw the German 88mm guns direct fire on several troops of 17-pounder anti-tank guns, as well as the infantry 6-pounders. 'The enemy fired phosphorus bombs into "A" company position. The next day, attacks patterned after the day before. "A" Company again came under heavy fire – *Nebelwerfers*, Moaning Minnies and a lot of heavy stuff.'

With the left, eastern flank reasonably secure, the main divisional attack started at midnight on 15 July under so-called Movement Light or Monty's

Moonlight. 227 (Highland) Brigade and 44 Brigade advanced in parallel south-west from Tourmauville and Baron towards Bougy and Evrecy respectively, the Royal Scots, KOSB, Gordons and Argylls from right to left (north to south). Both brigade TAC HQs were bombed and shelled and Brig Mackintosh-Walker was killed by a direct hit on his scout car. Lt-Col E.C. Colville of the Gordons took over his command of 227 Brigade.

There would be four phases: the capture of Esquay, already achieved by the Glasgow Highlanders; next the clearance of Gavrus and Bougy (by the Royal Scots) and the high ground between Bougy and Evrecy (by the KOSB); then the Gordons and the Argylls would advance in a straight line from Baron and capture Hill 113 overlooking Evrecy; finally, in the fourth stage, planned for 0530 hours on 16 July, 10th HLI would capture Evrecy and 2nd Argylls Ferme de Mondeville, south-east of Evrecy, on the way to Maizet. Reconnaissance beforehand was difficult. Enemy observation points still atop Hill 112 dominated the area. The little River Guigne, which ran west–east from south of Evrecy, was probably a barrier to anti-tank guns and almost certainly to the tank support. The opposition included 21st and 22nd SS Panzer Grenadier Regiments firmly dug in on all the reverse slopes.

The Royal Scots, with 153rd Royal Armoured Corps in support, developed a winning formula. Advancing along the south bank of the River Odon from Les Vilains, they attacked first Gavrus and then Bougy. The Royal Scots attacked each village from the front and the tanks from the rear. At 0800 hours Gavrus yielded seventy prisoners, and at 1000 hours Bougy yielded 100. The Luftwaffe rather surprisingly was very active, and heavy mortaring caused casualties, wounding Lt-Col Delacombe and the CO of the tank regiment. The KOSB indomitably fought their way south-west towards Hill 113. Lt Woollcombe described part of their battle. 'We went in with Bren guns firing tracer from the hip. We reached our first objectives to find them pulverised. The enemy fox holes were strewn with greatcoats, *Wehrmacht* caps, respirator containers, mess tins, even postcards and letters to the Fatherland, but grabbing their weapons and ammunition the defenders had got out of it.' Many enemy snipers hid in knocked out British tanks. 'For three days and nights our companies on Hill 113 stood to their arms under incessant mortaring and shelling. We hung on to Hill 113 by our eyebrows.'

Lt-Col Shillington had been severely wounded, and Maj Giles Richardson succeeded him. The KOSB counted seventeen Messerschmitts in one Luftwaffe attack. A squadron of Churchills was destroyed by 88mm guns, despite an artillery smoke-screen. The KOSB had a terrible time and had nine officer casualties in the three days of Greenline.

At one early stage on the 16th, 227 Brigade, with supporting Churchills, Crocodiles and AVREs and with the Gordons leading, was crammed into an area 1,000 yards deep and 300 yards wide. The Gordons, then the Argylls and the HLI (their brigadier had just been killed) were static south of Baron.

Mist and smoke shrouded the German observation points on Hill 112 and they failed to counter-attack. The HLI sensibly withdrew towards Baron, the

Argylls dug in and the Gordons eventually cleared minefields and opposition in front of them. At midday on the 16th five German Mark IV tanks (less of a threat than Panthers), followed by infantry, attacked the Gordons' HQ, and Maj Sinclair's anti-tank platoon knocked them all out. 131st Field Regiment dispersed the infantry. On the 17th the unfortunate Royal Welch Fusilier Brigade of 53rd Welsh Division had crossed the River Guigne and was advancing up the hill towards Ferme de Mondeville. Its first and second attacks failed against the enemy 276th Infantry Division. Although the Argylls on Hill 113 were under great pressure, the minor counter-attacks on the KOSB and Gordons were on a smaller scale. The Corps Commander ordered the relief of 46 Brigade (except for the Glasgow Highlanders still around Esquay) and 227 Brigade (less the Gordons). Early on the 18th 44 Brigade faced one savage counter-attack, with a further four during the day. On the morning of the 19th the KOSB sent fighting patrols across the Bougy–Evrecy road. Dennis Bunn, not quite 21, with 15th Recce, reported:

> My feelings on patrol were probably typical. We were the first of a two-car patrol followed up by Bren carriers. I cautiously drove the heavy Humber armoured car. Inside the car was intense heat and darkness, outside brilliant sunshine. I sat firmly and gripped the steering wheel with damp hands as I peered through a small aperture at the ground in front, the high hedge on the right, the ground sloping away to the left, at the trees, the bushes, seeing or suspecting danger in every blade of grass. We came on a straight piece of road about 600 yards – in front was a stone breastwork. Our Besa machine gun sent a stream of bullets down the road. Then the road, trees, sky, everything was gone. All I could see was red fire and black smoke. Something had exploded immediately in front. The Besa was still going, empty cases rattling behind me.

A stray shell had landed, but no damage.

44 Brigade was relieved that night and withdrew to Le Haut du Bosq. Greenline or the second Battle of the Odon, 15–19 July, was over. Monty was pleased, 'The enemy armour has been pulled back into the line [i.e. not diverted to the American front]. The fighting had been severe.' 1st SS Panzer Division was involved in counter-attacks round Esquay, where 10th SS was also heavily engaged; 9th SS Panzer Division was committed at Evrecy and Maltot. On 18–20 July the ill-fated three-armoured division attack south-east of Caen in Operation Goodwood came to a sad end with heavy losses in drenching rain.

During the Second Battle of the Odon the division suffered almost 1,000 casualties, with 8th Royal Scots, 6th KOSB and 2nd Glasgow Highlanders each with over 100.

CHAPTER 4

Operation Bluecoat: The Caumont Battles

The Scottish Division spent a few days out of the line. VIII Corps Rest Centre was now open at Saint-Aubin-sur-Mer, to which every unit sent leave parties. There were problems, however. The fine weather broke and drenching rain set in.

'The weather turned wet and nasty', recalled Lt MacLellan, 2nd Glasgow Highlanders,

> and the men were becoming miserable and ill at ease. All of my Boy Scout, Cadet and army training was needed to show them how to be comfortable and remain dry under such circumstances. We gathered everything we could lay hands on to provide rain proof shelter for slit trenches, even to grass, which we thatched to direct the rainwater to where it belonged. We dug draining ditches around the tops of the trenches and sump holes in the bottom, which we kept bailed out. We used old sacking or cloths to wipe the mud off our boots before entering the dry areas of the trench. We protected blankets and personal belongings with our gas capes or ground sheets, and, when above ground, we wrapped our ground sheets tightly around us for warmth and dryness. My men relied on me and we enjoyed a rich sense of mutual trust. I was very proud of them.

The KOSB received a big intake of reinforcements, a whole batch of Ulstermen, Inniskillings and veterans back from Burma. In the fighting for the Odon river, Epsom and Greenline, the division had suffered 180 officer casualties, mainly in the nine infantry battalions. And of course many more young NCO leaders at platoon level. The integration of LOB and reinforcements is never easy.

'We collected some new reinforcements,' MacLellan again, 'who were well trained but lacked experience. We had to fit them into a fighting team and I used to talk to and listen to them as often as possible, for only by knowing the character of the men you lead can you come to depend on them and them on you.'

Efficient infantry–tank cooperation was vital, and training before the Second Front tried hard to develop a good working relationship. Many infantrymen thought (and said) that tank support close to them brought down unpleasant enemy shelling and stonks. When giving signals or requests to a tank commander, the infantry officer or NCO was an easy target for the enemy to pick off. So REME welded boxes and phones to the back of tanks working closely with infantry.

For the next attack, Operation 'Bluecoat', every Scottish battalion had a tank partner. 2nd Argylls had the whole battalion of 3rd Scots Guards, with whom they had trained at Gandale and in the Dukeries. The KOSB and 44 Brigade relieved 10th US Regimental Group between La Vacquerie and Caumont. On their departure, 'We discovered in a farmhouse enough lavatory paper for a brigade, quantities of excellent tobacco and cigarettes, candy, various tinned foods and cigars,' Capt Robert Woollcombe recalled. 227 Brigade relieved 11th US Regimental Group between Caumont and Le Repos. The bocage country, thickly hedged, resembling Devon, was undamaged, and the German 326th Division was distinctly not belligerent.

Montgomery's plan for Bluecoat was for VIII Corps (15th Scottish, 11th and Guards Armoured Divisions) and XXX Corps (43rd Wessex, 50th Tyne-Tees and 7th Armoured) to exploit southwards towards Mount Pinçon and Vire.

Specifically, 15th Scottish line of attack was in a narrow corridor to Sept-Vents, Hills 309 and 361, and Saint-Martin des Besaces. On the right flank was 11th Armoured and, on the left, 43rd Wessex Division. 44 Brigade was now commanded by Brig Cockburn. Higher command had overlooked the fact that the German 326th Infantry Division held two strong-points, Lutain Wood (Bois Mondant) and the village of Sept-Vents, both situated 1,000 yards *before* the divisional start-line! There were only two good roads in front, one for 43rd Wessex and the other south through Saint-Martin des Besaces to Vire for 15th Scottish. The GOC ordered a two-battalion attack at 0700 hours on 30 July, with the Gordons on the left, Cameronians on the right supported by tanks of 4th Grenadier Guards, plus flails and Crocodiles. The RAF and USAAF sent 1,500 bombers to take out key defences in front. There was not a set-piece artillery barrage. 15th Recce Regiment was also in action, and two squadrons on the left flank enveloped Lutain Wood and went on to La Recussonnière and Les Loges. Their carriers followed the lumbering Guards Churchills and mopped up enemy pockets. Dennis Bunn noted, 'The carrier-borne troops went out on foot to investigate. There was a large anti-tank gun with dug-in German infantry. We lost three killed and five wounded in the ensuing action. As darkness fell and we drew back, I could not avoid driving the Humber over the bodies of two German soldiers sprawled in the road.'

The Gordons met heavy Spandau and mortar fire mainly from enemy entrenched in Lutain Wood, but Crocodiles belched flame on one side, Grenadier Guards Churchills from another and the Gordons came in from a third flank. By midday most of a battalion of 752nd Grenadier Regiment had surrendered. The Argylls followed up but kept well west of Lutain and then captured Les Loges.

The artillery plan of the day was a series of timed concentrations with codenames 'Laryngitis', 'Measles', 'Mumps', 'Pleurisy' and 'Pneumonia'.

On the right flank the Cameronians started from Villeneuve, a southern suburb of Caumont towards Sept-Vents. A heavily mined, narrow sunken lane held up all transport, and most of the supporting tanks were disabled. It took until 1500 hours to clear Sept-Vents, and the HLI took over the advance south and caught up with the Coldstream tanks that had crashed ahead to Hervieux. The Scots Guards tanks had also smashed ahead on the left flank from Lutain Wood to capture Hill 226, where the Argylls established themselves at 1500 hours.

Maj Kenneth had taken command after the CO, Lt-Col Tweedie, went sick for a slight operation with 153rd Field Ambulance. For the loss of twenty-four casualties the Argylls had advanced 6,000 yards, through three enemy positions, and negotiated a defended minefield on the way. A disaster occurred when three huge Jagd Panther tank destroyers and supporting 88mm anti-tank guns knocked out ten Scots Guards Churchills in a few minutes from the left rear of Hill 226.

Point 309, also known as Quarry Hill, was a key objective two miles south of Hervieux. At 1600 hours it was heavily bombed by two waves of Martin B-26 Marauders, and the Divisional GOC sent the 4th Coldstream Guards tanks on ahead to capture Point 309. At the same time 4th Grenadier Guards tanks would lift the Glasgow Highlanders from near the Hervieux crossroads to put infantry on the ground at Point 309.

Despite the bogs and springs of the source of the River Drome at the foot of the quarry, the Guards Churchills reached the crest of the hill. A traffic jam in Hervieux, an 88mm anti-tank gun in La Morichesse and Luftwaffe ME 109s delayed the Glasgow Highlanders' move south. By 0230 hours on 31 July the Glasgows had arrived on Quarry Hill, having marched through the dusk and night, fighting their way through the enemy in La Morichesse and La Ferrière. Lt-Col Campbell held an 'O' group and took over the defence of the hill. Lt MacLellan noted, 'I was given one of the finest defensive positions an infantier could imagine – beautiful fields of fire, covered approaches lots of aiming marks and an unobstructed panorama.' Brig Barber had ordered the Seaforths to make their way by a difficult night march to join the Glasgow Highlanders on the top of Hill 309. They arrived before dawn on the 31st.

Bluecoat had got off to a good start. VIII Corps had driven nearly six miles deep into 'Indian country'. Gen Lt von Drabich-Waechter, GOC the German 326th Division, had been killed. By 1100 hours on the 31st, 11 Armoured Division had cleared Saint-Martin des Besaces, which was then occupied by the Cameronians. Pte Alan Warburton, Seaforth Highlanders, wrote, 'Life became a mixture of walking, digging slit trenches, standing-to at dawn, hiding behind hedgerows and in ditches, dodging shellfire, bullets, mortar bombs and snipers. Sometimes a huge Tiger tank would come round a corner and start shooting us up or "Moaning Minnies" would come raining down on us. The armour could not get moving through the bocage country, so we foot-sloggers had the grim task of flushing out the enemy.'

The GOC ordered the Royal Scots to take the area north-west of the enemy, hold the large Bois du Homme and link up with the Argylls in Les Loges and the two battalions atop Quarry Hill. Despite friendly-fire attacks by Typhoons, they took their objective by 2200 hours. Meanwhile 15th Recce Regiment moved south-east from Saint-Martin on 1 August to help the Cameronians of 46 Brigade clear the hamlets of Galet and La Mancellière. But a considerable battle ensued when the old foe, 21st Panzer Division, had turned up in force in the Bois du Homme and launched a whole series of strong counter-attacks on the Seaforths' sector on Quarry Hill. The deluge of shelling started at 0530 hours, continued between 1100 hours and noon, with a final substantial attack at 1600 hours. Divisional and corps artillery, 4.2-inch and 3-inch mortars, medium machine guns, everything, was fired at the Panzers, who lost six Tigers in the fighting. The Seaforths had three company commanders wounded, and suffered more than forty casualties. 'It was a living hell and our numbers were severely depleted', noted Pte Allan Warburton. The KOSB were then ordered up to close the gap between the Royal Scots and Quarry Hill. It was Minden day and the KOSB wore roses in their hats as they advanced up the spur of La Ferrière on the north-west edges of Bois du Homme against 125th Panzer Grenadier Regiment. Capt Woollcombe wrote, 'We attacked the high sullen feature which crossed the main road Villers Bocage to Avranches, and gained the woods at the top to find several knocked-out Panther tanks and large numbers of enemy dead – most of them extraordinarily young – and the moaning of wounded among the trees.' Eight field regiments and RAF rocket-firing Typhoons had caused the slaughter.

Most of the fighting on the 2nd took place by 9th and 10th Panzer divisions trying to halt the advance of 11th and Guards Armoured Divisions. The leading armoured cars of 15th Recce took up positions in La Boulinière, Beaumont and Le Bressi. For the first time they encountered the joy of liberation for French villagers just free of *les sales boches*. Wine, calvados, eggs, flowers, certainly kisses from the ladies. On the 3rd, 44 Brigade's new task was to move forward from Le Tourneur (1½ miles south of Saint-Martin des Besaces), south-east to Cathéolles, east to Montcharivel, south to Estry, La Caverie and Lassy. 15th Recce had been halted outside St Pierre Tarentaine. Brig Cockburn ordered up the Royal Scots Fusiliers, lifted by 4th Grenadier Guards tanks, to capture Arclais and Les Haies east of Cathéolles. Streams feeding the River Soulèvre made it difficult for the heavy Churchills in support, but, starting at 2100 hours, the RSF had gained its objectives overlooking Mont Charivel.

The GOC, Maj-Gen G.H.A. MacMillan, who had led the division superbly through the attritional Odon river battles, was wounded by a shell splinter. So Brig C.M. Barber took command, as did Lt-Col R.M. Villiers of 46 Brigade.

The next day, 4 August, the Royal Scots and the KOSB swept eastwards along a ridge on the south bank of the River Soulèvre and by 0900 hours had cut the Montcharival–Montchamp Road. During the afternoon the RSF with Guards Churchills cleared Montcharival in the Soulèvre Valley below the ridge. 46 Brigade then came up to relieve 44 Brigade and stayed peacefully for two days in Arclais, Drouet and Montchamp (captured by Welsh Guards tanks).

On 2 and 3 August Orders of the Day arrived from Lt-Gen Sir Miles Dempsey, the Army Commander, and from Lt-Gen Sir Richard O'Connor, VIII Corps Commander, praising 15th Scottish Division and 6 Guards Tank Brigade for their magnificent partnership in Bluecoat.

During Bluecoat the Scottish Division suffered nearly 600 casualties, mainly in 2nd Gordons, 9th Cameronians, 10th HLI and 6th KOSB. 15th Recce in its first mobile battle had more than thirty casualties.

CHAPTER 5

The Battle for Estry

The enemy was still holding the line Vire–Estry–La Caverie–Mont Pinçon–Aunay-sur-Odon. On the 11th Armoured Division front, 9th SS Panzer Division was fighting furiously to hold the Vire–Vassy road. And 10th SS Panzer Division was on its way to Vassy.

Maj-Gen Barber's plan was for 227 Brigade to pass through 44 Brigade at La Caverie, in the direction of Lassy. The HLI reached Au Cornu on 5 August, half a mile east of La Caverie, and was heavily shelled. The Gordons south of Au Cornu were also under fire. 15th Scottish Recce Regiment encountered German troops in the woods near Danvou and Saint-Jean le Blanc on the eastern flank.

The next day would become known as 'Black Sunday' for the Cameronians. It was a misty morning as they moved towards the steep hill called Bois des Monts from La Bruyère. On the far side the ground drops sharply into a tributary of the River Orne. The hamlet of Le Codmet was taken without opposition, but the village of Gourney was strongly held. The going was bad for the Coldstream tanks, with intense shelling and machine-gun fire from across the valley. Three Cameronian companies were pinned down near Le Pont Soffrey, and during the day suffered almost 100 casualties. The Glasgow Highlanders behind took up positions in the Bois des Monts under heavy mortar fire. Military information about the enemy's movements and strength was inaccurate. Theoretically they were in full flight, but at Gourney, Lassy and specially Estry the defences were ferocious. At about 1500 hours the Seaforths with Coldstream tank support moved towards Lassy in the river valley south of Bois des Monts. On the open forward slopes the leading company was decimated, the CO, Lt-Col Robertson, was mortally wounded, and hidden 88mm anti-tank guns knocked out many of the supporting tanks. Two hours later two other Seaforth companies renewed the attack, but could make no progress. At about 1930 hours they were forced to retire with almost ninety casualties. The situation was so bad that the Divisional Commander ordered Brig Villiers to withdraw the three battalions under cover of darkness to La Druerie–Au Cornu–La Caverie.

Little resistance was expected in front of 227 Brigade's attack south by the Argylls to capture Hill 208, and south-west by the Gordons to take a crossroads two miles away near Estry. Finally the HLI would follow the Gordons, then move south-east towards Le Theil ridge. As usual, each Scottish battalion had tank support from the Guards.

The German High Command had by now organised the defence of what was soon to become the Argentan–Falaise Killing Grounds. A whole network of villages at the western end of the German corridor had become strong-points with nests of machine guns, dug-in tanks, many *Minnenwerfers* and a call on heavy artillery further back. Backs to the wall, the Panzer Grenadiers fought frantically. 9th SS Panzer Division had strongly fortified the Estry ridge.

Meanwhile counter-attacks by tanks held up the Scottish advance. The start-line of advance by 227 Brigade at La Caverie crossroads was rudely disturbed by two Mark IV Tiger tanks! The 15th Scottish Recce armoured cars reported that Estry was strongly held and the main road to Le Theil mined, and covered by German tanks and machine guns.

The Gordons ran into a minefield half a mile from Estry crossroads. 9th SS Panzer Division meant to hold Estry come what may. An SS regiment had a dug-in tank, 88mm guns, *Nebelwerfers* and *Panzerfausts*, machine-gun nests, mines, of course, and powerful artillery on call. Lt-Col Sinclair tried everything, a company head-on, another left flanking, another right flanking. The Grenadiers in their Churchills tried their best and a squadron was almost wiped out. Lt-Col Russell Morgan, CO 10th HLI, following up behind, made a plan with Lt-Col Sinclair. The 4.5-inch and 5.5-inch medium regiments available on call put in a concentration onto the German defences in Estry. A further attack by the HLI with Scots Guards tanks made some headway, but both the Scottish battalions dug in among the orchards on the eastern side of Estry, as 9th SS Panzer Division called in its medium guns to 'stonk' the brave but battered Scotsmen.

The Argylls' attack along the La Caverie–Vassy road due south to the village of Canteloup and Hill 208 also ran into predictable difficulties. Enemy guns and mortars 2,000 yards to the east around Lassy overlooked the Argyll axis, but by evening on the 6th they reached the slopes of Hill 208 and dug in. The German defenders remained on the crest 300 yards away!

The next day the dangerous stalemate continued. The Argylls made another attempt to capture Hill 208, so close. Maj Alan Fyfe, a much-loved 'B' Company commander, was mortally wounded, and Maj Moreton, OC 'C' Company, won the MC by arranging a truce in No Man's Land for both sides to bring in their wounded. During the night of the 7th a German counter-attack supported by tanks on Au Cornu, a mile behind the Argylls, was only just beaten off. As the Argyll historian wrote, 'With very little to show for it, the 93rd (2nd Argylls) had lost in killed and wounded 3 officers and 41 other ranks in the fighting on the Vassy road. Stalemate continued in Estry as the Gordons and HLI battered the Panzer Grenadiers and were themselves battered in turn. The supply road north-east to La Caverie was under mortar fire all day.'

Maj-Gen Barber, the GOC, was determined to capture Estry. He probably had the Corps Commander and perhaps the Army Commander breathing down his neck! His plan was carefully to withdraw the Gordons and HLI and put down, not a Divisional concentration but a massive Corps concentration of artillery on the Estry defenders. This would be followed by a determined attack by 44 Brigade, the RSF and KOSB attacking from Monchamp at noon. A large force of Funnies – Crocodile flame-throwers and AVRE Churchills with their Petards – led the attack, but were thwarted by the narrow sunken lanes and banks round Estry. The small town stood on rising ground, surrounded by very thick country with limited visibility. 6th KOSB on the right flank of the attack got its two forward companies across the main road from Estry to Vire. Capt Woollcombe, 'A' Company, wrote:

> We failed to capture the village itself. As the assault went in we discovered that the German outposts perched among the hedges and cross lanes above us must have watched our Recce parties clambering about in the early mist before the attack . . . casualties rose steeply again. Severe mortaring fell on us as the companies moved in. Marshy ground held up the tanks. 'Eight-eights', Spandaus, bazookas and riflemen opened up from close cover. The Fusiliers on our left were brought to a standstill and lost their colonel [Buchanan]. Our leading companies, struggling for the village, were met by heavy fire from Panther tanks. The Churchills were unable to clear the place.

CSM Millar stalked an enemy tank with a PIAT, destroyed it and was awarded the MC.

The Royal Scots Fusiliers on the left flank of its attack had a difficult time. Their supporting tanks never reached the startline. Led by three Mark IV tanks, a German counter-attack at 1300 hours drove the RSF back across their startline! However, 97th Anti-Tank Regiment took the Panzers on, destroyed two, and the survivor pushed off, followed by the Panzer Grenadiers. The RSF moved into Estry from the positions created by the HLI. By 1500 hours it was still stalemate in Estry with both sides doing their best to destroy each other. Capt Woollcombe again: 'So there we were. Poised. Neither side quite able to force a decision on the other. The 'Royals' waiting behind us to counter-attack if we got ousted back. And the curious thing was that the German resistance in Normandy was supposed to be crumbling.'

On 9 August the Argylls were pulled back and away from Hill 208 to Haute Oraille, 1,000 yards to the west, where they stayed for five days. The Royal Scots moved up in support behind the KOSB and RSF in Estry, where two more German counter-attacks were beaten off. 46 Brigade stayed in La Caverie, Au Cornu and La Druerie.

The indomitable 9th SS Panzer Division and assorted battle groups held half of Estry, Gourney, Bois des Monts and Hill 208. The stalemate continued until, on the night of the 12th, like thieves in the night, the Panzer groups decamped from Estry. The Royal Scots occupied the battered little town and pushed south to Le Theil. 15th Scottish Division was now relieved by 11th Armoured Division, and moved on 12 and 13 August north to Feuguerolles and Saint-Pierre Tarentaine. The division was not to be used in the hard fighting for Falaise and the ultimate sealing-off of the notorious

Pocket, but was kept in reserve to rest and refit for a possible assault crossing of the River Seine.

In the aftermath of Bluecoat, in the ferocious fighting that followed in the Estry area, the division suffered more than 1,000 casualties. The HLI, Gordons, Argylls, KOSB and RSF each lost more than 100, and 46 Brigade lost 280. For all the Scottish units, it was the end of their fighting in Normandy. Of the fifty days since they had first gone into action, there had been fighting on thirty-seven, and on the other thirteen they had been in shelling distance of the enemy, and altogether suffered more than 5,300 casualties.

Capt Woollcombe wrote of the enemy, 'With tight-lipped, bitter verve they fought . . . Above all we saw the dark face of the *Waffen SS*. And this we broke, in Normandy.'

CHAPTER 6

In Limbo: Operation Gallop

For two weeks in August the Scotsmen were out of action – in limbo, many of them in the valley of Bois Halbout, east of Thury Harcourt.

The Argylls spent a few leisurely days at Maltot on the far side of Hill 112, 'where the flies, the heat and the mosquitoes made the old soldiers talk reminiscently of tropical service, and the wasps throve on mosquito ointment and compo ration jam', according to the Argylls' historian. Pipe-Major Angus Graham composed two new tunes, 'The 93rd Crossing the Odon' and 'Fifteenth Scottish Division'. The kilts were unpacked for the first time in France and the pipes and drums beat Retreat twice. ENSA shows and the mobile cinema arrived. Other treats were the mobile baths and the rather better food, including fresh bread. There was a Corps (White Knight) rest camp on the beaches which was popular. Capt Woollcombe noticed the many German cemeteries of SS troops killed near Caen and the River Odon. A huge Iron Cross proclaimed *SS-Unsere Ehre Heisst Treue.* Maj-Gen Barber took many of his senior officers on a tour of the Odon battlefields to view the hostile points of view. By very bad luck six enemy dive-bombers appeared at midnight on the 20th and struck the Argylls HQ, causing twenty-five casualties, including Maj Kenneth, the padre and the mortar officer.

Capt Woollcombe noted, perhaps a trifle bitterly, 'the leisurely turmoil of the myriads in uniform that seemed to dwell like ants behind the fighting line: lines of Communication, Rear Bases, Main Bases, Depots, Dumps and Roadheads of all descriptions, until the actual fighting troops resembled some remote minority away at the tip of this fabulous supply system'. It was ever thus. Winston Churchill was always trying to get the CIGS and all the Army Commanders to reduce their long, long tail of non-combatants. The German Army, he noted sharply, had a far smaller admin/supply tail; why could not the British Army do the same? The divisional Recce Regiment shared Amaye-sur-Orne and then Fresney-le-Vieux with a plague of insects. They bathed in the River Orne, and field bakeries, mobile canteen, excellent ENSA shows and an imaginative race-meeting (with wooden horses, taped squares, the bookies being the CO, Lt-Col Grant Peterkin, Maj MacDiarmid and the RSM), all these activities were welcome distractions. 15th Recce was briefed for Operation 'Gallop', the peaceful advance to the River Seine. Star route in the north (Falaise to Louviers), Sun route in the centre (Trun to Emanville) and Moon route in the south (Vignats also to Emanville by a different route). The squadrons were accompanied by Royal Engineers (who defused mined bridges), bulldozers (which cleared wrecked German AFVs and tracks, and dead horses off the roads), bridging equipment (AVRE Churchills with Bailey bridges on top) and recovery vehicles.

The two truly startling aspects of Operation Gallop east of the Argentan–Falaise gap were the appalling carnage inflicted on the retreating *Wehrmacht* and the intoxicating welcome of liberation by the French villagers. In the campaigning zones, enthusiasm for the liberating troops was muted. The RAF had (with a great deal of help from Army Group Royal Artillery (AGRA)) flattened every town and most villages in front of Montgomery's troops. Farmhouses had been wrecked, fields poisoned by minefields and herds of cows killed, and so farming communities were distinctly lukewarm in their reception. But between Falaise and the Seine the towns and villages were relatively undamaged and the population turned out *en masse*, throwing flowers and fruit (often solid apples, which hurt) and offering wine and calvados, while the children waved flags. There were speeches from the mayor and posturing by the French Forces of the Interior, who appeared out of the undergrowth looking dangerous. Their exploits were recounted and their forecasts of either vacant or occupied villages ahead were usually inaccurate. The small boys everywhere came up with the chant 'cigarettes pour papa'. By and large the young Scottish crusaders enjoyed the jubilant scenes of liberation.

The young Canloan officer, Lt Roger MacLellan of the Glasgow Highlanders, wrote:

> Our next move was to be a mad dash to the River Seine. On the move continuously, we suffered delay after delay caused by roads blocked with rubble or with heavy traffic. The towns of Falaise and Trun and many villages were smashed beyond description. The road was rough and treacherous. On nearing the River Seine, we came upon the aftermath of the retreating German army. Convoy after convoy had been caught on the roads and tracks, and were smashed beyond belief, by our aircraft. Many vehicles were completely burned, they ranged from bicycles, to horses and carts [the *Wehrmacht* surprisingly relied considerably on horse-drawn transport], wheeled vehicles, half tracks and tanks. Some of the half tracks had six to ten dead German soldiers, slumped over and badly burned. Many of the vehicles were still in the middle of the road, deadly evidence that drivers were completely surprised by the sharpness of the attack. The bodies of enemy soldiers lay everywhere – on the road, the verges, the ditches, along hedgerows, up side roads, alleys and tracks. The stench was beyond description – and even belief. The closer to the river we got, the closer together were the vehicles and the greater the carnage.

The rocket-firing Typhoons had more or less demolished divisions of the German Seventh Army in what became known as Dead Horse Alley.

On the evening of 24 August 44 Brigade was in harbour on 'Star' route east of Vimoutiers, 46 and 227 Brigades in harbour on 'Moon' route, west and east of Trun respectively. The next day 44 headed for Le Neubourg via Orbec and Bernay. The River Risle's bridges were blown, but a detour south showed a small bridge standing. 227 Brigade reached Emanville, and the HLI and

Gordons were sent to Louviers, and 46 on 'Sun' route halted near Beaumont le Roger. On the same day American and French troops entered Paris and 43rd Wessex Wyverns began their four-day battle at Vernon to force the River Seine. The Glasgow Highlanders camped at Vieux Villers near the Seine. According to Lt MacLellan, 'While waiting we practised assault crossings by water, first on dry land, then down to the waterfront itself. It was valuable training. The assault boats had wooden frames with canvas sides and outboard motors and were manned by Royal Engineers. Each boat could carry about fourteen soldiers, so each platoon needed two for the crossing.'

Staff College would have taken a week to plan the assault crossing of a major river obstacle. The Scottish Division carried out the planning in six hours, between the Brigade Commander's initial order and H-hour for the actual crossing. The necessary build-up of storm boats and material for Class 9

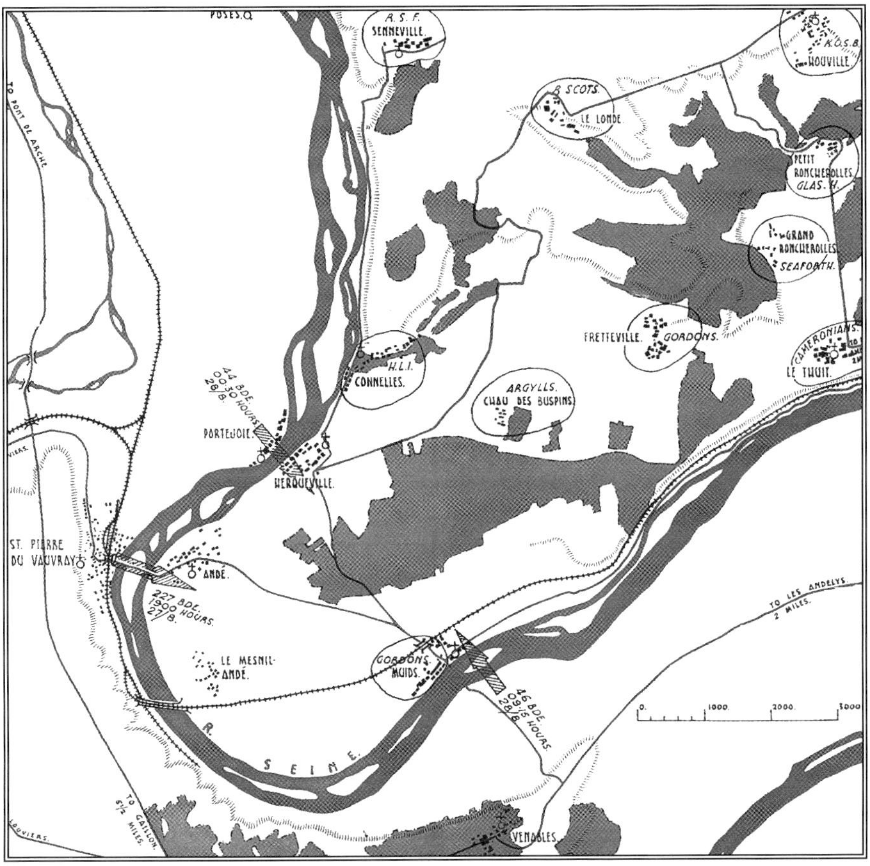

End of Operation Gallop – assault crossing of the River Seine.

and Class 40 bridges (for light and heavy vehicles respectively) was complicated by the fact that the main supply route from Le Neubourg to Louviers was shared with the US 10th Corps, so the 'redcaps' of the Military Police were vital for the smooth running of the build-up.

At Saint-Pierre du Vauvray, the chosen site for the assault crossing, the River Seine meanders between steep escarpments, some 400 feet high. The average width of the river was about 300 yards. The plan was for 227 Brigade to assault in the centre at Saint-Pierre, 44 Brigade after dark at Port Joie on the left flank, and 46 Brigade on the right opposite Muids.

15th Scottish Recce Regiment had been very active with extensive patrolling on the south side of the River Seine, which did not draw serious fire from the enemy. Lt John Wheeler took a small patrol across by rowing from Port Joie to Herqueville, accompanied by a member of the FFI. Lt Shirley and some of his troop crossed in an assault boat, to the island opposite Muids, where it was proposed to build a bridge. The lack of serious opposition enabled the river to be crossed without all the very detailed preparations.

At 1900 hours on 27 August, 10th HLI and 2nd Gordons crossed just south of Saint-Pierre. All three leading boats were sunk by machine-gun fire and the Gordons lost fifty-four casualties, while thirty were taken prisoner. Brig Colville, whose 227 Brigade had also secured a bridge, decided to reinforce the successful HLI crossing, so he switched the main Gordon thrust by DUKWs to follow up behind the HLI. The HLI also succeeded in liberating some of the Gordons who had been captured. The Argylls crossed at 2300 hours into the HLI/Gordon bridgehead and went on to the loop area between Andé and Le Mesnil Andé.

The 44 Brigade assault on the left from Port Joie to Herqueville was completely successful. By 0200 hours the RSF in assault boats was across, and three hours later it had established the bridgehead. By dawn the sappers were rafting over the RSF vehicles. By 0800 hours the Royal Scots were across and by 1100 hours the KOSB. 44 Brigade linked up with 227 Brigade near Andé. The Gordons moved out of the Saint-Pierre bridgehead at Andé, south to Le Mesnil Andé, and moved inland to Muids, enabling the rest of 46 Brigade to cross west of Muids in assault boats and Class 9 rafts. The sappers soon had bridges (Class 9 at Muids, Class 40 at St Pierre) operational. Lt MacLellan, 2nd Glasgow Highlanders, wrote of his crossing on the second day, 29 August: 'There were only 12 boats and the plan was for two companies to cross at a time. But as soon as a boat was loaded, the sapper in control started the motor and left without waiting for anyone else! Ahead was an island which was used for cover, before dropping downstream with the fast current, coming around the end of the island then heading back upstream on a tack.'

15th Scottish Recce Regiment's armoured cars had been rafted over and were now in their rightful *métier*. 'A' Squadron headed for Les Andelys, Fretteville and Le Thuit. Cpl Whiting was awarded the DCM for conspicuous bravery in an action near Fretteville. Lts Blount and Kerridge each earned the MC for aggressive and successful forays.

'B' Squadron also shot up Germans in Les Andelys, Connelles and Heudebouville. The Maquis (FFI) was now very valuable with information and often rode in the Recce's armoured cars. Capt Woollcombe made a grand foray with a large band of Maquis who needed protection as they retrieved an arms dump hidden in a forest. Undoubtedly, apart from shaving the heads of young ladies who had fraternised with the young blond *Herrenvolk*, the FFI was helpful in rounding up and guarding German stragglers.

CHAPTER 7

Liberating Northern France and Belgium

The attritional form of warfare 'Epsom' style seemed to have vanished, and certain distinguished soldiers claimed that the war would be over by Christmas. After all, the German Seventh Army had been almost destroyed. About 60,000 escaped from the Pocket and were now north of the Seine, having had about 90 per cent of their tanks and transport captured or destroyed. Nevertheless, the hot pursuit by the three armoured divisions towards Brussels, Antwerp and Ghent often left the infantry to follow up and subdue small towns and villages with German garrisons that had been bypassed. This, of course, required different techniques. Lt MacLellan, 2nd Glasgow Highlanders, wrote: 'In clearing buildings, I had trained my men to get to the uppermost floor as fast as possible and clear downwards. I personally raced for the third floor of one building and found a dormitory that had obviously been evacuated in a hurry.' He did find a young scantily clad French girl abandoned by her *Wehrmacht* lover! 'We found no Germans in the area, quickly consolidated outside, then I sent up the success signal. The rest of the battalion came forward in jeeps and carriers, the priest and his flock emerged from the Church and were despatched to another locality. That was always the way, it seemed. We would liberate the village, be moved out to protect the perimeter and the troops behind us would get the credit, the wine and the revelry.' Somewhere near Roncherolles and Couverville, German mortars caught 'B' Company Glasgow Highlanders, at a crossroads and their company carrier, with ammunition, mortar bombs and other explosives, received a direct hit. There was a terrible explosion, which inflicted thirty-four casualties, including at least six killed.

The 15th Scottish Recce Regiment spent three pleasant days at Marlers, resting and working on their vehicles, before resuming the chase on 5 September. The Argylls too had four days peacefully at Buspins, whilst 227 Brigade and the rest of the division waited inactive in the bridgehead.

Maj-Gen Barber and Divisional HQ were in Herqueville in a charming house with a charming host. The Scottish staff were 'At Home' to the leading *citoyens*, and danced eightsome reels and drank to the 'Auld Alliance'. It was lovely countryside, with bathing parties, good food and wine, and there were frequent FFI 'parties' or war-games, usually when the

SS prey had melted away. Much of the divisional transport was lent to support the 'Great Swan' north. The Welsh 53rd Division passed through the bridgehead following up behind 11th Armoured in their amazing race to capture Amiens and Antwerp. Suddenly, on 2 September the Argylls were detached and sent on a twelve-hour, 120-mile ride in troop-carrying vehicles to Bernaville on the River Somme to hold a crossing point. Thence to Saint-Pol for three days, where their pipes and drums beat 'Retreat' to an enthusiastic, often tearful Belgian audience.

The division set off north and covered 25 miles on 3 September, 15 miles on the 4th and 75 miles on the 5th, through the chalklands of Picardy and Artois. Lt MacLellan, 2 Glasgow Highlanders, noted, 'We passed through Amiens, Arras, Vimy Ridge and Lens, skirted Lille and entered Belgium on 5 September through the little town of Belleghem, where we received a terrific welcome', and the next day on to Oudenarde. The KOSB crossed the Somme west of Amiens on the way to Saint-Pol, then over the Calais–Arras highway, north-east to Bethune and La Bassée towards Lille and the Belgian frontier. They stopped at one First World War cemetery, where KOSB soldiers lie buried. In Halluin on the border, the KOSB had a riotous and happy welcome, and then into Belgium across the River Lys to Wevelghem. It was a royal procession with banners proclaiming 'Welcome our liberators'. 15th Scottish Recce Regiment went through Doullens, Houvin, Arras, Lens, Carvin, Seclin and Roubaix. Whenever the armoured cars or carriers halted, girls and children chalked on them the names of their towns, their own names, slogans. There were kisses, flowers and fruit. On the frontier French and Belgian gendarmes cheered side by side. The Recce had come 300 miles through France in fourteen days, and now drove on beneath the red, yellow and black Belgian flags. On their mapboards, blue circles showed that not far ahead the enemy waited, so they now headed for Belleghen, Kirkhove and Avelghem.

In the area west of the line Antwerp–Ghent–Lille–Bethune–Hesdin, some 160,000 German troops who had been expecting the main Allied invasion to come in the Calais area were now streaming northwards. Some of them would attempt to break into the area Thielt–Deynse–Courtrai–Menin–Roulers. So 'Lys Force' was formed with the Seaforths, Royal Scots and the Recce Regiment, plus a company of Middlesex and backed by artillery. The Seaforths took over Courtrai, but, as 7th Armoured Division, who with the Poles had captured Ghent, had blown up all the bridges over the River Lys, the risks of serious counter-attacks diminished. North and west of Vichte the Recce had a brisk skirmish, ambushed a bus full of German troops and captured 130 prisoners near Gruyshautem. Lt Kerrridge led his troop of three armoured cars and two carrier sections to reconnoitre Waereghem. 'We passed through tanks and motorised infantry outside Kirkhove and mooched comfortably on for about eight miles. Sgt Ramsay went into Waereghem and out again, reporting many Germans there with anti-tank guns. On the road he met and knocked out a German lorry but did not molest two German ambulances.' Soon afterwards Lt Roy Higgs, 'armed with the tracks [carriers] immediately deployed and the half track with the six-pounder [gun], was brought into action to cover the road. The small-arms and mortar fire was heavy and a shell landed under the back axle of my [armoured] car. A German observation point was eliminated, but enemy infantry and a SP attacked us from left and right.' Sgt Hughes's car was put out of action by an anti-tank gun and Lt Kerridge's was hit in the radiator. Owing to the built-up nature of the area, the wide, deep ditches and the two woods, their arcs of fire were narrowed. Each day the brave Recce cars and carriers scuttled briskly ahead, drawing fire and taking casualties and always reporting back by wireless contact. Many small towns and villages changed hands, which made the inhabitants extremely anxious, as the Germans always carried out reprisals if they returned. The RSF occupied a village astride one of the escape routes. 'After killing or capturing all the Germans there, the RSF company had an amusing night ambushing enemy convoys which unsuspectingly kept driving into the place', relates 44 Lowland Brigade's account. The Argylls crossed the Belgian frontier on 7 September at Moucron, and had a carnival evening at Bossuit. The troops were loaded with apples, pears, plums, tomatoes, eggs, wine and coffee. There was an orgy of kissing!

During the 7th, the Royal Scots crossed the River Lys canal and then fought their way to Roulers, taking many prisoners. The RSF crossed the Courtrai–Bossuyt Canal and took Deerlyck, ambushed enemy columns in buses and returned with seventy-five prisoners. Capt J.S. Cunis, Forward Observation Officer, of 181st Field Regiment, occupied a comfortable observation point in a tall block of flats in Courtrai. He had a hot bath, eggs and bacon, and when the morning mist lifted he got to work. On three roads clearly visible, not more than a mile away, were long columns of slow-moving stolen country carts piled high with loot. These targets of opportunity continued throughout the day as Cunis kept his 25-pounder gun teams busy. On the 8th, the Recce Regiment led the RSF to capture Deynse, the KOSB to Zulte and the Royal Scots to Harlebeke. 227 Brigade moved south of Ghent, mopping up pockets, and stayed in the area until 11 September. Antwerp and Brussels had been captured a week before and some leave parties were sent off to the fleshpots of Brussels. 46 Brigade was echeloned along the Escaut Canal for eleven miles north of Oudenarde and remained there until 10 September.

In Deynse near Mechelen, Maj Moreton of the Argylls, acting as Town Mayor, was entertained to a champagne dinner in the town hall, a dance was held and the pipes and drums beat 'Retreat' in both towns. The pipe-major received bouquets from the Belgians, which he laid on the local war memorials.

The Glasgow Highlanders were sent off to help the Queen's Infantry Brigade of 7th Armoured Division clear a large factory area across the Canal du Nord. The German force had been resisting the Polish Armoured and the Desert Rats for nearly a week in Ghent. A large, well-defended town, it needed a lot of infantry to clear it, and it became a platoon commander's battle. '"B" Company lorries were just in front of us', wrote Lt MacLellan, 'and the second truck ahead of mine got a direct hit killing and wounding several soldiers. Shelling in a built-up area is a frightening experience, even more so than on a reverse slope. You cannot tell where the shells will land with any degree of accuracy and when they explode, besides shrapnel, there are also splinters of glass, wood, concrete, dirt and metal coming at you.'

No. 17 Platoon took 200 prisoners out of the total bag of 6 officers and 233 prisoners. By the morning of the 11th Ghent was free at last, but the Glasgows took sixty-six casualties in their two days of street fighting and factory clearance. The division had spent 10 September near Malines. The town burghers celebrated by playing a recital of Scottish tunes on the famous carillon.

The Gheel Bridgehead

The German Gen Student commanding 1st Parachute Army was responsible for the defences of the Meuse–Escaut Junction Canal. He had under his command 719th Infantry Division, 51st and 53rd GAF Regiments (grounded Luftwaffe troops), supported later by the Hermann Goering Training Regiment sent post haste from Rotterdam. They were provided with SS officers and NCOs. He also commandeered all the various

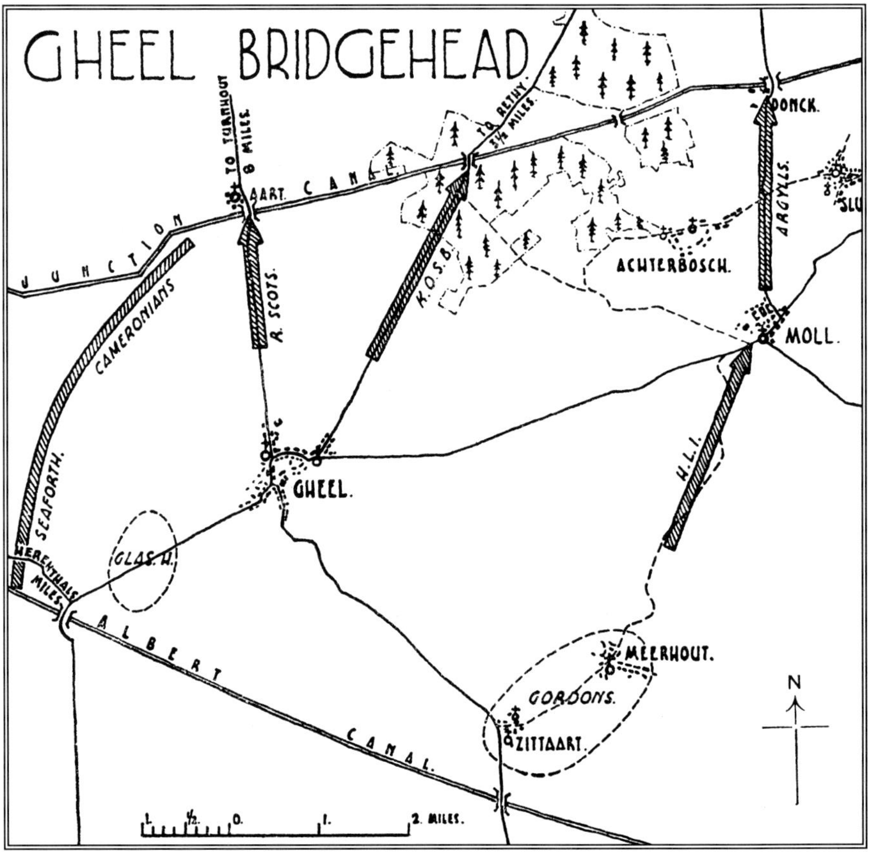

The Gheel bridgehead and assault crossings of the Escaut and Junction canals.

artillery weapons at the Bourg Leopold training centre. The crack NCO instructors came with their guns! The Germans still held the artillery practice ranges at Turnholt, eight miles due north from Aart, and deployed accurate and expert bombardment on the bridgehead. In the autumn of 1944, the German commanders were brilliant at quickly cobbling together disparate troops into a cohesive, efficient fighting unit. Marines, Luftwaffe, policemen and soldiers on leave were scooped up and integrated, as well as the 'sick' formations of 'deaf' soldiers, 'stomach' units who needed a special diet to keep them going, plus a small tough minority of SS to provide the backbone NCOs. And Tiger tanks and self-propelled guns were still reaching the front from the Ruhr factories.

As part of the huge complicated plan for Operation 'Market Garden' – the bold thrust for the Rhine crossings – 15th Scottish Division was to relieve 50th Tyne-Tees Division in the Gheel bridgehead beyond the Albert Canal. It was like a series of chess moves. 50th Tyne-Tees, when relieved, would move east into the De Groot bridgehead, which would then enable Guards Armoured to lead XXX Corps advance north to Arnhem. On 12 September 44 and 46 Brigades moved embussed from Malines, to debus south of the Albert Canal and to cross over into the Gheel bridgehead.

The bridgehead was quadrilateral in shape, with the Albert Canal, six miles of it, at the southern end. The little towns of Gheel, Aart, Donck, Moll, Meerhout and Zittaart lay north of it, before the Escaut Junction Canal is reached between four and eight miles north-west and north-east. The German 16th GAF Division had pushed 50th Division out of Gheel itself. 15th Scottish's task was to clear the whole of the countryside between the Albert and the Junction canals.

The battle plan was for 44 Brigade to clear Gheel up to the railway, and move north to Junction Canal. 46 Brigade would extend the bridgehead north-west towards Herenthals. 227 Brigade would then extend it north-east and capture Moll and seize the bridge at Donck. 15th Recce Regiment had sent patrols deep into the bridgehead north of Gheel, as far as Moll, where two of its armoured cars were knocked out.

By 0800 hours on 13 September the Royal Scots occupied Gheel shortly after 200 GAF troops had moved out. The GOC, Maj-Gen Barber, decided to use the tactics so successfully employed at the crossing of the River Seine. He ordered 44 Brigade, with comprehensive sapper support and bridging material, to go headlong for the Junction Canal defences. From Gheel, the Royal Scots would take the three-mile road north to Aart and the KOSB the road north-east towards Rechy. On the left flank 46 Brigade, led by the Cameronians and followed by the Seaforths, would advance three miles west of Gheel in a defensive role to prevent enemy movement out of Herenthals. 227 Brigade would extend the bridgehead on the right-hand flank, HLI leading, through Meerhout towards Moll and Donck, followed up by the Gordons.

All went well to start with. The HLI liberated Moll, empty of opposition, and the Argylls reached Donck. The Gordons were in Meerhout and

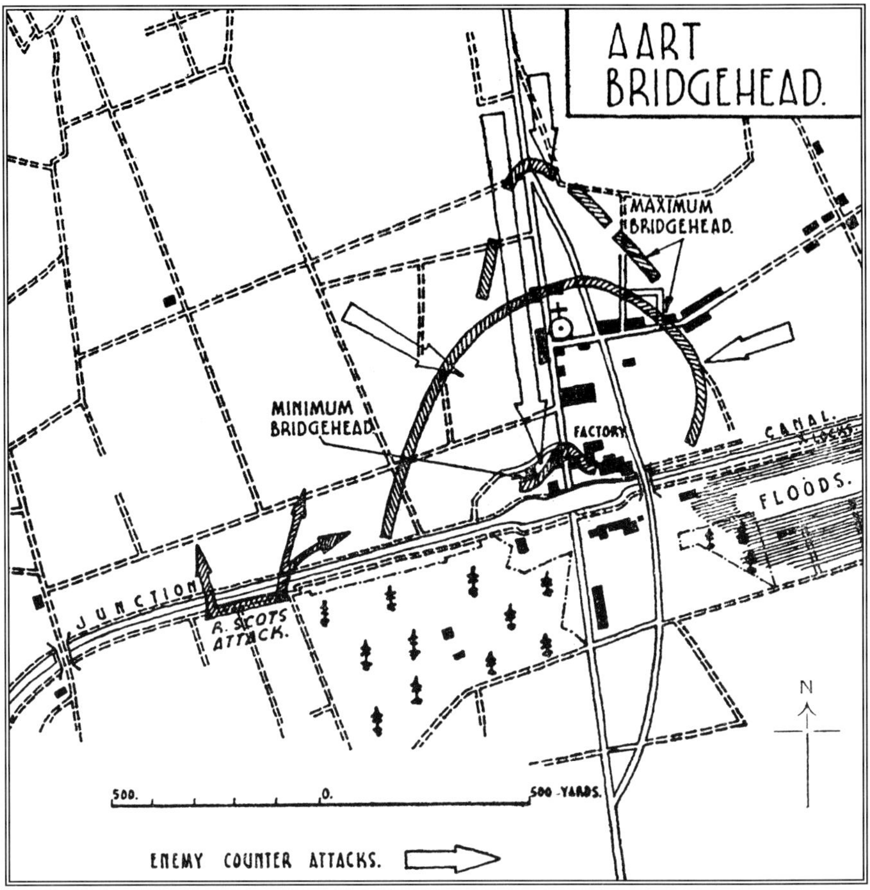

The Aart bridgehead.

Zittaart. Both 46 and 44 Brigades closed up on the Junction Canal, and 15th Scottish now held the nine-mile line of the Junction Canal with predictably all bridges blown ahead of them.

The KOSB incursion during the dark night of 13/14 September was a gallant failure. A platoon crossed over the damaged lock on the road to Rethy and was cut off and captured, as mortars and 88mm guns swept the canal in enfilade. Maj Rollo, who had won the MC in Normandy, was fatally wounded. The German defenders then manipulated the canal locks and flooded the battleground. The CO, Lt-Col Richardson, ordered his forward companies to withdraw – through three feet of water.

Two miles to the west lies the village of Aart, with its road, bridge, church, crossroads and a large, square factory. Lt-Col Lane Joynt, CO of the Royal Scots, organised an assault to capture Aart, using assault boats provided by 279th Field Company RE. Starting at 0400 hours, the whole battalion went over the canal, although 'A' Company suffered heavily from twin-barrelled flak guns firing in a ground role. The sappers under Maj P.T. Wood endeavoured to bridge another nearby lock site, but the enemy's flooding destroyed their efforts. On the evening of the 14th, Wood succeeded in rafting 6-pounder anti-tank guns over to the Royal Scots. Confused fighting went on in and around Aart, with support for the beleaguered Royal Scots from tank, SP guns and artillery. By nightfall they had captured 100 prisoners from the Luftwaffe regiments attacking them.

Gen Student now sent in his Herman Goering Training Regiment, who launched a ferocious attack at 2200 hours down the main road from Turnhout. The Luftwaffe troops, led by SS, attacked the Royal Scots from the east under covering fire. An hour later two well-handled SP guns with infantry support came in from the west. Confused fighting, much of it hand to hand, went on all night in the bright light of burning houses and haystacks. 'A' and 'C' companies were torn apart, 'D' only just held and 'B' was surrounded. On the morning of the 15th the bridgehead had been reduced in size, with a few Royal Scots platoons on both sides of the main street holding out. At about 1000 hours the Germans disengaged to allow a bombardment of the tiny bridgehead. Brig Cockburn sent the RSF by assault boats to reinforce the battered Royal Scots, landing on the north bank of the canal to the east of Aart.

They soon expanded the bridgehead by 1430 hours, but the Hermann Goering Regiment put in two heavy counter-attacks and compressed the area held by the Scotsmen. Finally Brig Cockburn sent the KOSB across to try to expand it to the north and east. They arrived to find the Scots and RSF in considerable confusion, fighting for their lives.

Maj-Gen Barber then ordered 227 Brigade to a concentration area near Donck to make an assault crossing seven miles to the east.

While 44 Brigade was fighting to avoid being overwhelmed, Field Marshal Montgomery arrived at Divisional HQ to present medal ribbons: 'I hope that you will tell your folk at home that I came here today and told you that the 15th Scottish Division had done magnificently.' The Recce Regiment provided the guard of honour and was complimented by the GOC on its smartness and bearing. It was a crazy war. In Gheel the officers of 2nd Glasgow Highlanders held a mess dinner in the basement of a building, dressed in kilts brought up to the front by the Quartermaster. Their CO praised three of the Canloan officers for their deeds in Ghent – Russell Parke, Louis Boudreau and Roger MacLellan (who was awarded the MC for his successful actions in Ghent).

Meanwhile the three gunner regiments fired DF targets and concentrations around the bridgehead. The Recce Regiment stayed south of the canal, quartered among the hospitable people of Moll and Meerhout, patrolling the factories, straggling suburbs, woods and marshes in the canal area to prevent German infiltrations. At 0400 hours on 16 September, the Gordons tried to cross the Junction Canal near Donck but were pinned down by intense and accurate machine-gun fire. Brig Colville withdrew them after several hours of intensive fighting. Throughout 15 September, despite the KOSB getting across the Rethy bridge to help the RSF and Royal Scots, the enemy held the initiative and mounted several fierce counter-attacks. The heaviest came in at 2000 hours, and the RSF was pushed back but held on – just.

Early on the 17th, the survivors of the Royal Scots were pulled out of the bridgehead and ferried to relative safety. In their three-day battle they had lost 230 officers and men (31 killed in action, 53 captured) and went back – poor devils – to Gheel to reorganise. In the early afternoon the Scottish Division watched the Dakotas, Stirlings and gliders flying towards Arnhem through puffs of anti-aircraft shells. It was the beginning of the ill-fated Market Garden operation.

After dark the Argylls crossed in assault-boat ferries into the Aart bridgehead to relieve the battered 6th RSF, who were withdrawn at 0730 hours on the 18th. They too went back east of Gheel, having suffered 172 casualties in three days (18 killed in action, 50 captured).

Gen Student was obviously determined to contain the Scottish threat and his battlegroups hammered away all day on the 18th at the KOSB and the Argylls. 'We lived like moles, clinging to our slit-trenches in the sandy soil and beat off thirteen counter-attacks,' wrote Capt Woollcombe, 6th KOSB, 'several of which came in battalion strength supported by tanks. Our gunner observation points were shot out of the church spire and shot off the factory roof – or at least they should have been – only they just stayed on. Our perimeter was ringed with defensive fire tasks laid from the gun areas around Gheel town.' Shells were rationed for 44 Brigade, with ammunition priorities given to Market Garden. 'The Lord's Prayer, the Creed, the

The battle for the Gheel bridgehead, 12–15 September, cost 15th Scottish Division about 540 casualties, including 141 killed in action.

General Confession – they were my repertoire. If the shelling still continued, I started over at the beginning.'

The divisional forward observation officers from 181st and 131st Field Regiment observers were ensconced in the large square factory in the centre of Aart and helped greatly to break up the German assault with their dedicated calls for defensive fire. During the night of 18/19th, the Gordons were ferried across to relieve the KOSB.

44 Brigade had lost 26 officers and 513 ORs in the Aart bridgehead. Nine officers and 134 ORs were killed. The Germans lost 200 prisoners, the Scots 160. But the German cemetery outside Aart is very full – with more than 200 tombstones.

On 19 September, Lt-Gen Neil Ritchie, 12 Corps GOC, wrote to Maj-Gen Barber explaining that a high proportion of the enemy's available reserves (Gen Student's 1st Parachute Army) had been drawn against 15th Scottish in the Gheel bridgehead. 'The Division has had some very tough fighting and has suffered casualties as well. It is small consolation, but the initial success of Market Garden operation does owe a lot to what the 15th Scottish Division has achieved.' So the sacrifices made at the Aart bridgehead had not been in vain. 'We were puzzled as to what was being achieved by the severe fighting here and by the vehemence of the enemy's reaction,' wrote Capt Robert Woollcombe. 'The idea had been to force a way of advance into Holland for Second Army. The brigade fought for three days and four nights, lost over 500 men [actually 900 in the division] and in the meantime the main thrust of the Army developed elsewhere. Finally the bridgehead was abandoned altogether. However we undoubtedly slew many enemy.' 6th KOSB had 166 casualties. It certainly was not a victory for the Scotsmen. Gen Student had contained the Gheel bridgehead despite terrible German losses. 'Sagged about and scattered down the village street the lone bodies of German paratroopers slowly rotted, sacrificed and mutilated through hopeless acts of bravado. You stepped over them every time you went back to the command post at the canal.'

CHAPTER 9

End of Operation Market Garden: The Actions at Best

Later that day we [Glasgow Highlanders] packed our kilts and left by truck to move toward those voluminous air drops. The roads were full of traffic – tanks, lorries, jeeps, guns, the whole works of an army on the move. The going was painfully slow, we would pull over to allow ambulances to pass to the rear and for ammunition trucks to pass to the front. We'd be stopped until rivers or canals were bridged – some by Baileys, others by floating Kapok – and again move slowly forward. We pulled into

Maj-Gen 'Tiny' Barber, the tallest general in the British Army, receives a bar to his DSO from Field Marshal Montgomery, 16 September 1955.

hospital grounds south of Eindhoven. But when the town was bombed that night we dug in deeply. The next day [22 September] we moved up to the Wilhelmina Canal for the attack on Best and were allotted a wooded area just south of it.'

Lt Roger MacLellan wrote without, of course, realising that in two days time he would be wounded rather badly and flown back to a Canadian hospital in Farnborough.

Market Garden was in its sixth day, and, although the Airborne Division in Arnhem was still holding out bravely, the long thin corridor via Eindhoven and Nijmegen was also under immense pressure from German battlegroups. The XXX Corps centre lines were being cut by Gen von Rundstedt's 1st Parachute Army to the east and the German 15th Army with fifty tanks to the west. The area of the centre line between Eindhoven and St Oedenrode had already been cut, but the axis restored again.

7th Armoured Division temporarily took over the Aart bridgehead with 227 Brigade under command, while 46 Brigade was to spearhead 15th Scottish Division through the 53rd Welsh Division bridgehead at Lommel. The Recce Regiment on 21 September passed through Lommel (fifteen miles east of Aart), crossed the Escaut Canal, entered Holland and drove on to the Eindhoven area. A mile or two north the Welsh Division – to be relieved by the Scottish – faced the enemy across the Wilhelmina Canal. 9th Cameronians moved at once to take over the defence of the Class 40 bridge. The main objective of the division was to strike north towards s'Hertogenbosch to relieve pressure on the left flank of the Market Garden corridor.

The town of Best, six miles north of Eindhoven, was in the way and heavily defended, as the Seaforths found to their cost. Both road and railway bridges across the canal had been blown. Despite its steep twenty-foot banks, men could wade across the sagging structure of the bridge. This was almost the Peel country of Holland – dead flat, desolate heath, many ditches, small streams, occasional woods, orchards and hamlets. The slit-trenches were half filled with water and tracked vehicles had to stay on roads, often raised above the countryside. In front of 46 Brigade, on its right, was the large Zonsche Wood. Straight ahead was the so-called main road from Eindhoven to Boxtel via the straggling village of Best. A lateral road went half right for three miles to the town of St Oedenrode. A railway line was parallel to, and half a mile to the west of, the road to Boxtel. Best is dominated by a church and monastery, and near the railway line south-west of the town centre were parallel sheds known as the Cement Factory. By dawn on the 22nd the Seaforths were across the Wilhelmina, with jeeps and anti-tank guns, and Lt-Col Hunt sent 'D' Company to occupy Best, which it did in a rather casual way. Every house was occupied by the enemy, and the Seaforths quickly lost thirty-three casualties. Brig Villiers immediately sent the Glasgow Highlanders across and the sappers completed a Class 9 bridge. But no tanks could get across. Intense mortar fire and Spandau bursts halted Lt-Col Campbell's Glasgow Highlanders. All the 46 Brigade patrols in the darkness of the day before had

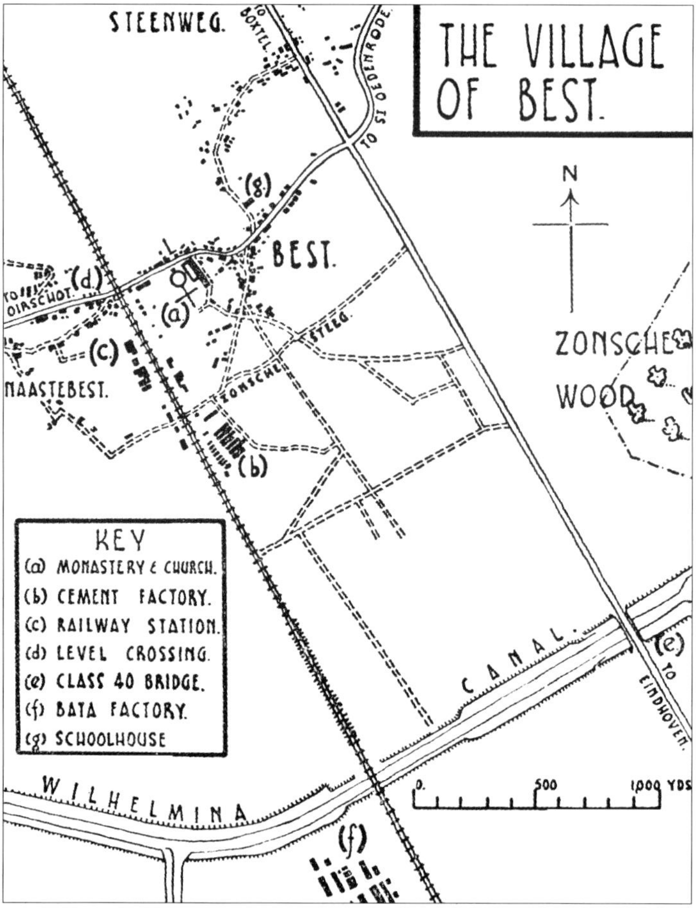

The grim battlefield around Best.

failed to bump the enemy defences, which were firmly dug in along the railway or snug in the Cement Factory and the cellars of the houses in Best.

By dusk on the 22nd the Glasgow Highlanders were scattered in and around Best, having taken the church and monastery. The KOSB arrived during the afternoon and went right-handed through Zonsche Wood, cleared by American paratroopers at the start of Market Garden, and occupied Steenweg, a village 600 yards east of Best. The enemy garrison of Best was estimated at two battalions, with the same mix that Gen Student had sent against the Aart bridgehead.

44 Lowland Brigade had moved up through Eindhoven past the huge Philips radio works and across the Bailey bridge, KOSB leading. Capt Woollcombe noted the grim evidence of overrun guns and equipment lying about in the Zonsche Wood, and 'enemy dead packed the ditches. The Yanks had certainly laid about them. We moved through a mass of empty

weapon-containers, ration cartons and the big white flutters of discarded parachutes.' In daylight the KOSB relieved the German corpses of their fine (looted) watches and wads of German and Dutch paper money, but not, unfortunately, valid Allied currency!

On the 23rd Brig Villiers put in a three-battalion attack. The KOSB was to link up with the Glasgow Highlanders holding the eastern part of Best; then the Glasgows and the Seaforths would put in a two-battalion attack westwards, with the railway line, station and Cement Factory as their objectives. It took all day for the KOSB to advance 400 yards, with house-to-house fighting, so at 1530 hours the second attack from Best started over the Zonsche Steeg (the inter-battalion boundary). Despite a barrage from one medium and two field regiments, Middlesex 4.2-inch mortars and medium machine guns, the joint attack failed to take the Cement Factory, but captured the railway station. Lt MacLellan's 'A' Company Glasgow Highlanders started its attack with three officers, including Maj 'Andy' Anderson and 2/Lt Tom McLaren (who had been commissioned from sergeant in the field). The platoons were commanded by sergeants and had to advance through a cemetery. No one had anything to eat that day, the wireless sets were not working and it was raining! The enemy had turned the Cement Factory into a fortress and was dug into the railway embankment and under the railway wagons in the sidings. By 1845 hours the Seaforth attack had failed, with six killed and thirty-three wounded. 46 Brigade was ordered up to help. The RSF came across the canal and moved through the KOSB round Steenweg (the hamlet north-east of Best), thence towards Vleut, another hamlet on the road north-east to St Oedenrode. The Royal Scots closed up south of the Wilhemina Canal, and so did the HLI, who had been left behind just south of Aart. A patrol discovered that Gen Student's forces had abandoned the bitterly contested Aart bridgehead! Near the railway line south of the canal was a large Bata shoe factory, which provided an excellent observation point for the Middlesex and Field Regiments.

On 24 September Gen Student's forces cut the main Army centre line between St Oedenrode (five miles north-east) and Veghel – hence the necessity for the Scottish Division to keep hammering away at the enemy defences in Best. It was pouring wet and a strong enemy counter-attack more or less overwhelmed the Glasgow Highlanders. 'B' Company under Maj Millar was over-run. Lt MacLellan was now acting OC 'A' Company, as Maj Anderson had been wounded, as had several of MacLellan's Canloan friends. 'My men came under deadly crossfire and I ran over to assist.' A machine-gun bullet hit his knee. 'I was shaken and so terribly angry at myself for being so careless as to get myself shot and felt sad that I had let my men down when they needed me most.'

Maj Briggs now took command of 'C' and 'D' companies and withdrew to the church and monastery. Later they withdrew into Brigade reserve, having lost nine officers and 138 men, of whom one officer and fifty men had been captured. Only six men were left in 'B' Company. 44 Brigade was tasked with a drive north-east towards St Oedenrode. At 0730 hours, as the ferocious German counter-attack came in on Best, the Royal Scots pushed rather painfully for a mile towards Vleut, which was later occupied by the RSF. The next day, the 25th, 227 Brigade moved across the Wilhelmina Canal with its objective Naastebet, a mile west of the railway line near Best. Despite RAF Typhoons smashing up the Cement Factory (but not its tough defenders), the Gordons were brought to a standstill with heavy casualties. The Cameronians on their right made little progress towards the railway. At 1630 hours Brig Colville called off the attack. However, on the right flank, Lt-Col MacKenzie's RSF, having cleared Vleut and Hoefke, reached Donderdonk.

Capt Rosdol, the Division's Intelligence Officer, made the first of several 'surrender' broadcasts to the German defenders. Usually a German deserter got a bullet in the back before he had gone twenty yards! Capt Woollcombe was detached with 'A' Company KOSB to move briskly along the northern bank of the canal eastwards to protect the bridge at Zon, which was guarded by one Dutch Resistance sentry with a rifle! An LAA battery took over from the KOSB as 'sentries'. On his return, Woollcombe encountered the immensely tall GOC, Maj-Gen 'Tiny' Barber, who told him the KOSB 'got a bloody nose today'. Woollcombe noted, 'A dour atmosphere had been cast over everyone. This had been a vicious little affray. "D" Company, advancing to some miserable farm buildings, had been caught in the open by intense Spandau fire and three parts destroyed.' That day Field Marshal Montgomery admitted defeat at Arnhem and decided to withdraw the remnants of 1st Airborne Division. Gen von Rundstedt turned his attention to the Nijmegen bridge and bridgehead, 'the gateway to the Reich', as he called it.

On the 26th, 46 Brigade made a determined attack out of Best to clear the fortress of the Cement Factory. Together with four SP guns, the gallant Seaforths did just that and cleared the fortress, but lost in the process four officers and thirty-eight men. On their right the Cameronians with considerable losses cleared the western sector of Best up to the railway line. For the next six days Seaforths and Cameronians stayed where they were, exhausted, reduced in numbers, but unbeaten. The GOC now decided to bypass the German resistance in Naastebest with a three-battalion drive towards St Oedenrode and the Dommel river west towards Liemde. So, with the Argylls in the centre, HLI on the right and RSF on the left, and with RAF Typhoon support, they moved off initially into thick scrub and then into dense woodland south of Liemde. All went well until 'B' Company Argylls met opposition in the forest and a Spandau burst killed Maj Robertson and Capt Shaw. CSM Davies, later awarded the DCM, crawled out under fire to retrieve Maj Robertson's maps and orders. Later the Argylls pulled out and spent a week near Vleut, then to Bakel.

The Recce Regiment had been busy each day. 'A' Squadron had patrolled forward from the bridgehead, up forest tracks, plotting the enemy's positions. 'C' Squadron guarded the main bridge built by the sappers across the canal, and its assault troop, the Bata shoe factory observation posts. 'B'

Squadron could not move far west, so nipped up to St Oedenrode and patrolled between the river Dommel and 'A' Squadron's patrols in the dense woods north of Vleut. At night the woods were alive with the chatter of small arms and the glow of tracer bullets. Night was the time of foot patrols. On one night Cpl Elliott and two others from 'D' Company Argylls brought forty-three prisoners, two Mongols but also forty-one Germans! The HLI and the RSF in their sweep north on the 26th took eighty and seventy-three prisoners respectively, and the KOSB got into the hamlets of Kremsel and Boschkant, south-west of St Oedenrode. Early on the 27th the whole of 227 Brigade was in defensive positions between Donderdonk and the Boxtel road north of Best. Lt-Col Richardson sent 'C' Company KOSB against Gasthuishoef, under cover of an artillery concentration. 'D' Company was badly mauled and 'C' Company was counter-attacked from Fratershoef. Difficult fighting went on till 2000 hours, when 'A' Company rejoined from the Zon bridge patrol and helped restore the situation.

Later that night, RSF put in an attack north of Kremsel, lost a number of men but took a small hill near the river Dommel with forty-five prisoners. Back at Best, the Seaforths sent a patrol to the railway wagons south of the Cement Factory and found it clear. The enemy, however, still held Naastebest. The next day – the 28th – the Royal Scots led out of Gasthuishoef, held by KOSB, to attack north-west on Fratershoef, taking forty prisoners. But a heavy counter-attack came in on the Royal Scots from a Luftwaffe GAF unit, which was met with artillery defensive fire targets and withdrew under a smokescreen. The German defenders were scrupulous in allowing Scottish RMOs and stretcher-bearers to bring their wounded in, and Lt-Col Lane Joynt, CO Royal Scots, reciprocated at Fratershoef. On the divisional front on the 29th little of importance occurred except for the usual intermittent mortaring and shelling. On the 30th it was not so: at 1830 hours a strong counter-attack came in on the three battalions of the Lowland Brigade south of the River Dommell, which after an hour's fight was repulsed with heavy losses. Further south the Cameronians got their patrols into Naastebest. But there was a sting in the tail on 1 October. A fighting patrol of the Cameronians was ambushed just outside Best; five were killed and eight wounded.

Operation 'Haggis' now followed, a peaceful and perhaps unique handover by 15th Scottish Division to 51st Highland Division over 1–4 October. In the eleven days of fighting to clear Best and the north-east to St Oedenrode, the division had lost 925 casualties, including 120 killed in action and 279 taken prisoner. The Glasgow Highlanders, KOSB, Seaforths and Gordons came off worst. In the words of Capt Woollcombe:

> The heavy grey days passed. Days of infiltration and counter-attacks, perpetual stand-to and artillery fire churning along drear tree lines. God-forsaken tracks that led nowhere or anywhere. The snarl of the hidden Spandaus in a fir plantation, RAF Typhoons circling in the sky. And lonely derelict farms, more dull names – Gasthuishof – Fratershof – for these names were now the work of the devil. And thoughts turned with persistence to when relief might come.

CHAPTER 10

Operation Pheasant: Capture of Tilburg

Mirabile dictu! To everyone's surprise, probably including the GOC, 15th Scottish was out of the line for nearly three weeks in and around Helmond, ten miles east of Eindhoven. At first Field Marshal Montgomery had intended to carry on the Rhineland battle without a pause. So recce parties went off after two days to plan an attack on Gennep in a joint operation with 3rd British Division, which had suffered similar casualties to the 15th! Two infantry divisions were to be broken up to provide reinforcements for the huge losses suffered by 21st Army Group since Overlord had started. In three months the division's casualties had reached 7,000, including 860 killed and 2,230 missing. Some of those wounded in earlier battles had recovered and rejoined, so training and integration of the newcomers – very many non-Scots – proceeded apace. Rifle companies, of course, trained in battle drill and the firing of weapons – boring to the veterans of the Odon, Aart and Best. Several staff majors joined the division as company commanders to get experience of infantry fighting. There were exercises in canal crossing by assault boat and with the Scots Guards tanks and practice with Kangaroos (armoured troop carriers – Canadian 'Ram' tanks without turrets).

Another possible operation for an assault crossing of the Wessem Canal was cancelled, although recce parties went to visit the US 7th Armoured Division near Weert, which was guarding the canal. Reinforcements poured in from many sources. By 5 October, 2nd Argylls, ensconced at Bakel, had only eleven officers left from the battalion that had crossed to Normandy. Despite best efforts, drafts of reinforcements were insufficient, so they and other formations could not maintain four complete rifle companies. Instead they formed a 43-strong 'battlegroup' with seven Bren guns, two mortars, two PIATs and a sprinkling of riflemen.

The Recce Regiment 'spring-cleaned' its vehicles and stripped down its weapons. One squadron was billeted in a large monastery. The bearded monks were fascinated by the armoured cars, but none was recruited. There was more sleep than usual, hot baths, ENSA shows and cinemas. Everybody played football, not only against other units but against the local Dutch sides. The Argylls just beat Bakel town. The massed pipes and drums of the division gave an impressive display in the grounds of Helmond Castle. The next Sunday the Recce Regiment marched to church, piped by 2nd Gordon Highlanders. On

Field Marshal Montgomery talks to 15th Scottish Division troops after investiture.

17 October at Geldrop the beating of the 'Retreat' was played by the pipes and drums of three battalions of Argyll and Sutherland Highlanders – the 2nd, of course (resuscitated from 93rd Highlanders), 91st Anti-tank and 7th Battalion. They played 'Cock o' the North', and the 'Retreat' programme included 'The Green Hills of Tyrel', 'My Home', 'The 79th's Farewell to Gibraltar', 'Because he was a Bonnie Laddie', 'The Highroad to Linton', 'The Blue Bonnets', 'Hielan Laddie', 'The Campbells are Coming' and 'Dovecote Park'.

But the war caught up again, with the planning for Operation 'Pheasant', in which the division as part of XII Corps, with its old friends 6th Guards Tank Brigade, would clear the triangle Best–St Oedenrode–Boxtel and then advance and capture Tilburg (west of Helmond and close to the Wihelmina Canal).

Various moves took place on the 19th and 20th, and, when the Cameronians revisited Best, the enemy was still on the far side of the railway and in Naastebest. For three days artillery and mortar shelling and night patrols resumed their deadly pattern. But the German defenders were now almost surrounded, and the strong positions at Liemde and Naastebest were abandoned on the night of 23 October. The Recce Regiment occupied Oerschot, also found to be empty.

It took three days to approach and liberate the large town of Tilburg. The division suffered 150 casualties during Pheasant, mainly in 46 Brigade, with the Seaforths and Cameronians coming off worst. 15th Recce Regiment pushed, probed and prodded ahead to Oirschot (having cleared obstacles and mines), and, with great help from the Dutch Princess Irene Brigade on bicycles, progressed to Moergestel, where the bridge, of course, was blown. The Recce troops then scooted north to Oisterwijk. This straggling village was heavily defended, as were the road bridges over the Voorste Stroom. The Seaforths moved up with the Scots Guards tanks on the night of 25 October. Meanwhile the Cameronians moved west from Moergestel and found the road and rail bridges two miles ahead, over the Wilhelmina Canal, duly destroyed. The main divisional road axis Oerschot–Moergestel into Tilburg was nearly always hopelessly congested. Brig Cockburn sent his 44 Brigade Royal Scots through forest tracks; KOSB, led by the Recce cars, followed the canal bank to Biest, a crossing point. The Glasgow Highlanders, following the Seaforths, were in Moergestel.

Early on the 26th, Lt-Col Hunt, CO of the Seaforths, organised a classic assault over the Voorste Stroom's two bridges, one a footbridge, the other a minor roadbridge. The Scots Guards tanks and artillery support provided cover and by 0900 hours a substantial bridgehead had been established. The Seaforths had forty-one casualties, had captured forty-four prisoners and killed many of the defenders. The Glasgow Highlanders came up in support but met heavy resistance from a large convent and a factory area.

With the help of Wasp flame-throwers, the northern part of Oisterwijk was taken, but the Glasgows lost seventeen casualties. On the southern flank the KOSB's patrols found the villages of Hilvarenbeek and Voorst empty.

The GOC, Maj-Gen 'Tiny' Barber, had by the 27th planned a four-pronged attack on Tilburg: the KOSB, through Broekhoven to the south, the RSF, who had found a covered route across moorland beside the Wilhelmina Canal, the Cameronians and Glasgow Highlanders, and, from Oisterwijk from due east, the Seaforths. Tilburg was found empty of German troops, who had demolished powerhouses, railway workshops, anything of military value. But they had left behind the 120,000 Dutch inhabitants. Capt Woollcombe, KOSB, wrote: 'Tilburg was now a mass of wild humanity and chaos swallowed us. The entire population must have been packed along our route. All these delirious people cheered and cheered. They showered fruit at us and storms of petals of the House of Orange. Men, young and old, ran up to shake us by the hand. Women with tears on their cheeks lifted little children to be kissed by "Tommy".'

One KOSB company reported over the wireless 'heavy civilian opposition'. Tilburg was divided into three brigade areas. Early on the 28th the GOC declared that Tilburg had been officially liberated. The celebrations by the people of Tilburg continued for 36 hours – laughing, dancing, singing (their National Anthem, of course), flirting and offering hospitality. The pipeband of the RSF went to the main square to play selections. 15th Scottish Division will never forget Tilburg.

There were, however, two sour notes. Part of the opposition to the Scots had been by a Dutch SS regiment. And it was learnt that the Germans had launched a spoiling counter-attack with two Panzer and one Paratroop divisions against the thinly held sector where 7th US Armoured Division was in the line, capturing Meijel and threatening Helmond.

CHAPTER 11

Meijel: Abomination of Desolation

The American 7th Armoured Division had been holding a dog-leg front about twenty-eight miles long in the empty Peel country between Wessem, up the Wessem Canal towards Nederweert north along the Noorder Canal and Deurne Canals. Opposite them were the two battlegroups, the Hubner and Hermann, part of the German 344th Division. Von Rundstedt on 27 October ordered up 9th Panzer and 15th Panzer (47 Panzer Corps) to cross the canals in front of them and push hard for Antwerp. Hitler knew that Antwerp port was crucial for supplies to 21st Army Group and Eisenhower's armies further south. If he could deny this use of Antwerp to the Allies, they would not have sufficient *matériel* to invade the Reich. His fortresses guarding the Scheldt could not hold out much longer and his V-Bombs that were hitting Antwerp could not close the port.

Meijel to the east and Ospel to the south were chosen as the initial objectives and quickly taken. Helmond was only thirteen miles away and could be reached by two roads, one through the small town of Asten, the other north through Liesel and Deurne. By the 28th the Panzers had made such progress that British 2nd Army HQ began to evacuate Helmond.

15th Scottish Division was ordered to make all haste to deploy in the Asten area. Curiously enough, the first two regiments in action were 131st Field Regiment RA and 25th Field Regiment from 8th Army Group Royal Artillery. They both fired almost non-stop for twenty-four hours, with a FOO with the US infantry two miles down the Asten–Meijel road. The GOC rushed up 227 Brigade to hold and block the Asten–Meijel road to Heusden, 44 Brigade the Asten–Liesel Road and 46 Brigade the Deurne–Liesel road. In the next two weeks, battles in and around Liesel, Hutten, Heitrak and the approaches to Meijel would take on Normandy severity. The two Panzer divisions were kept to the few roads, but they had immense artillery support from east of the Deurne Canal. 15th Scottish battalions were soon on the receiving end of huge mortar and shellfire concentrations, helped by accurate enemy observation from beyond the canal. The American combat groups had been swept aside.

The GOC realised Liesel was the key objective for the protection of Asten and Deurne and ordered a two-brigade attack on the 30th.

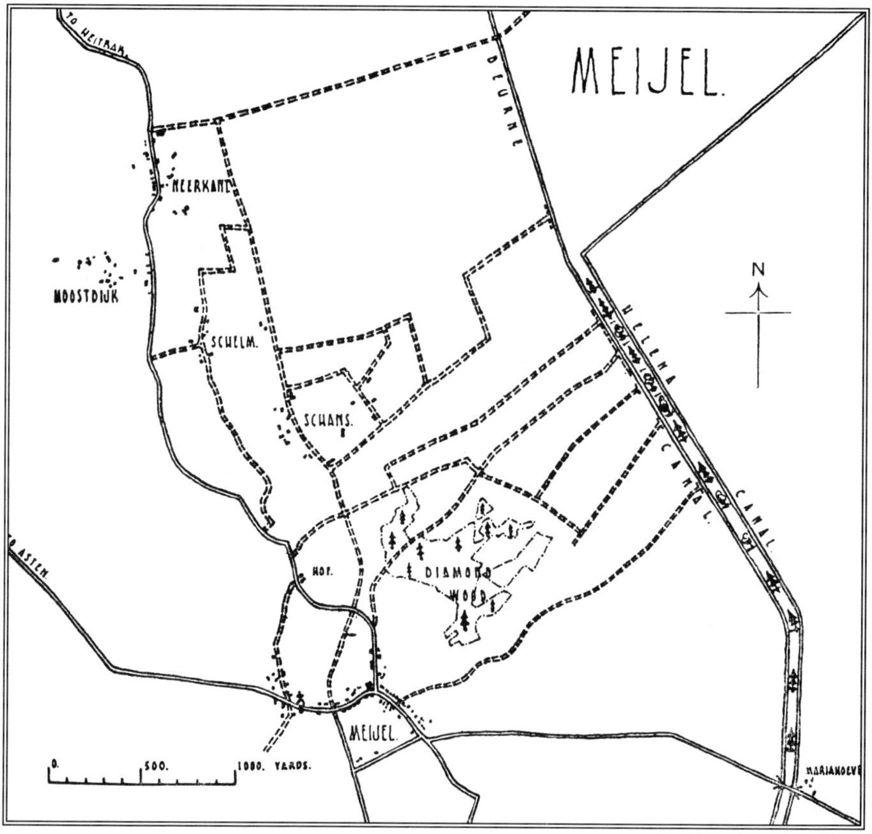

Meijel battle with Hubner and Hermann battlegroups.

From Leensel the RSF and Glasgow Highlanders, with Grenadier Guards tank support, advanced through woods a mile or so west of Liesel. Despite heroic support from the Middlesex medium-machine-gun platoon, German tanks and infantry overran a Glasgow platoon. The German tank support was Mark IVs, as the heavier Tiger and Panthers could not cross the canal bridging. The Royal Scots came up to support the Glasgows. The RSF with tanks got into the north-west part of Liesel, but strong-points around the church held them up. From the north, the Seaforths took Loon, but were halted in the northern suburbs of Liesel by SP 88s and fire from across the Deurne Canal. The predictable German counter-attack in the evening was just fended off by RSF and Seaforths. In fact von Rundstedt called his 47th Panzer Corps back across the canal that night, having lost twenty-five tanks and three SP guns. During the 30th the Glasgow Highlanders battlegroups suffered more than eighty casualties.

The next day, the 31st, after severe fighting, Liesel and the village Slot just south were painfully captured. The Parachute Regiment Battlegroup Hubner fought for every yard on a beastly black and lowering October day. 'D' Company of the Cameronians lost nearly seventy casualties including their CO, Lt-Col Sir Edward Bradford. The Luftwaffe made a rare appearance and bombed the Scots at night with shrapnel bombs. The KOSB's attack on Slot was successful and two Mk IV German tanks were destroyed.

On 227 Brigade's flank south of Heusden strong enemy infiltration during the night of 30/31 October caused the CO of HLI to bring down a divisional 'Uncle' target, scale 5, on a large wood ahead. On the morning of 1 November the Cameronians and Seaforths moved east of Liesel and Slot towards the Deurne Canal and found that the enemy had departed rather quickly and left a lot of equipment behind. KOSB patrols found Hutten empty, but 15th Recce found the enemy still in Heitrak and guarding the Hoogeburg bridge. On the 2nd the four-day battle for Moostdijk and Meijel started. In their withdrawal the Hubner battlegroup and 6th Parachute *Lehr* Regiment Hermann laid mines and booby-traps everywhere. On the roads, verges, tracks, they sowed Teller (anti-vehicle) mines, and anti-personnel 'R', 'S' and the new and deadly wooden-cased Schu mine. In thick mist south of Hutten, three flails and one Churchill tank were blown up on mines. Sgt Dobson, 15th Recce, noted: 'The road to Meijel was suicide. Everyone knew that. It was dead straight for the first mile beyond the infantry positions. It ran across open peat bogs and marshes and was banked up several feet above ground level. Within a couple of hundred yards of the village we pulled three strings of Teller mines off the road. We saw many Germans milling about in a wood 1,000 yards behind and to the right.' Snipers and four 88s in the village, firing indirectly, caused casualties. Evidently Meijel itself and Vieruitersten (Diamond Wood) to the north-east formed the enemy's defences. Deep minefields, ground too boggy for digging and merciless mortaring and shelling meant that progress south on the 2nd and 3rd was slow and very painful. Many more flails and Guards Churchill tanks were blown up or firmly bogged down. Both 46 and 227 Brigades adopted a system of two battalions at a time in the line, while the third spent five days at rest or in reserve. The Princess Irene Dutch Brigade had a comfortable training camp in the woods between Liesel and Deurne made available to 46 Brigade. 227 Brigade rested in Asten.

Combat teams 'A' and 'R' of the American 7th Armoured Division were still fighting vigorously, now approaching Stokers Horst, a village on the Noorder Vaart Canal south-west of Meijel. Large quantities of smokeshells were dumped on the 4th. The enemy had enjoyed – weather permitting – clear visibility for gunfire targets from the east side of the Wilhelmina Canal. Smokescreens would diminish that accuracy. On the 5th the Grenadier Guards tanks had a disaster as they advanced from Schelm south-east towards Diamond Wood – ahead lay a bottomless peat bog salted with mines. No. 2 Squadron of Churchills then had only two left battleworthy.

No. 1 Squadron with the RSF lost five tanks in a minefield. The division's gunners laid a thick smokescreen to help the crews of twenty-three Churchills, bogged down, to reach safety. At midnight on the 5th the GOC called the attack off.

Static warfare conditions prevailed in every sector of the Meijel front, and for ten days, with patrolling on both sides, slow and deadly mine clearance and 'stonks' and counter 'stonks' took place. The flat peat bogs were dotted with the wreckage of German and American (and now Scottish) armoured vehicles, half tracks and armoured cars. Almost every house that was not totally ruined was booby-trapped, and every hamlet was a German mortar registered target. On the 11th, 12th and 14th, KOSB patrols found Meijel empty, but so thoroughly mined and booby-trapped that it was a danger for weeks afterwards.

The battle for Meijel cost the division 750 casualties, mainly from the KOSB and RSF. 46 Brigade lost more than 200 and 227 Brigade 120.

Out of the line there were billets in Asten for hot baths, a change of clothes and a good, long sleep, and the Red Lion Club opened as a Divisional Rest Club in Tilburg. This, together with 48-hour-leave passes in Brussels, offered some comfort at the start of the winter of abomination and desolation.

Closing up on the Maas to Blerick

XII Corps was now made responsible for clearing the rain-swept, sad, boggy Peel country up to the River Maas between Blerick (a small town facing Venlo across the river) to Wessem, twelve miles further north. 15th Scottish was tasked with clearing the country round Helenaveen and Sevenum, the Horst, Tienraij, Lottum and finally Blerick. It would be a battle against rearguards, mines, craters and demolitions. The historians of the Recce Regiment wrote: 'Surpassing all else, mud – November mud, which clogged and clung or squelched and oozed and spread so wide and lay so deep that it soon obliterated the poor tracks which were the division's only eastward roads. These were strewn with bogged vehicles.' The RE companies laid miles of double Corduroy track, which helped a bit for road maintenance. Since the division's troops would be carried in Kangaroo armoured-personnel carriers, road and track maintenance was vital. Another new vehicle appeared – the Weasel – a light unarmoured, broad-track vehicle which was guaranteed to cross the mud. Unfortunately the scale of six per brigade was not nearly sufficient. The GOC planned two axes of advance: the northern (left) axis, called 'Ayr', from Liesel over the Class 40 bridge at Hoogebrug to Helenaveen and east by the Achterste Steeg to Stevenum; the southern (right) axis, called 'Skye', from Meijel over the Class 9 bridge at Mariahoeve, Beringen, north-east to Sevenum.

227 Brigade was allocated 'Skye' and 346 Brigade 'Ayr'. The German rearguards carried out a scorched-earth policy. Farmhouses, barns, shelters and haystacks were burned and the Scots infantry met a pitiful army of refugees who moved west with their few possessions in handcarts, in prams or on their backs. Old men and women and children trudged through the mud – abject human misery – as the *Wehrmacht* battlegroups slowly and painfully retreated.

Anti-personnel mines, Spandaus, mortars, of course, and a few determined SP 88s slowed down the Scottish advance. On 20 November the Cameronians, then the Glasgow Highlanders, then the Seaforths fought their way along 'Ayr' and the Gordons and Argylls along 'Skye'. On the 21st and 22nd weather conditions were appalling, and the rain turned all used tracks into mudbaths a foot or more deep. Churchill tanks were stuck, carriers and jeeps bogged. Sometimes a man got stuck in potholes and needed several others pulling a rope to extract him. The sappers even fed whole tree trunks into the morass on top of Sommerfeld and Corduroy track. The bog swallowed the lot and asked for more. One night the six Weasels of 46 Brigade made fourteen trips each bringing up rations, blankets, cooking sets and possibly mail.

By last light on the 22nd, Horst, Vorst and Sevenum were reached on 'Skye' route. But the bogs on 'Ayr' were so widespread and deep that the GOC ordered Brig Villiers to send his transport and guns to the north on 11th Armoured Division's axis, which went through Amerika. The author's armoured group went through Amerika that day. Beside the apology for a track were dead German soldiers, most of them booby-trapped.

Cpl Ridge, driver for Lt-Col K.C.C. Smith, CO of the Recce Regiment, wrote:

> Going to visit 'C' Squadron [at Horst] we put the jeep into four-wheel drive and low-ratio bottom gear and started to plough our way through [from Beringen]. We passed many bogged vehicles, but got through to Squadron HQ in Sevenum. We left about three o'clock and on the way back were stonked by mortars. After two miles we came to the sea of mud. The wheeled track and the tank track were now both pretty deadly. We tried the tank tracks. After 20 yards the jeep sank up to its axles. I dug but the mud came back as fast as I dug it out.

Rescued by an infantry carrier, the jeep sank again, and so on.

On 24 November the infantry of all three brigades remained halted. General Mud had won! The sappers repaired several bridges on the canal system north of Horst. The weather was better on the 25th and 227 Brigade pressed north; the Gordons occupied Swolgen, the Argylls Tienraij and the HLI remained south in Eikelenbosch. The enemy shelled each battalion severely. The Recce Regiment found white flags hanging from the church in Tienraij, and pushed a troop to the outskirts of Broekhuizervorst on the banks of the River Maas, where the enemy was using one of the remaining ferries. Sgt Millroy's armoured car in the lead was nearly hit by a bazooka and became ditched. Lt Richford on the wireless ordered, 'Bale out, bale out'. 'Bale out be b . . . ered,' said the old cavalryman. 'I've got a thousand fags in here and they're not for the bloody Jerries.' So under cover of smoke not only were Sgt Millroy's fags kept safe and the car towed away, but, furious at these indignities, the sergeant ran up to the house where the bazooka had come from and pitched grenades through a window. He attacked another position on foot with a Bren gun and his patrol then supported the Gordons in storming the main strong-point. Millroy received an immediate award of the DCM.

The enemy had fortified half a dozen towns and villages on the west bank of the Maas, which they now proceeded to defend in their traditional manner. These were ferry sites that the Cameronians at Lottum and the Gordons at Broekhuizervorst did their best to capture or destroy.

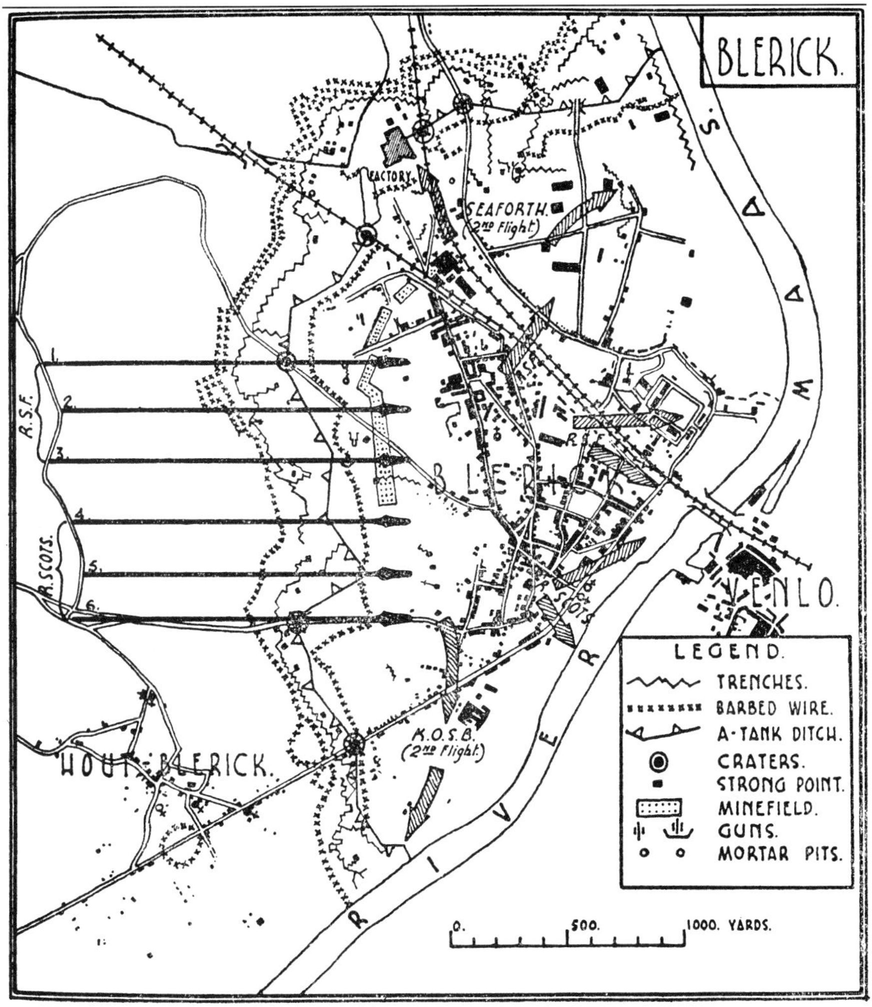

Operation Guildford – the capture of Blerick.

The Argylls' historian describes the scenes: 'Tienraij presented the now familiar picture of ruined houses, mined roads and felled and booby-trapped trees, but by now most of the troops had become pretty wary and skilful at negotiating such things without casualties. The shelling was at times intense . . .'. But it was now the turn of 44 Brigade to close out the Scottish drive to the Maas, with the capture of Blerick. Codenamed Operation 'Guildford', it must rank as one of the most intelligent and carefully planned assaults on a defended town in the north-west Europe campaign. The case history of Guildford was later written up in a War Office pamphlet. Situated on the west bank of the Maas, Blerick was in effect a suburb of the larger Venlo, separated by 150 yards of water. Venlo, of course, dominated the Guildford battlefield, with German observation points in tall buildings and higher ground to the east. The defences of Blerick were formidable. The approaches from the west were 2,000 yards of flat ground without cover, leading to an anti-tank ditch over three miles long, covered with a belt of wire and a minefield. Massed German mortars and artillery covered – from Venlo – all the approaches to Blerick, itself a confusing place of tortuous, winding narrow streets. There was almost no chance of the paratroop defenders of Blerick escaping.

Brig Cumming-Bruce, 44 Brigade, and Brig Knight, 31st Tank Brigade Group, planned Guildford carefully: a mock but realistic attack from the north in the Glasgow Highlanders' sector, with fighting patrols and sound effects of tank noises; breaches blown in the wire defences with Bangalore torpedoes; massive artillery support from three AGRAs, 3rd, 8th and 59th, totalling more than 400 guns; and, for the first time on land, Canadian 'Mattresses' of rockets that could saturate an area 200 yards square.

The real attack would come in from the west in two phases. The Armoured Breaching Force would assault in six parallel lanes, 300 yards apart. Gen Percy Hobart made a name for himself in the Second World War by his brilliant formation of three armoured divisions. His 79th Armoured was composed of a magnificent collection of armoured vehicles, nicknamed the 'Funnies'. In Brig Knight's command were 22nd Dragoons with Sherman flails for mine clearance, part of 81st Armoured Regiment RE with bridge-laying Churchill tanks, a squadron of 1st Fife and Forfar flame-throwing Crocodiles. These were backed by 107 Royal Armoured Corps Churchill gun tanks and two squadrons of Kangaroos. With skilful deployment of this specialised armour, breaches could be made in the defence, under the formidable barrage of artillery, rockets and of a smokescreen. The Scottish infantry would be in Kangaroos, the RSF in the three lanes on the left (north) and the Royal Scots in the three lanes on the right (south). The Kangaroos would decant the RSF and Royal Scots in the centre of Blerick and then return to collect the KOSB and Seaforths to bring them into battle. At the last moment on the evening of 2 December the rain came down on already soaking ground, with the serious risk of the armour getting bogged down before breaching the defences. The decision went all the way up to the Corps Commander. Luckily the rain stopped at 2100 hours. At 0525 hours on the 3rd the mighty AGRAs and Mattresses started up Guildford. The armour moved off at 0745 hours and predictably five flails were bogged. By 0925 hours the AVREs had laid bridges on Lanes 1, 2, 5 and 6. The Royal Scots drove straight through into the town outskirts, but the RSF decided at the last moment to march over the extremely boggy terrain in front of them. By early afternoon the Royal Scots, with the RSF and KOSB following up, were in the heart of Blerick, albeit under heavy shelling. By 1600 hours the battle had been won for a cost of only fifty casualties. More than 250 prisoners and a large amount of equipment were

Royal Scots Fusiliers hunt snipers in the streets of Blerick, 5 December 1944.

captured. Nearly 3,000 Dutch civilians emerged pale, shaken but enthusiastic from their cellars and shelters. The rain came down again and all six lanes were soon impassable. The history of 44 Brigade notes:

> Each time the recipe was the one learned at Blerick – meticulous preparation and planning, concentration of all available fire power, use of the 'Funnies' [and not the infantry] to overcome the obstacles and a quick, bold use of the infantry to exploit the advantage won by the success of the armour – if possible by moving straight into the heart of the enemy position. This recipe brought quick success at little cost.

After the terrifying battles in the Gheel bridgehead and at Meijel, the success at Blerick gave the whole division a psychological boost.

CHAPTER 13

Watch on the Maas: Winter 1944/5

From 4 December until the end of January 1945 the Scottish Division held – rather defensively – the line of the River Maas from near Grubbenvoorst in the north to Kessel in the south. Across the 150 yards of river, 'No Man's Land' was an aggressive, first-class Parachute division. It had, of course, taken with it all the Dutch ferries and boats of all descriptions. The divisional assault boats were meant for canals, not a wide fast-flowing river. Apart from the division's artillery and mortars, there was little aggressive activity. Observation points were manned in Blerick and regularly exchanged fire with the paratroops in front of them. The German patrols were exceedingly bold, active and elusive and they often lay up on the Scottish side during the day. One Recce Regiment outpost was rushed at night and lost nine prisoners. The division's tactics were aimed at protecting their outposts with wire, minefields and constant standing and recce patrols at night changing routes, locations and timing. Holding twenty miles of line in the Dutch bleak midwinter against a very aggressive enemy was always a duel of wits. The Recce Regiment historian wrote:

> From slit trenches, from the houses the squadron look-outs spied all day on the Germans across the 150 yards of water, and watched the distant white vertical trails which showed where rockets were being fired at Antwerp. The Germans looked out from similar hiding places on the other side. Sometimes their shells shrieked over, ripping into the woods. Nights were tense. Look-outs were replaced by listening posts close to the river. Ears were strained for the sound of a German patrol coming across by boat. Eyes peered into the darkness until familiar bushes became crouching men. It was not the policy to cross to the German side, but the German patrols crossed frequently at night and slipped easily through the thin screen of outposts.

At first, 44 Brigade was in the line holding an eleven-mile front astride Blerick, with its reserve at Rooth and Maasbree. Then 227 Brigade held a sector south of 44, with battalions on the Maas at Baarlo and Kessel and reserve at Helden. On 17 December 46 Brigade came into the line at Haelen and Buggenum with reserve at Roggel. All three brigades rang the changes on their battalions at regular intervals.

Capt Baggaley, KOSB, quoted this doggerel verse:

> As I sit on the banks of the Maas
> I reflect it is really a farce
> At my time of life
> and miles from my wife
> To be stuck in the mud on my arse.

On 13 December Field Marshal Montgomery visited the division again at Zomeren for a presentation of medal ribbons. The Recce Regiment received twelve. 'I remember very clearly,' he said,

> visiting your Division in England when I came back from Italy, and I well remember your division landing in Normandy when you came over just after D-Day. You were untried then, though you had some veterans with you. I remember the first time your Division went into battle at the River Odon, and I remember feeling anxious that the division should acquit itself well. One can't help feeling anxious at those times, though there is no need to. Your division did very well indeed, and you have never looked back since. You have only to look at the Battle Honours on the stage behind me – I have noticed well-known names like Caumont – to realise how much you have done.
>
> I expect that today there are representatives here of every unit in the division. When you go back I would like you to tell the others that I came here today, and that I think this division has done awfully well. In this fighting no division has done better, and it is a first-class show. We did not expect anything else, but it is very creditable for all that.

Leave to the UK would start from 1 January 1945 to some of those, chosen by draw, who had six months' or more continuous service overseas. By mid-December the weather had turned bitterly cold and snow had fallen; the canals were iced over, with nights of temperatures below zero. White snow 'zoot' suits were issued. All transport engines had to be run at regular intervals to prevent freezing up. Even wireless batteries froze and burst. Instead of the autumn mud, the tracks now had deep iron ruts in them. There was alarm in case the Maas itself should freeze. The enemy patrols came over and bazookad the Middlesex vehicles and blew up the Ferry House near Baarlo. In Blerick, held by the KOSB, a house on the waterfront was observed to have a large Swastika flag flying. The KOSB, were bombarded by leaflet shells printed in English, which ended 'Death in the Meuse'. Once a whole paratroop company came over and stayed near Tienraij for several days. The Ardennes Battle of the Bulge came, and eventually went, in late December, over Christmas and into the New Year. There was a convincing rumour that the German paratroopers were planning a comprehensive raid or raids over Christmas, which made it a muted, watchful period for the Scots. Just opposite Kessel, the paratroopers put up a mass of fireworks at midnight, nipped across (they were even known to have swum across in freezing water) and captured four Scots from a forward post. Nevertheless, belated Christmas dinners were duly eaten (in reserve positions), with excellent tinned turkey, plenty of beer and of course the nightly rum ration. On New Year's Day the Luftwaffe appeared in force, and several were shot down in the divisional area.

Behind the lines, many Scotsmen made firm friends with Dutch families, particularly in Helmond. A Dutch concert party came to Lierop to entertain the Recce Regiment. One poem entitled 'To our Liberators' was read with great feeling by its author. 'We sighed and sighed in slavery; we cursed the horrid Huns.'

> Then after years of pining, hark! The sound of saving guns.
> Our trembling hearts cried out for joy in spite of bomb and shell.
> For was not Heaven coming after years and years of Hell.

In reply to that four-line tribute, a Scotsman penned another poem reproduced in a Helmond newspaper:

> Our stay with you, so short has been
> but you have made us feel
> t'was worth our while in freeing you
> from the yoke of the Nazis heel.

Plus another four verses.

Between 20 and 26 January, now that the Ardennes campaign had been tidied up, 6th Airborne Division moved up from one severe combat zone to a more peaceful one, by relieving 15th Scottish. The Army Commander and the Corps Commander inspected most of the division and had a good look at the enemy positions in Venlo from the observation points in Blerick. Just before they departed to Sevenum, then to Goirle, south of Tilburg, half a dozen RAF Spitfires dived and machine-gunned the Argylls' transport. It was the end of the Watch on the Maas.

CHAPTER 14

Operation Veritable: Closing up on the Rhine

Having successfully masterminded a significant part of the eventual victory in the Ardennes, Field Marshal Montgomery now devised Operation 'Veritable', the destruction of all the German forces between the Maas and

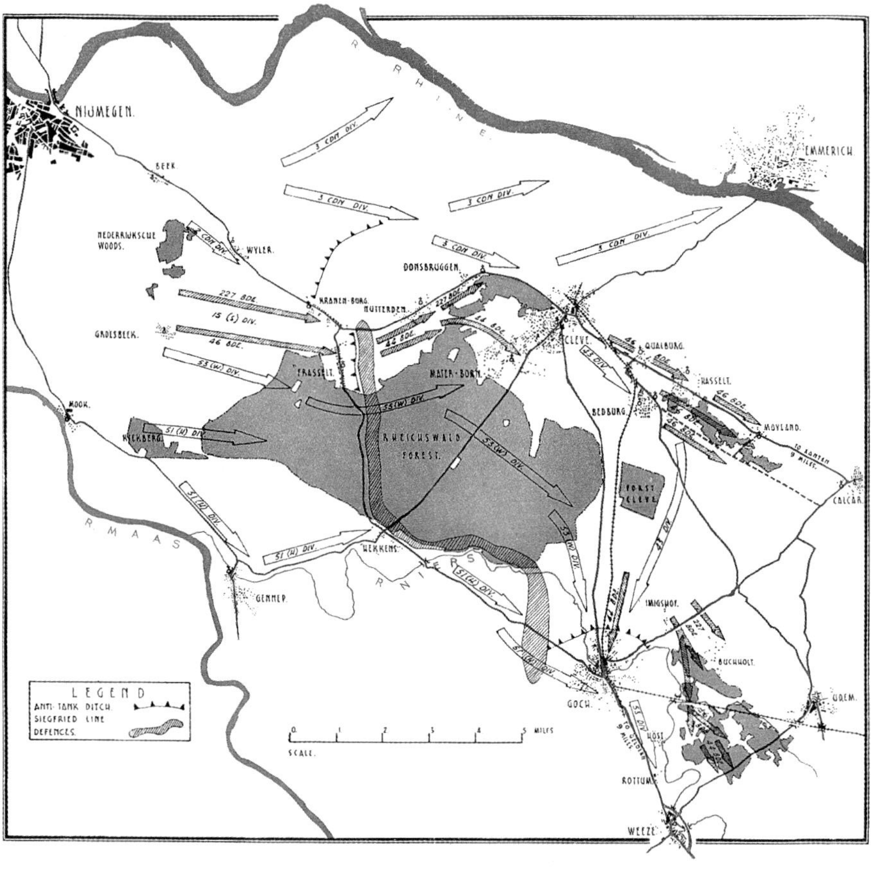

Operation Veritable, through the Siegfried Line to the Rhine.

Lt-Gen Horrocks, Field Marshal Montgomery and Maj-Gen Barber, GOC 15th Scottish Division, confer during Operation Veritable.

the Rhine. This of course meant the invasion of Germany and the breaking of the Siegfried Line defences. The First Canadian Army with the British XXX Corps under command would launch a massive offensive from the Nijmegen bridgehead, south-east, with the final objective the line of the Rhine between Geldern and Xanten. Specifically the XXX Corps offensive would start a five-divisional front, from north to south 3rd Canadian, 2nd Canadian, 15th Scottish, 53rd Welsh and 51st Highland. The first phase for 15th Scottish would be to breach the Siegfried Line north of the Reichswald Forest and seize the high ground overlooking Cleve, an advance of about eight miles. Four hundred and forty-six freight trains lifted a quarter of a million tons of stores to the railheads near Tilburg. Four hundred miles of existing roads had to be repaired and a further hundred miles of new roads constructed. Eight hundred thousand special new maps had to be issued and a half a million air photographs taken of the battleground up to the Rhine. Thirty-five thousand vehicles took part in Veritable, and five bridges had to be built across the Maas leading to the forward assembly areas. 1st Canadian Army deployed nearly half a million men. The German defences ahead eventually totalled eleven divisions. No fewer than 1,334 guns in five AGRAs had been concentrated to support Veritable, with initially 600 rounds per gun. And 1,500 tanks would be in support from the Guards

'B' Company 2nd Argyll & Sutherland Highlanders aboard their 'big friends' in Kranenburg, 8 February 1945, at the start of Operation Veritable, in which 15th Scottish Division suffered over 1,500 casualties.

Armoured Division, three armoured brigades and no fewer than eleven regiments of 79th Armoured Division's Funnies.

The mighty Siegfried Line between the Maas and the Rhine was organised in three zones of defended localities, minefields, hedgehog defences, pillboxes and an anti-tank ditch. Half a dozen small towns and villages had been fortified and integrated into the various zones of defences. The initial German garrison was 84th Infantry Division, reinforced by three parachute battalions – a total of thirteen battalions with 100 guns. In mobile reserve were three Panzer-type and two Parachute divisions within a few days' march to the front. Support for 15th Scottish would come from 6th Guards Tank Brigade, 2nd Household Cavalry (Recce) Regiment, 22nd Dragoons (flails), 101st RAC (Crocodiles), 6th Assault Regiment RE (scissors bridges and fascines to fill craters and trenches), 1st Canadian Armoured Personal Carrier Regiment (Kangaroos), a searchlight company, two SP field regiments, two SP anti-tank batteries and a medium 5.5-inch artillery regiment. The RAF 2nd Tactical Air Force would bomb enemy railheads, bridges and ferries in the areas behind the immediate front. It was an overwhelming military array.

For a week the division enjoyed the hospitality of Tilburg in friendly Dutch billets. The divisional Tam O' Shanters, ENSA and cinema shows, battalion canteens and dances were all exceedingly good for morale. During the day, training or dealing with deep wire entanglements, minefields, concrete pillboxes, studies of aerial photographs, maps and cloth model exercises were part of the rigorous countdown. The Recce Regiment was billeted in a cold Trappist monastery where the bearded monks wore brown or white robes and brewed Trappisten beer in silence. 'C' Squadron, the traffic police force for the difficult

10th HLI on Kangaroos in Kranenburg, in Operation Veritable, 9 February 1945.

but successful attack on Blerick, was to do the same through the Siegfried Line. The other squadrons were tasked with the reconnaissance from Cleve to Calcar and Udem and to find roads between Cleve and the Reichswald for the Household Cavalry armoured cars to make a dash for Goch.

Brig Cumming-Bruce had told each battalion of 44 Brigade, 'The other two brigades are going to reach the Siegfried Line, and then our brigade is going to go through the Siegfried Line.' It was reassuring to be told that the northern extension of the Siegfried Line along the Dutch frontier was mainly earthworks without the concrete fabrications to be encountered further south. In the first phase of attack D-Day, 8 February, starting from Groesbeek, 227 Brigade on the left flank and 46 on the right would advance some three miles to secure the general line Kranenburg to Frasselt. The second phase would start at 2100 hours on D-Day when 44th Brigade Group, repeating the successful Blerick combined operation, would breach the Siegfried Line north of the great Reichswald forest and penetrate to Nuttenden, a long straggling village along the Cleve–Nijmegen road. This would be illuminated by 'Movement Light' or Monty's Moonlight. The immense Corps fireplan had twelve phases, of which many would be specific barrages ahead of the Scots, with a series of 300-yard lifts every twelve minutes. Hundreds of Lancaster and Halifax bombers roared over the troops during the night of the 7th to smash Cleve and Goch. But the soaking rain caused the medium bomber strikes on the villages of Nuttenden and Materborn to be cancelled. For 46 Brigade, the Glasgow Highlanders led, through Boesteeg, across the German frontier to reach Haus Kreuzfuhrt and Hettsteeg, their objectives. They took 150 prisoners in a successful advance, despite flail and Coldstream tanks getting bogged. The Cameronians took over, reached the Galgensteer spur, the woods round Auf Den Heovel, and by dusk had captured Frasselt. 'B' Company took heavy losses in a minefield, but forty-eight prisoners were taken and a battery of 88mm guns captured. Many tracked AFVs were bogged down. The Crocodiles burned down many enemy-occupied houses in Frasselt, which greatly helped the Cameronians.

On the left flank, the Argylls led, with the HLI in support on their left, in their advance to capture Klinkenbeg and the road–railway triangle beyond Kranenburg. The Argylls, whose CO was on UK leave, were commanded by Maj Goodwyn in their first set-piece action since Normandy. They set off riding on the Churchill tanks of 3rd Scots Guards, from the thick woods near Hooge Hof. After an early breakfast and a tot of rum, they moved through an American minefield. A stream then bogged down all the armoured fighting vehicle (AFV) support. 'B' Company ran into a thickly sown anti-personnel minefield, which caused seven casualties. 'A' Company received heavy defensive fire, which killed or wounded all the officers. CSM Green took command and rallied the company and was awarded an immediate DCM. Elsenhof strong-point was taken after a hammering by the Canadian Mattress rockets, and eighty prisoners were taken. 'C' Company also took eighty prisoners, but also lost some of its own men to heavy enemy DF. Then the Argylls and the HLI, after a difficult afternoon's fighting, cleared Kranenburg, and to everyone's surprise the customary German counter-attack failed to materialise.

By 1830 hours the Scots had achieved Phase One of Veritable with complete success. By nightfall the mediocre tracks, saturated with heavy rain and thirty-ton AFV movement, simply gave up. First 227 Brigade's track became impassable; by 9 February 46 Brigade's narrow unmetalled track, with deep ditches on either side, was completely useless. The main Nijmegen–Wyler–Kranenburg road was cleared only by the neighbouring Canadian Division late at night on the 8th. It was by heroic efforts that AVREs of the Armoured Breaching Force (ABF) (of which 44 Brigade was part) reached a key anti-tank ditch east of Frasselt, and laid a scissors bridge and fascines. By dawn 'C' Company of KOSB had crossed it and established a bridgehead in Schottheide and Konigsheide, and was soon joined by the other rifle companies. The ABF was twelve hours late because of the diabolical bogs and morasses that had once been reasonable tracks.

The KOSB had spent twelve hours in their Kangaroos. They noted the slogans painted in big white capitals on the battered buildings: *Wir Glauben an Adolf Hitler* and frequently *Ein Volk, Ein Reich, Ein Führer.* Captain Robert Woollcombe recollected:

Lt-Col B.A. Pearson, CO 8 Royal Scots (44 Brigade) and Lt-Col de Wilton, 2 Gordons (227 Brigade) consult a map on the way to Cleve, 10 February 1945.

> It was one of the great moments of the campaign. We were the first British unit to breach the main belt of the Siegfried Line. The mist had cleared and the rain was holding off for a while. The sky was dull and overcast. Tactically it was mighty ground . . . various small hills, or knolls partly wooded stood about, the chief of which, named Hingst-berg, was near Nuttenden, which gave its name to the whole sector.

The Gordons, under command of 44 Brigade, had a similarly traumatic journey – ruined tracks, mines, roadblocks and trenches – so that it was only at dawn that they passed through the HLI in the ruins of Kranenburg. They then captured intact the road bridge over the main anti-tank ditch and by 1000 hours had cleared Nuttenden, capturing 200 shell-shocked prisoners lurking in deep concrete bunkers.

Lt-Col Richardson sent 'A' and 'B' companies of KOSB in their Kangaroos on to Wolfs-Berg, where whole bodies of enemy with their NCOs in front came doubling across the fields in perfect columns to give themselves up. Medium guns were overrun and ten enemy officers and a Battalion HQ surrendered. The Royal Scots then occupied Hingst-Berg, half a mile to the north-east, the link between the Gordons and the KOSB. The second phase of Scottish Division's part of Veritable was completely successful, albeit nearly twelve hours behind schedule. The GOC kept up the pressure against the Materborn feature, two hills south-west of the key objective of the town of Cleve. The Gordons, Royal Scots and KOSB pushed east in Kangaroos supported by Grenadier Churchill tanks. The Esperance feature, Bresserberg and Donsbreuggen were then cleared.

2 Gordon Highlanders pass knocked-out German AFVs, advancing from Donsbruggen towards Cleve, 11 February 1945.

The old spiteful enemy in Venlo, 7th Parachute Division, had been rushed into the defences of the Siegfried Line and met the KOSB head on in the straggling hamlet of Bresserberg. The ABF 'Blerick fashion' was in full flow; Churchills and Crocodiles belted BESA fire and flame at the defenders in the wrecked buildings. 'So our first night in Germany came down in utter destruction and the crackling of fires. It is hard to reflect the violence of it. Always there was one more river, and during the opening days of the Veritable offensive, a wave of bitterness swept through the troops as never before. At last it was Germany. The thought never left you: Germany. It did not matter what damage we did,' wrote Capt Woollcombe.

Damage indeed had been done to Cleve. Gen Horrocks asked for a heavy bombardment, and 700 Lancasters duly dropped 1,384 tons of high explosive. The streets were blocked with craters and rubble. Horrocks now made a rare mistake. 15th Scottish was in the western suburbs when 43rd Wessex was ordered up to complete the capture of the town, even though 15 Recce with tank support had pushed right through. A Wessex brigade took a wrong turning and also found itself in the centre of Cleve. Soon there was the most monumental traffic jam. The story gets worse. 43rd Wessex artillery bombarded the RSF near Stern-Berg and caused casualties in all four rifle companies. Two more enemy divisions now appeared, one of them 6th Parachute Division commanded by Gen-Lt Plocher. Eventually 43rd Wessex was persuaded to remain in the Materborn area in the southern suburbs, and the KOSB and Royal Scots took over. The Gordons under Lt-Col de Wilton, with Scots Guards tank support, entered Cleve from Donsbreuggen along the main west–east road. The Gordons cleared the northern sector over the canal west of Cleve railway station. The HLI arrived at dusk and almost had a pitched battle with their friends! The Canadian 3rd Division sent a small task force, 'swimming' with their Buffaloes, down the west bank of the Spoy Canal into the very northern suburb of Cleve – finally captured on 11 February. All this time the Recce Regiment had been probing hard. Capt Boynton and Lt Gillings led a patrol with six Sherman tanks. 'On the far side of Cleve, the commander of the column called a halt until daylight. After an eternity, dawn broke and we went forward past the leading tanks. Sgt Grice's car had been swallowed by an enormous crater, but during the night he and his crew had taken more than 30 prisoners, put them into a cellar and guarded them with a Bren gun.'

The next objectives were Moyland and Calcar, five and seven miles south-east, on the road to Xanten and Goch, a town eight miles due south of Cleve.

The Germans had now breached the winter dykes on the Alter Rhine, and a huge area in the Canadian sector was under two feet of water.

46 Brigade set off early on the 12th, with the Seaforths in Kangaroos, a Coldstream tank squadron, a battery of SP guns, and sappers, under command of Lt-Col Hunt of the Seaforths. In a dramatic action in Qualburg, a mile south-east of Cleve, 'B' Company had four Kangaroos knocked out by bazookas and an SP gun. They quickly debussed and cleared house by house, killing twenty-five, wounding many more, taking sixty-five prisoners – but at a cost of twenty-five casualties. The rest of the division was not in action in or around Cleve. Meanwhile 15th Panzer Grenadier and 116th Panzer Divisions were reported further south. For five days 46 Brigade fought a savage, brutal battle to take Moyland, with its crossroads, woods and Schloss. Brig Villiers sent the Cameronians and Glasgow Highlanders south-east from Bedburg. The Seaforths were still on the main road south-east of Hasselt.

Lt-Col Baker-Baker's Glasgows advanced through thick pine woods from Rosendahl to the village of Tillemanskath against ferocious shelling, mortaring and SP guns and took heavy losses. Lt-Col Remington Hobbs' Cameronians were tasked with the capture of two knolls in the woods half a mile west of Moyland, and suffered just as severely. On the 18th and 19th, 46 Brigade and the HLI were pulled out for a brief rest in Cleve. Despite AGRA support, Typhoons with 'Limejuice' and WASP flame-throwers, the bravery shown by the infantry was not enough. The paratroopers fighting in their *Reich* and supported by immense artillery and mortar fire had been ordered – come what may – to defend the axis Cleve–Calcar, as being the key to the defence of the Rhineland.

It was now 44 Brigade's turn for a major assault on the town of Goch, which is on the River Niers. It had a population of 10,000 inhabitants and, like Cleve, was a major defence point in the Siegfried Line. Battlegroups of 2nd, 7th and 8th Parachute divisions and 180th and 190th Infantry divisions were known to be defending Goch, although they would have lost heavy casualties in the first ten days of Veritable and the RAF bombing. Nevertheless, there

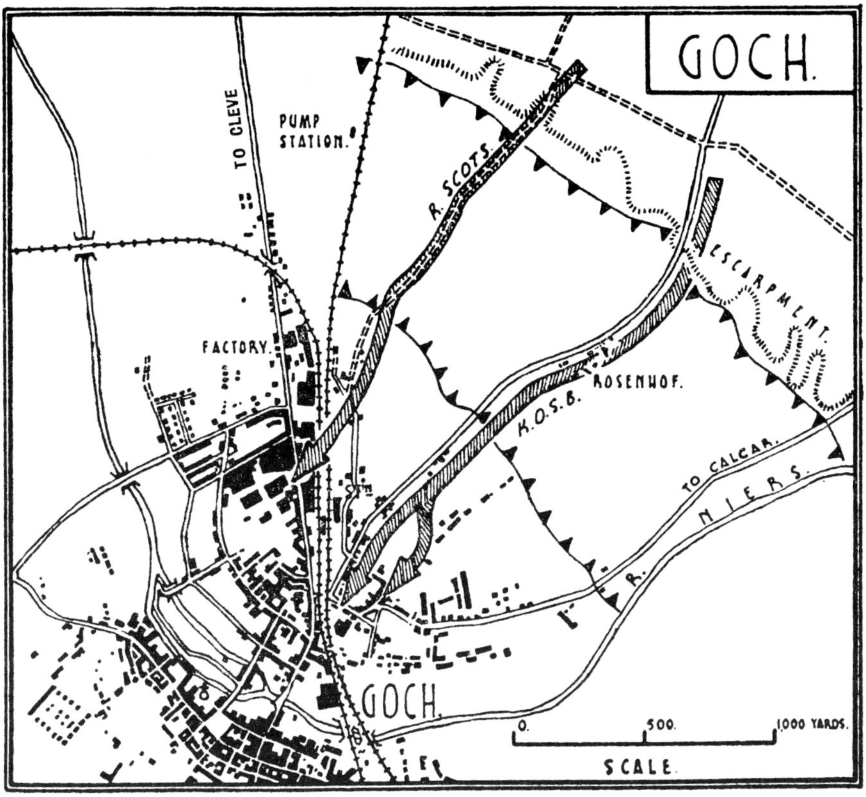

Goch, a major defence point in the Siegfried Line.

were two anti-tank ditches dug around Goch. Gen Horrocks's plan for Veritable had been delayed and he was anxious to capture Goch quickly. 51st Highland Division would attack from the south-west, 53rd Welsh from the north and 43rd Wessex from the north-east, and 15th Scottish would take Goch in the sector north of the River Niers on the eastern side of the town.

The Armoured Breaching Force of Grenadier Guards Churchill tanks and an array of Funnies moved from Cleve to the assembly point near Pfalzdorf. Brig Cumming-Bruce's plan was that the Royal Scots on the right (northern) flank, and the KOSB on the left (southern) flank, in Kangaroos, would follow the Funnies, under the usual huge barrage, including Mattresses. The anti-tank ditches were ten feet deep and, in key places, twenty-five feet wide, so that bridging or fascine laying would be difficult but essential.

The floods had endangered the whole system of supply. One of the main artillery shell dumps was submerged. The RASC drivers splashed their three-tonners through from Nijmegen. For two difficult days they drove red-eyed for want of sleep, over treacherous roads often two feet deep in flood water, to deliver shells and rations. The set-piece artillery plans required thousands of shells to be in place for the three field regiments' fire programmes.

During the 18th, despite many vicissitudes, both the Royal Scots and KOSB fought their way across the ditches into the eastern edges of the town, clearing the defended houses and large factory site. They worked closely with the Grenadiers, who shot up each house in turn, and soon white rags waved from every doorway. By 1800 hours on the 19th 600 prisoners had been taken, mainly from 190th Fusiliers, who had arrived post-haste from Venlo on their bicycles! The RSF, following up behind the KOSB and into the north-east sector of Goch, were very heavily shelled and casualties were rather heavy. It was probable that the Germans were firing off their huge Siegfried Line ammunition dumps before they were forced back over the Rhine.

The next divisional objective was for 227 Brigade Group to capture the village of Bucholt and the Schloss Calbeck, on the east side of the River Niers three miles east of Goch. The brigade had been in Corps reserve for a week, and plans changed almost hourly – for an attack on Calcar, or on Goch, but in fact to Imigshof, the start position for the attack on Bucholt. On the right (east) flank were the Glasgow Highlanders, and on the left (west) flank the Argylls being driven in Kangaroos or on the backs of the Coldstream tanks, with a troop of Crocodiles in support. Three hours after the 1000 start all the objectives had been taken, despite intense German defensive fire, and 350 prisoners had been captured. Most of the 15th Scottish battalions were now using WASP flame-throwers mounted in a Bren carrier with considerable success. A cumbersome Crocodile with its dangerous fuel towed behind would bog down in this semi-flooded ground, but a WASP would stay mobile. When the Gordons went through to tackle the fortified Schloss Calbeck, all the AFV support got bogged down, but the Gordons' WASPS flamed part of the Schloss buildings.

'A' Company crossed the railway and established a small bridgehead over the Nier. The RSF were withdrawn from Goch to leapfrog through the Gordons on the 21st, for a night attack to extend the bridgehead. This they did in a costly attack with fierce resistance from mortars, small-arms, and SP guns defending the minefields. During the night the RSF dug-in under violent shelling by enemy tanks and SPs. At dawn on the 22nd enemy paratroopers launched a vicious attack on 'B' Company RSF inflicting casualties. The RSF held the area around Hooesaat with great difficulty – it was touch and go. The Recce Regiment sent out patrols every day, but it was difficult to map-read the tortuous tracks in the huge pine woods. Lts Browne, Buck, Shirley, Gillings, Falloon and Jellinek all led dangerous patrols, with casualties lost to German SP guns, Spandau fire, mortars, of course, and the horrible Schu mines.

Capt Liddell commanded 'C' Squadron during Veritable.

> The journey down from Goch was comparatively peaceful until I reached the Schloss [Calbeck] which was being used as temporary HQ by infantry, artillery observers, engineers, signallers . . . Our old friend Doc [RMO] Pooley was running a casualty collecting and clearing station, and he was a very busy man.

> Several carriers were burning in the middle of the courtyards. Every few seconds another load of shells would crash down.

The Gordons lost four Bren-gun carriers in Schloss Calbeck. One had Bangalore torpedoes aboard and exploded the HQ cellar and knocked out the rear link wireless. During the 22nd, the Gordons tried to clear the woods down to the Goch–Wesel railway line. All day, attacks and counter-attacks went in amongst furious 'stonks' from both sides. The various FOOs were Maj G.C. Campbell, Capt Meredith, Maj Cornwall, Maj Sam Ginn, Capt Shaw, Capt Whitton and Maj Wingate – to name some of the twenty-seven brave forward observation officers who brought down concentrations, barrages and DF tasks for 'their' infantry. The situation south-west of Bucholt was so serious that two battalions of 46 Brigade, the Cameronians and the Seaforths, were now rapidly brought into action, arriving from Cleve. At about 1400 hours the Cameronians were across the Niers bridge and passed through the RSF at the crossroads. The Seaforths followed to clear woods to the east and finally Brig Villiers ordered the Glasgow Highlanders to clear the village of Hooesaat. 46 Brigade achieved all its objectives and took 100 prisoners. At first light on the 23rd, the Gordons, supported by Scots Guards tanks, finally took the enemy-held Schloss Calbeck, south-west of the railway line. The GOC then sent Brig Cumming-Bruce's 44 Brigade south – the KOSB on the right, Royal Scots on the left with Grenadier tank squadrons. During a day of fierce opposition from tanks, SPs and 20mm guns, the fortified hamlets of Saarbrockshof, Fasanenkath, Heishof and Vasenhof were captured. The Lowland Brigade took 150 prisoners and 8 self-propelled guns from the Battlegroup *Graefing* and 901st Panzer Grenadier Regiment.

The Luftwaffe bombed and strafed from time to time and attacked the Royal Scots, and some of the new jet fighters were heard and seen. The RAF bombed 'C' Squadron of the Recce Regiment, who were on the whole quite pleased. Nobody was hurt but three of the unpopular, elderly Carden Lloyd carriers were burned out and were subsequently replaced with more popular, modern carriers able to tow anti-tank guns. The final action in Veritable took place on 24 February. From the Heishof–Vasenhof spur in the eastern loop of the Niers, the KOSB had a commanding view of enemy targets to the west in front of 53rd Welsh Divison. So Brens, mortars and medium machine guns had many excellent targets and fired on them with impunity. 15th Scottish was relieved on the 25th and 26th and began its move back to peace and quiet in the Tilburg area. 46 Brigade's history relates: 'We had been told to fight ourselves to a standstill and we had done so. The limit of human endurance is an unknown quantity and can only be gauged by experiment. We had very nearly reached this limit in Operation Veritable.' In its part in the storming of the Siegfried Line, the division had suffered more than 1,500 casualties. 46 Brigade lost an appalling 620, 227 Brigade 415 and 44 Brigade 390. Altogether 232 were killed in action and 215 taken prisoner. The severity of Veritable was nearly on a par with the Epsom battle.

Operations Torchlight and Plunder: The Rhine Crossing

The Scottish Division had a remarkably pleasant week out of the line in and around Tilburg, where the Red Lion Club, the Tam O' Shanters, ENSA, cinema shows, sport and the friendly Dutch helped dispel some of the memories of the mud and ferocity of Veritable. Bullshit reigned of course. Lt-Col Morgan, CO of 2nd Argylls, insisted on a superb turn-out for the GOC's inspection on 1 March. The pipes and drums of the Argylls were in

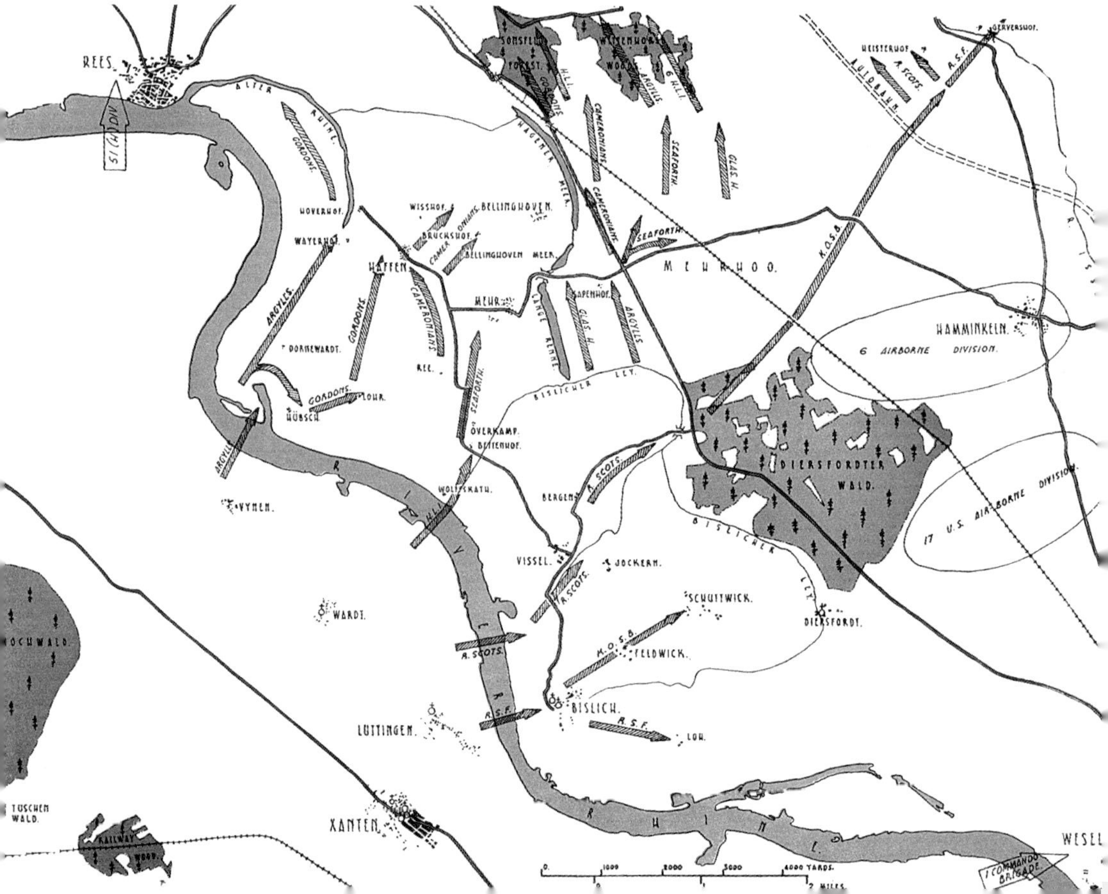

The Rhine crossing by 15th Scottish in Operation Torchlight.

great demand, under Pipe-Major Kerr. The Retreat March, Slow March, Quick March, Strathspey, Reel and Final March were traditional tunes. Every officer and man had forty-eight hours' leave in Brussels. There was no work after 1500 hours. Field Marshal Montgomery on 9 March issued his orders for the crossing of the Rhine north of the Ruhr. The XII Corps night assault, Operation 'Plunder', would task 15th Scottish with a crossing directed on Bislich and Mehr. The former was four miles west of the large town of Wesel and the latter three miles south-east of the town of Rees. Two airborne divisions would land in front, in the area of Hamminkeln and Diersfordter Wald three miles inland from Mehr and Bislich, to secure the bridge crossings of the River Issel. D-Day would be 24 March. The 15th Scottish operation was named 'Torchlight', and would involve 227 Brigade, with Gordons and Argylls leading on the northern flank, making a bridgehead in the area Haffen-Mehr. 44 Brigade further south would cross from Xanten, led by the RSF and KOSB, with Bislich as their objective. Each attack would have tank support, 11th RTR and East Riding Yeomanry respectively. Each assaulting battalion would be lifted in Buffaloes or Landing Vehicle Tractors (LVTs), large amphibious vehicles capable of carrying twenty-eight men or a carrier or jeep with its team. 46 Brigade was in reserve with the DD tanks of 44th RTR in support. They would cross the 500-yard-wide Rhine in the 'ferry wave' of LVTs, storm-boats, rafts and DUKWs.

The Gordons, then the Cameronians and Glasgow Highlanders, would concentrate east of Haganer Meer and on the high ground south-east of Sonsfeld Forest, south of Haldern. But first of all Operation 'Buffalo', two full-scale practice crossings of the now peaceful River Maas, took place at Reckheim, near Roermond. A dry-shod exercise, loading and unloading Buffaloes, took place on the evening of 9 March. A daylight exercise on 14 March was followed by a night exercise on 15 March. Although the Maas was narrower than the Rhine, it was also faster flowing (about four knots). The Argylls' historian wrote, 'The Yeomanry responsible for the actual crossing were a delightful lot to work with, with a fine cavalry dash and a persistently horsey outlook, even in the water, when squadron commanders were heard urging their drivers to "get their whips out".' A week of intensive study followed – of cloth models, maps and air photographs of the area just south of Rees. Both banks of the Rhine were protected by summer Bunds, 10–15 feet high, parallel and close to the river. Often there was a second line of winter Bunds a mile or so further inland. The ground between was mostly flat but intersected with pools and watercourses. The tracks on top of the Bunds, though exposed to enemy fire, would provide better going. To protect the Allied forces' immense preparations coming up to the west bank of the Rhine, Montgomery had organised a huge fifty-mile-long smokescreen, which prevented both sides from seeing what was happening. Gen Blaskowitz's Army Group H was composed of four parachute divisions and three infantry divisions in the front line of defences. In reserve were 116 Panzer, 15th Panzer Grenadier and an infantry division, all of whom were fully aware that a massive Allied onslaught was being prepared. The German 7th Parachute Division was guarding 227 Brigade's objectives, and the battered 84th Infantry Division was opposite the 44 Brigade crossing-place at Xanten.

Montgomery's plan for Plunder relied initially on the successful airborne drops and landings, and secondly on the deployment of 1,300 guns firing from close to the banks of the Rhine. 15th Scottish Recce Regiment was quartered in farms around Winnekendonck. Their historian wrote: 'This area near the river was already an amazing sight; almost every hedge and wood sheltered the bridges, rafts and boats in which 60,000 Royal Engineers and men of the Royal Navy were to carry an army across 500 yards of water. Each of the regiment's squadrons was to supply six half-tracks to tow assault-boats and bridging materials to the banks of the Rhine on the eve of the attack.' Six carriers would transport military government detachments over the river to administer occupied German territory gained in Plunder. The scale of the assault over the Rhine was almost unimaginable. On the ground there were 400,000 vehicles of every possible description – tanks, SPs, AVREs, carriers, half-tracks, Crocodiles, Wasps, DUKWs, LVTs, DD (swimming) tanks, field ambulances, signals trucks, REME vehicles and more.

Col R. Foster commanded 11th Army Group Royal Engineers, responsible among other things for the initial assault-boats, rafts, ferries, river booms, and the follow-up 'serious' pontoon bridges (Class 9, 12 and two 40). The First Airborne Army was composed of more than 1,700 planes and 1,400 gliders. The 1,300 guns – field, medium, heavy and AA – needed careful disposal and coordination of a myriad fire plans. The Royal Navy supplied, manned and put in place huge river boats and barges for later river patrolling. Dumps of ammunition, petrol and lubricating oil rations had also to be coordinated. At 1700 hours on 23 March the XXX Corps counter-battery artillery programme commenced, and an hour later the guns of XII Corps opened up. 51st Highland started its assault crossing on Rees at 2100 hours, and an hour later 1 Commando Brigade assaulted Wesel, twelve miles south-east. The two Scottish brigades launched their assault crossing at 0200 hours on 24 March. The Seaforths would cross behind 44 Brigade, and the Cameronians and Glasgow Highlanders behind 227 Brigade. So they waited for their ferries. At 2330 hours the 700 guns in support of 15th Scottish opened up, and at 0100 hours the Divisional 'Pepperpot' fired their curious mixture of tank guns, heavy mortars, LAA guns, medium machine guns and anti-tank guns. And the deadly, noisy Canadian Mattress rocket salvoes were in play again. The 44 Brigade assault astride Bislich was completely successful. By 0400 hours the RSF, Royal Scots, KOSB, Seaforths and 44th RTR DD tanks were across. The casualties were few, some caused by Schu mines, others by 'friendly fire'. The engineers started their bridge building with pontoons. The 44 Brigade history quoted:

> The scene at the river was like the Thames at Oxford in Eights Week. The banks were crowded with men and vehicles . . . the assault-boats, rafts and Buffaloes

6 KOSB over the Rhine, near Bislich.

> plied backward and forwards with their loads, every moment landing stuff on the east bank, while the DD tanks, like strange canvas boxes, dived into the water and swam slowly across, emerged on the far bank, shook themselves, deflated and then miraculously appeared as Sherman tanks again.

At dawn the KOSB entered Bislich and met some resistance from 1062nd Grenadier Regiment, but by 1000 hours reached Schuttwick hamlet a mile further inland. The Royal Scots with 44th RTR Shermans captured the villages of Vissel and Jockern, also a mile inland, taking prisoners. The air armada arrived overhead at 1000 hours, the artillery barrage silent, as the bombers, Dakota tugs and gliders soared serenely over the Rhine. The parachutes opened like hundreds of flowers, and the gliders disappeared behind the huge Diersfordter Wald. The enemy Flak was very heavy, and shot down seventy aircraft and fifty gliders, and the Airborne Divisions suffered badly. But their objectives, the seizing of the bridges and crossing points over the River Issel seven miles inland, were taken. At about 1500 hours the KOSB and RSF met up with 17th US Airborne Division, and the Royal Scots, moving from Feldwick to Jockern, linked up with 5 Parachute Brigade of 6th Airborne Division at the bridge over the Bislicher Ley. At dusk the KOSB marched north-east to Bergen. 44 Brigade had captured over 1,000 prisoners for the loss of fewer than 100 casualties.

On the 227 Brigade front, the enemy paratroopers (with grim, efficient women snipers) put up one hell of a fight against the HLI around Wolffskath, Bettenhof and Overkamp. In confused and bitter fighting, the HLI, under Lt-Col Bramwell Davis, suffered nearly 100 casualties. 'A' Company lost all its officers and CSM John Wright took command and was awarded the DCM. In front of 'B' Company were no fewer than a dozen Spandau posts. The entire observation point party of Maj J. Oliver's 131st Field Regiment RA was ambushed and killed. Afterwards the enemy, who lost heavily in killed and wounded, including over fifty prisoners, were identified as a parachute battalion.

But by 0900 hours the area was sufficiently clear for assault echelons to cross the river, and for the sappers to start bridging. The Argylls crossed from Vynen, two miles north, towards Hubsch, although five out of six LVTs had to make a detour, and lost many men fighting another enemy paratroop battalion. At daybreak there was an unplanned gap of 2,500 yards between 'B' and 'A' clearing Hoverhof and Wayerhof on the northern flank. 'D' and 'C' eventually took Hubsch and with help from 'A' Company of the Gordons captured Lohr against fierce resistance. The whole of the British High Command was waiting for the success of the initial assault in Plunder. From Army Commander, Corps Commander, Divisional Commander, Brigade Commander – all eyes (and ears on the wireless set) were urging the hapless HLI and Argylls to 'push on regardless' to link up with the airborne troops. Memories of Arnhem were still very vivid. Moreover, the battles for the key towns of Rees, by 51st Highland, and Wesel, further south, by 1 Commando Brigade, were still in the balance. Some Sherman DD tanks were now across and helped clear Lohr. The recce armoured cars, too, were over, as their historian relates:

> When 'C' Squadron made its way through the bridgehead, it found everywhere evidence of the accuracy and deadliness of the airborne attack. Some of the landings had been in the middle of the enemy gun lines and the guns now stood, intact, but silent, beside their dead crews. So great had been the effect on the German artillery that under a cloudless sky not a single shell interrupted the busy ferries, although there was fierce fighting only three miles ahead.

At about 1000 hours the Divisional Commander ordered the Seaforths across, followed later by the Cameronians and the Glasgow Highlanders with DD tanks. The Seaforths cleared Sandendorf, pushed inland through the HLI in Overkamp to clear Mehr, and tried but failed to capture the bridge over the Bellinghoven Meer. The German 7th Parachute Division was determined to hold (and eventually to destroy) this vital bridge, between two miles of lakes and waterways, carrying an important road east to Hamminkeln. Haffen, a large village 2½ miles south-east of Rees, on the northern flank of the attack, was half taken by the Gordons with the bayonet, capturing seventy prisoners. At nightfall on the first day of Plunder, the Cameronians were fighting hard to capture the eastern half of

Haffen, and the Seaforths were still fighting vigorously around Mehr. The Royal Engineers had by then built three bridges across the Rhine.

During the night of 24/25 March, two companies of paratroopers counter-attacked the Seaforths in Mehr and with Spandaus and bazookas inflicted heavy casualties. Two artillery forward observation officers, Maj Wingate and Capt Whitton, brought down defensive fire stonks on Mehr itself and forced the paratroopers to retreat.

It was now essential for the Scottish Division to capture two important road bridges – the one at Bellinghoven Meer and another four miles further north-east across the half-finished autobahn, at Gervershof, west of Dingden, crossing the River Issel.

The latter was the task for 44 Brigade, which had done so well on the first day. At 0730 hours the KOSB set off from Bergen (north of Bislich), with two companies lifted on the Sharpshooters (3/4th CLY) Sherman tanks, the other two marching. Their route lay through the large pine forest Diersfordter Wald, over the main railway line to within 2,000 yards of the Wissmaan bridge over the Issel. This flat open country was under fire from enemy SPs, which quickly knocked out three Sherman tanks. So Lt-Col Richardson decided on a silent night attack, starting from the Autobahn. The KOSB, now with the Royal Scots behind them, worked their way to within 800 yards before heavy resistance was met, and the advance temporarily halted. Nevertheless the KOSB and Sharpshooters had penetrated five miles through enemy defences.

Brig Villiers and 46 Brigade had to capture the Bellinghoven Meer road bridge. A head-on attack would be suicidal, so the Glasgow Highlanders and Argylls were sent right-flanking in choking dust, due south, west of the lake Lange Renne. Then round it and clear through woods on the eastern side to cut off the German defenders of the vital road bridge. By nightfall the Seaforths advancing from Mehr met the Glasgow Highlanders, and captured the bridge, which of course was thoroughly demolished. The Argylls consolidated round Kapenhof half a mile east, whilst the Cameronians, west of the lakes, beyond Haffen were twice counter-attacked. They in turn captured the hamlets of Brukshof and Wisshof. The Royal Engineers meanwhile had built a Class 40 Bailey pontoon bridge at Xanten, in half the time originally planned.

The German 7th Parachute Division was still full of fight, and tanks and SPs of 116th Panzer Division were reported ahead.

On the night of 25/26th, the KOSB were sharply counter-attacked by a parachute battalion, which overwhelmed 'C' Company and the Regimental Aid Post. Pte Howe and most of No. 12 Platoon were wiped out, but no less than ninety-eight dead Germans were found the next morning in the KOSB orchard. By 0630 hours the whole of the Sharpshooters' Sherman tanks had arrived to stabilise the situation. Unusually, 132 Germans surrendered to 'D' Company a few hours later, and the KOSB recovered their wounded in the captured RAP. Nevertheless the KOSB suffered seventy casualties that night. At midday ten tanks from 115th Panzer appeared but were driven off. Two enemy SPs disturbed a patrol by the Recce Regiment.

> After meeting the KOSB, Lt McFall's carriers went forward to the woods where we found the HQ of the 3rd Parachute Brigade in a large building, surrounded by dead Germans. During the night Brigade ordered us to patrol through the wood to the Autobahn north of Hamminkeln. We arrived to find our forward troops under fire from SPs and several Shermans burning.

Brig Cumming-Bruce next launched the Royal Scots Fusiliers in Kangaroos supported by Sharpshooters' tanks and Crocodile flame-throwers to clear the west bank of the Issel and capture the bridge at Geyershof, by now, of course, destroyed.

It was a brilliant operation. Lt-Col MacKenzie sent his RSF off at 1600 hours. The Shermans moved out to the flanks and took seventy prisoners. The Crocodiles flamed the defences in front and by dusk 'D' Company had collected 160 prisoners. Sgt Urie, the RAP medical sergeant, was captured, but persuaded forty-five of his captors to come in and surrender. Despite heavy mortar and Spandau fire, the other three RSF companies managed to debus in the midst of an enemy position, charged the river crossing (the Issel, a small weedy river, was about ten yards wide and three feet deep), waded across, climbed the far bank and, still under fire from both sides of the river, charged – incredibly – with four enemy 20mm guns firing viciously at them. By 2200 hours they had taken all their objectives, and 200 more prisoners for a cost of sixty-two casualties. The Brigadier now made another audacious plan. The pathetic little Issel had to be bridged, and quickly, that night. A counter-attack would have destroyed the RSF in their little bridgehead. A bridging 'train' was ordered up along the main road from Hamminkeln. It was met halfway by the KOSB carrier platoon, and escorted north through enemy patrols on the road. By 0600 hours on 27 March the Issel bridge had been built. On the left flank the Royal Scots had a nerve-racking night at Heisterhof between the autobahn and the River Issel. They were counter-attacked during the night by paratroops with bazookas and Spandaus. 'A' Company was nearly overrun and fighting went on all night. They were saved by the Royal Scots artillery forward observation officer bringing down DF targets.

The GOC now had orders to link up with 51st Highland Division, which had just cleared Rees, so Brig Villiers sent Glasgow Highlanders and the Seaforths north towards Haldern. With the help of the flame of Crocodiles and WASPS many defended farms were taken, plus several hundred prisoners.

Late on the 26th, the Gordons mopped up around Haffen and linked up with 5/7th Gordons (51st Highland), a mile or so south-east of Rees. Another bridge was completed over the Rhine, a Class 12 Bailey pontoon at Hubsch. The next day there were five desperate hours on the Issel

Royal Scots Fusiliers move through woods over the Rhine under shellfire.

bridgehead, but the RSF with half of KOSB just held firm. The gallant 44 Brigade had smashed up the German 84th Division in almost four days of non-stop fighting and had captured 2,000 prisoners, and then had fought against the seasoned 7th Parachute Division. It had linked up with both Airborne Divisions within five hours of their landing – a very fine performance.

46 Brigade had two more days of fighting to clear two large forests south-east of Haldern, the Sonsfeld and Wittenhurst Woods. Both the Glasgow Highlanders and Cameronians bumped the enemy in strength, and the Crocodiles and artillery support knocked out troublesome 88mm and 20mm flak guns. The Seaforths were sent up to help but the paratroopers had had enough. Fifty surrendered, tired, hungry and dispirited. White flags were hanging from all the farms and the countryside was strewn with abandoned equipment. The bridgehead between Rees and Wesel had been cleared for the loss of almost 1,000 casualties. Six of the infantry battalions lost over 100, fighting the German paratroopers to a standstill. One sour note was struck by the prevalence of friendly fire. The Argylls were heavily shelled by artillery, either Corps or from another division. Nevertheless it was 'a great achievement', wrote Gen Dempsey to the GOC, Maj-Gen Barber. 'I send you and the Division my very sincere congratulations. I am sure you are all very proud of what you have done. A great achievement.'

CHAPTER 16

The Advance to the Elbe

On 29 March the weather broke and 15th Scottish rested, refitted and absorbed reinforcements, while occupying undamaged farms and houses. Current policy was that fraternisation with the enemy was absolutely *verboten*. The Germans were to be taught the lessons of defeat. The area of the bridgehead was crowded with refugees from the bombed cities and from Eastern Germany, fleeing the Russians. The Jocks found most of the German children irresistible (not, however, the 14- and 15-year-old *Jugend* who had recently been taught how to use a *Panzerfaust*, and, if he was very good and keen, a Spandau). The historian of the Recce Regiment wrote:

> In the low land beside the Rhine, the regiment waited while the spring flowers opened and the battle which had become a chase swept farther and farther into the heart of Germany, away from this battlefield littered with broken-backed gliders, burnt-out planes and the weapons and vehicles which the Germans had abandoned

Support Company 2nd Argyll & Sutherland Highlanders advance over the Rhine, April 1945.

> under assault from across the water and out of the air. The tanks were in full clatter with the infantry astride them . . . For the time being there was nothing for the Scottish Division to do. Its part had been to open the flood gates for the pursuit.

The Argyll War Diary for 3 April read, 'Companies resting and training. Weather very good. No word of move. We are now mile behind the line.'

Field Marshal Montgomery had unleashed 21st Army Group across the Rhine, directed to the River Elbe on a three-corps front: on the left XXX Corps advancing towards Bremen and Hamburg, in the centre XII Corps advancing towards Luneburg, and on the right VIII Corps aimed at Osnabruck, Celle and Uelzen. 11th Armoured Division and 6th Airborne Division were the two spearheads of VIII Corps, with 15th Scottish in reserve to tidy up behind them. On 3 April 46 Brigade moved east of Bocholt, and 227 Brigade eight miles west of Ibbenburen. Each morning a brigade column would set off, usually with the Recce Regiment in front, the leading battalion riding on the Churchills of 6 Guards Armoured Brigade, and behind them the whole Brigade Group, some Funnies, a battery or more of 25-pounders, sappers for the occasional minefield and frequent booby-traps and the remaining infantry either in troop-carrying vehicles or somehow distributed among the group's vehicles. A blown bridge would hold up the entire column until it could be repaired, or a Scissors bridge laid, or the recce cars had found a feasible detour. The long column, nose to tail (for rarely was the Luftwaffe in action), was often double-, or even treble-banked, despite frenzied instructions from the 'Management'. If a battalion was not in the lead, there were always the mopping up tasks: combing woods for stray enemy, either in uniform or dressed as civilians, searching farms and cottages for firearms and hidden weapons or supplies (poultry, milk, bacon, eggs were often found), sorting out displaced persons (here the regimental interpreter was invaluable) and members of the SS, and collecting all men of military age who could not produce medical discharge papers from the German armed forces. Through Bocholt, Borken and Oisterwijk to Altenburg: this was the longest and swiftest 'swan' since northern France into Belgium and Holland – but how different! No cheering crowds in the towns and villages, no flowers, certainly no kisses, no wine, no calvados. In the small neat, high-roofed towns and villages, the peoples of the Third Reich stayed behind their curtains with occasional white sheets or flags of surrender. Only the very old or the very young civilians were to be seen, or the badly wounded *Wehrmacht* veterans with bitter faces. Occasionally the Poles, Russians and displaced slave workers from France, Holland and Belgium cheered as freedom came to them. The Recce Regiment were soon under command of the 6th Airborne Division, passing through Greven, Lengerich and Mundrop, Bad Essen and Oldendorf.

Lt-Col K.C. Smith, CO of the Recce Regiment, describes how 6th Airborne Division with only nominal transport of its own – mainly jeeps – was capable of astonishing advances. 11th and 7th Armoured Divisions –

thrusters to a man – could not understand it. The Airborne commandeered any vehicles, including steamrollers, to keep the red beret troops moving.

> The Airborne normally advanced on one centre line, the leading brigade clearing to about 500 yards on either side. On the flanks our task was to sweep through the country, dealing with minor pockets and informing Airborne HQ of any major concentrations or any other threat from the flanks. Our [Recce] assault troops and carriers were invaluable in overcoming minor opposition, even to the extent of clearing a village. If resistance was too strong, a brigade was immediately deployed. When the 6th Airborne troops arrived, they immediately attacked. The speed with which the Airborne worked on these small operations had to be seen to be believed. They had the drill absolutely cut and dried. No hanging about – their commander merely wanted to know what we had found out and at once deployed the infantry on either side of the road. The tanks followed up and between them they could clear a fairly large village in about twenty minutes.

On 6 April the Airborne stormed the River Weser at Petershagen, despite a rare Luftwaffe attack. Across at Wegholm, the Recce was given the key task of dashing ahead for the River Leine and seizing the bridges at Bordenau and Neustadt.

'The airborne colonel said to me [Lt Gillings], "Sonny, I want you to go like hell for the bridge and don't stop for anyone. I'll be right behind you." I had a Humber scout car – with twin K guns – and two Daimler armoured cars, with five carriers following. We did the first two miles in 20 minutes and reached Rosenhagen village.' The battle there lasted an hour.

> The leading car shot past three German soldiers, wounding all three, and engaged another six immediately. Soon all three cars were in the village and we were having the time of our lives. Having pinned the enemy to the houses, we used our 2-pounders, and the Besas started the usual fires. Three hundred yards behind us the carriers were engaging two Spandau positions with such good results that they never troubled us at all.

Six bazookas damaged two of the armoured cars, 'but we were able to sit tight and continue burning the village. Within twenty minutes the Airborne and tanks arrived, the Airborne colonel leading on the bonnet of a jeep. They just rushed up to the scene of the firing, dismounted from the tanks and were in action almost immediately – such beautiful drills. What confidence it gave us to see them in action.' Lt Gillings and three Daimler armoured cars then tore off down the road to Hagenburg and encountered fifty German defenders and roadblocks. 'We stayed in the village – quite comfortable – until the Airborne arrived 35 minutes later. The cars went backward and forward all the time, firing at anything that moved.'

In those two actions 300 prisoners were taken. Luftwaffe planes in a hangar were peppered by the Besas and 2-pounders. Then on, bypassing Wunstorf towards the River Leine, where a headlong rush of armoured cars and tanks crossed and captured the Bordenau bridge, and removed demolition charges. That night an attack to capture Neustadt bridge was foiled when it was blown up in the faces of the infantry trying to rush it. The next day, 8 April, Lt Arthur Buck, 'C' Squadron, was ordered to try to capture the third bridge over the River Leine two miles south of Bordenau at Ricklingen. Several Tiger tanks and SPs were giving the Airborne deep trouble in Luthe, a mile west of Ricklingen. The River Leine and its large metal suspension bridge lay midway between the two villages. Lt Buck's carrier and assault troops therefore travelled south on the east (enemy-held) river bank by a track. By 0930 hours they had captured the bridge intact, cut all the fuse wires of the demolitions, and forced the enemy prisoners to dump the explosives in the river. Buck placed his 6-pounder anti-tank gun covering the road to Luthe, put his forces into slit trenches and the enemy prisoners into cellars, and sat tight on and around the bridge until the Airborne came to the rescue. It was not to be. First enemy shelling started, and Buck asked for, and got, supporting Scottish artillery fire. At about 1400 hours, 'about forty yards away, just coming round the corner was a terrible looking monster with Tiger written all over it. The 88mm gun was pointing at us and the muzzle-brake looked the size of a railway engine.' The PIAT firer got off two or three shots but caused no damage; the 6-pounder anti-tank gun was covering a different road. 'By now the Tiger was shooting up our vehicles one by one, followed by two SPs, which had already shelled us from a distance, and three or four armoured half tracks.'

The Tiger destroyed eight carriers, four half-tracks and the 6-pounder anti-tank gun and forced the recce parties to retreat on foot. All the vehicles and wireless sets were out of order. But the Tiger tried and failed to destroy the bridge, and eventually the Parachute Brigade doubled for two miles from Luthe, led by their brigadier, to clear the enemy from Ricklingen. On the same day, 8 April, the Argylls' pipes and drums beat the 'Retreat' in Bohnhorst village square, to a startled German audience. Piper Fyffe Christie, 9th Cameronians, a notable artist, wrote:

> After the Rhine crossing, the nature of the fighting changed. Gone were the cheering crowds welcoming the liberators, replaced by the sullen inhabitants of the villages and towns – many in ruins – through which the Cameronians leapfrogged in their advance to the Elbe. Each farm and wood was fanatically defended not only by the German 7th Parachute Division, but by newly thrown-together infantry battalions formed of U-boat crews and Luftwaffe personnel. We saw the bodies of the boy-soldiers of the Hitler Youth and the old men of the *Volksturm* [Home Guard].

On 10 April the division as a whole now came up and over the River Leine to take over from the gallant Airborne Division. They had been in action constantly for two weeks since the crossing of the Rhine, and, despite huge casualties – almost 40 per cent – they had been magnificent. The objectives now were to take Celle and then Uelzen.

Celle stands on the River Aller behind a screen of forests, about fifteen miles north-east of Hanover, which had just been taken by the XIII US Corps.

The GOC ordered a two-brigade advance: 227 Brigade from Fuhrberg had eight miles to go due east, and 46 Brigade from Grosse Burgwedel a twelve-mile advance towards Celle from the south-west. Scots' and Coldstream Guards' tanks would support each advance. At 1930 hours on the 11th, the Cameronians under Lt-Col Remington Hobbs had a thoroughly unpleasant action with fifty-plus young officer cadets in woods near Ehlershausen, six miles south of Celle. Further north the Gordons, via Neustadt, had by dusk reached the canal two miles south-west of Celle. All the many bridges around Celle on the canal and River Aller were blown, except for two wooden bridges found at Altencelle, two miles south-east of Celle. Rather carefully, the Gordons and the Argylls and their tanks crossed. The HLI had cleared Celle and crossed the Aller by assault boats, and the sappers finished a Class 40 bridge across by midnight. Celle was not defended. There were many hospitals and a small gruesome concentration camp was found – a subsidiary of Belsen, which lay seven miles south. The ADMS Col F.M. Richardson – the chief divisional medical officer – ordered the citizens of Celle to remove the several hundred corpses and provide medical supplies and attention to the survivors. The advance continued on the 13th, north-east to Eschede and Uelzen, with the HLI leading. Two miles ahead of them, slowly retreating, was a highly efficient German demolition team, who blew up bridges and created colossal craters across the main road. One time-bomb destroyed a sapper vehicle, causing eleven casualties. Each crater was covered by fire from SP guns, small arms and bazooka fire. Nevertheless Brig Colville, 227 Brigade Commander, ordered two skilful, and lucky, detours through thick pine woods, north and parallel to the main road. The first one on the way to Eschede, ten miles out of Celle, eventually yielded 800 prisoners, mainly youngsters from GAF, the Luftwaffe ground troops. The second detour was even more startling: fourteen miles through the woods by the HLI and tank support – through the night. They started at 0100 hours on the 14th, the HLI in front, with two reputed members of the German Resistance movement as guides. There was faint moonlight strengthened by some searchlights. The HLI raced through a series of small villages, shooting up any vehicles in their way. They reached Holdenstedt by rejoining the main road, three miles short of Uelzen – at dawn. It was to be nearly a disaster. Uelzen was a key communication centre, as part of the German defences before the River Elbe. Fresh troops had just arrived from Denmark, including reserves of Panzer Grenadiers and a Flak regiment with 20mm cannon mounted on trucks. They – the defenders – were fresh, full-fed and truculent, undefeated and longing for a fight. Despite the fire of the Guards' Churchills and a troop of 131st Field Regiment 25-pounders firing over open sights, the HLI were torn apart. Their transport was destroyed and within a few hours they suffered more than 100 casualties, including thirty-two taken prisoner.

The Recce Regiment had since the Rhine crossing acquired some additional exotic transport vehicles, including sleek limousines, a German ambulance, speckled camouflaged German half-tracks and even a fire engine.

2nd Gordon Highlanders cross a temporary bridge north of Celle, 12 April 1945.

On 'Black Thirteenth' at Unterluss they came across a German artillery training centre, an ordnance dump, an enclosure of *Wehrmacht* ladies and considerable resistance. Lt Green became Mayor and Military Commander of Unterluss (for a day). Beyond Eschede, they captured old Field Marshal von Mackensen, an intrepid First World War veteran. His mansion contained cellars, which in turn contained enough wine to supply the division.

46 Brigade's task was to mop up on both sides of the divisional axis on a very broad front. The Glasgow Highlanders were on the right (south) side of the main road and the Seaforths on the left (north). By nightfall on the 14th, the former had reached Stadensen, five miles south of the HLI battle at Holdenstedt, having taken several hundred prisoners *en route*.

It was to take 15th Scottish Division – all of it – with supporting arms nearly five days to take Uelzen and Stadensen. The latter was defended by a heavily armoured battlegroup from Panzer Division Clausewitz.

CHAPTER 17

The Battles for Uelzen and Stadensen

At dawn on the 14th the HLI had been devastated around Holdenstedt, two miles south-west of Uelzen. Brig Colville sent up the Argylls, who cleared woods on the right flank, and planned a four-battalion attack during the night to try and clear Uelzen. The RSF would come under command to protect the rear of 227 Brigade, the HLI would take Veersen, a western suburb, the Gordons would go down the main road and clear the main town, and the Argylls would continue to protect the right flank. Seven quite important roads and a railway feed into Uelzen, which has the small River Ilmenau flowing through the centre. The GOC moved 227 Brigade along the northern road closer to Uelzen, and 46 Brigade on the southern road. At Bokel the Recce Regiment had a field day, as Lt McFall reported:

> We decided to loop along some high ground and broke from the woods. There in the valley was a company [of Hitler Youth] marching east with a wagon of bazookas. Sgt Jacques and Sgt Dullaway blocked the road, while the Dingo and I covered from the crest. Sgt Coe did some wonderful three-inch mortar shooting. We took one hundred and seventy prisoners. Cpl Lavery bumped off a staff car killing both occupants.

The Glasgow Highlanders reached Stadensen, six miles south of Holdenstedt, with 'C' Squadron Recce in Nettelkamp, a mile to the east. Panzer Division Clausewitz attacked at midnight on 14/15th and overwhelmed the recce squadron, with sixty casualties, including thirty-nine captured. Thirteen carriers, armoured cars and a half track were captured or destroyed. The German infantry led the attack, quietly, in rubber boots, while half-tracks with 20mm cannon followed them down the main street. SPs circled the village. Some of the attackers were French SS troops, and most of them were drunk or drugged; they howled, screamed and took crazy risks. Eight days later 11th Armoured Division released the Scottish troops taken prisoner. In nearby Stadensen the Glasgow Highlanders had an RASC troop of 3-ton supply lorries with them, a squadron of Coldstream tanks, a 17-pounder SP troop, a platoon of engineers and RHQ of 190th Field Regiment RA. All this mass of vehicles and troops crammed into the streets and alleys of Stadensen. At about

0400 hours the Panzer Division Clausewitch attacked, with infantry riding on armoured half-tracks supported by SP guns, and came crashing into the large village. Most of the houses were soon burning furiously, and close-quarter fighting went on for four hours. Several ammunition trucks blew up and the crews of the Scottish tanks and guns struggled to get into action. Maj J.H.M. Stephenson of 530 Field Battery won the MC by knocking out two enemy half-tracks with a Piat and then manning a 25-pounder field gun in an anti-tank role. The dreadful ordeal went on until dawn. The Glasgow Highlanders had fifty-four casualties, including twenty-two taken prisoners. Sixty-three vehicles and two 17-pounder guns were destroyed. Scores of German civilians were also killed. But the enemy left behind twelve SP guns and ten armoured half tracks destroyed, and very many killed and prisoners. It was an appalling battle. Stadensen was, of course, a ruin; with the end of the war in sight, it was incredible that the German Army was not only so full of fight, but prepared to destroy their own citizens so cold-bloodedly. The Cameronians came up and moved to Nettelkamp – the scene of the recce debacle – and took eighty prisoners without much trouble.

At midday on the 15th, the battered HLI resumed their advance into Veersen, the southern suburb of Uelzen. The Light AA group from Denmark had plenty of Spandaus, SP guns, bazooka squads and machine carbines. They counter-attacked the hapless HLI, whose CO, Lt-Col Bramwell Davis, was wounded, and overran a forward company. The Gordons attacked on the right in the southern suburbs and fared no better. The HLI and Gordons spent the day pinned down by fire.

The next day the Cameronians relieved the HLI, and the Glasgow Highlanders took over from the Gordons near the railway level crossing. The Seaforths remained four miles back, south-west of Uelzen. The RSF and KOSB reached Hambrock, another southern suburb. The GOC made various plans for attacks on the 17th, but Lt-Col Richardson's KOSB upset them by probing and pushing into the south-east of Uelzen, capturing the important bridge over the River Ilmenau in the centre of town. Late that afternoon the Cameronians also found resistance slackening in Veersen, and by dawn on the 18th captured it. By the end of that day, after hard house-to-house fighting with tank versus SP duels, the Seaforths and Glasgow Highlanders cleared the west and north of the town and linked up with the KOSB, RSF and Royal Scots. The Cameronians also liberated a PoW camp that contained 51st Highland survivors from Saint-Valery captured in 1940.

On the 19th the Argylls led 227 Brigade out of the ruins of Uelzen, and reached Volkstorf a few miles south-east of Luneburg – the wild, sandy, sparsely inhabited Luneburger Heide, the equivalent of Salisbury Plain. At the end of the day the Argylls had reached Hittbergen; the HLI, Scharnebeck; and the Gordons, Barum, a few miles from the great River Elbe. It was a 20–25-mile advance, with many minor hold-ups. The recce

Seaforth Highlanders clearing houses under fire in Uelzen, 18 April 1945.

found a large American and British PoW camp at Bavendorf, and in Neetze an international circus with the lions and bears missing. A performance – highly enjoyable – was given to the Scottish troops and 11th Armoured, who had already reached the river opposite Lauenburg. During the 20th, the HLI captured 200 German policemen at Artlenburg. Field Marshal Montgomery had hoped to 'bounce' the Elbe, but the vital railway bridge was blown up (250 yards from the author, forward observation officer with 11th Armoured Division).

It had taken just a month for VIII Corps to advance from the Rhine to the Elbe. It had covered more than 200 miles of country and captured 700 German officers and 30,000 men. The Scottish Division had suffered just under 600 casualties, mainly to the HLI, Glasgow Highlanders and the Recce Regiment. While the gunners were preparing for the next river crossing, Capt T.J. Stokes, 181st Field Regiment, wrote:

> While at Ludersburg, we sent all water trucks which could be spared to the Belsen concentration camp. The drivers had heart-rending stories to tell of the horrible conditions there. An armed guard watched each truck as it entered the camp, to prevent hundreds of starving inmates from clambering on, to get any drops of water they could. The people were dying as you looked at them. The German guards were made to dig the graves and accompany the loads of dead bodies to the burial ground.

The Scottish Division had been fortunate not to pass directly through Bergen–Belsen, where Kramer and Irma Grese, and the male and female SS guards, controlled the terrible fate of more than 50,000 prisoners.

Towards the end of April news came that the Russians had encircled Berlin and on 26th had linked with the US 9th Army.

For a week the division was resting and preparing for the last of four great river assaults – the Seine, Escaut, Rhine and now the Elbe. The war correspondents christened the division 'the Crossing Sweepers'.

Operation Enterprise: Advance to the Baltic

For a week very complicated plans were being drawn up for the assault crossing of the River Elbe. VIII Corps was given the honour of establishing a bridgehead, initially 1,500 yards deep and 2,500 yards wide. This would be the responsibility of 15th Scottish with 1 Commando Brigade under command. And 11th Armoured would then pass through and thrust north for Lübeck, Kiel and the Danish frontier.

The complications arose because the northern bank of the River Elbe is a substantial steep escarpment, which would make Buffalo or DUKW landings difficult. Moreover, enemy observation points had clear observation of the southern-bank activities for several miles. No vehicle movements were allowed in the forward positions during daylight. The River Elbe in April is about 300 yards in width in the Artlenburg–Lauenburg stretch and flows at about two knots. There was only one road into Artlenburg, a small town with narrow side streets with gardens and woods, and another from Scharnesbeck to Lauenburg. Enemy strength was estimated at about nine battalions of very mixed provenance with about 100 guns, and rather surprisingly supported by daring Luftwaffe jet plane attacks.

The final plan for Operation 'Enterprise' was for a two-brigade attack at 0200 hours on 29 April, under 'Monty's Searchlights', supported by a substantial barrage from seventeen artillery regiments.

1 Commando Brigade was tasked with a crossing west of Hohnstorf, to capture Lauenburg from the rear. 44 Brigade, led by the Royal Scots and RSF on board the LVTs of 11th RTR, would attack through the Grun Hof forests to capture Schnakenbek, starting from just west and east of Artlenburg.

Col R. Foster, Commander of 11th Army Group Royal Engineers, who had masterminded the complex Rhine crossing so successfully, was in charge of the plan for the Elbe crossing: suitable DD tank and LVT approaches, river entries and exits; a DUKW crossing; two 12-boat assault-boat ferries; at the Lauenburg crossing a Class 9 raft ferry and a Class 9 bridge of folding-bridge equipment; for the Artlenburg crossing a Class 40 raft ferry and a Class 40 Bailey pontoon-bridge. Col Foster also had to provide boom protection above and below the crossing places.

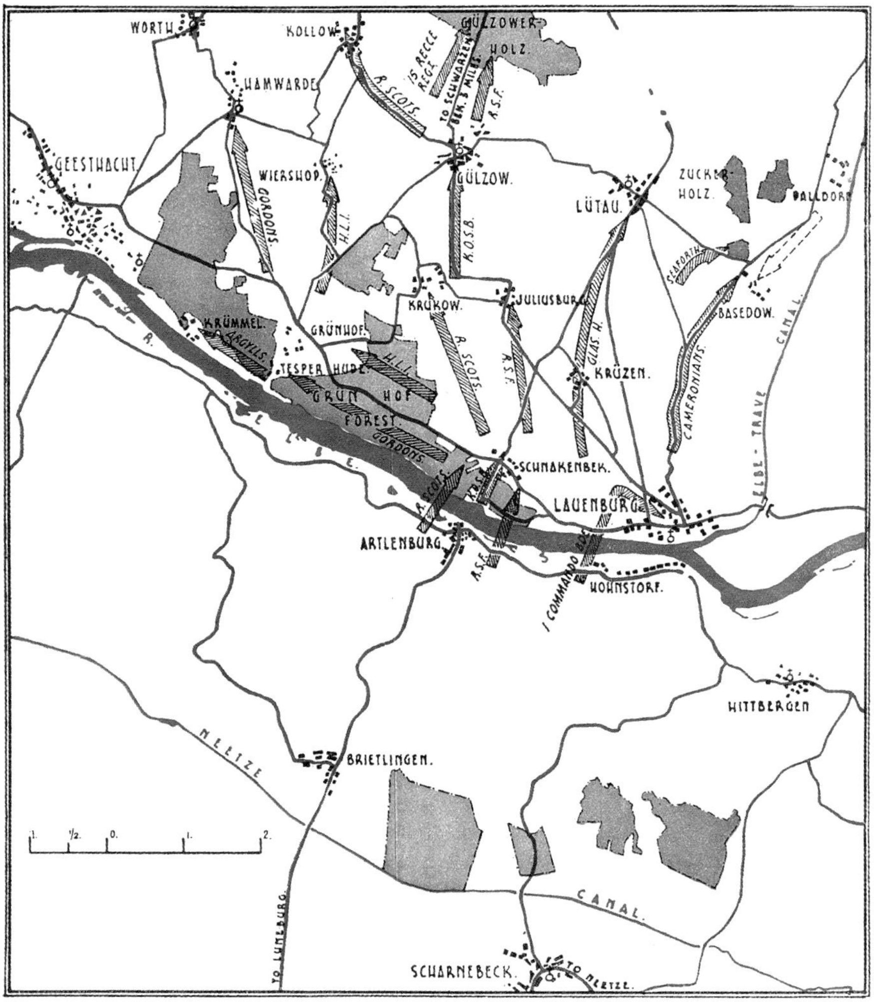

Operation Enterprise – assault crossing of the River Elbe.

The follow-up plan was for 46 Brigade to go through the Commando bridgehead, and for 227 Brigade through 44 Brigade. The Recce Regiment would land its armoured cars and carriers in the van of the assault and push out patrols to the north, west and east. The Recce Regiment's historian wrote:

> The bridgehead was a country of field and farm, deer forests and lakes, lonely castles, villages and little country towns, and west, along the Elbe, the outskirts of the sprawling, mangled port of Hamburg. The only civilian traffic on the

Operation Enterprise: 10 HLI troops have crossed the River Elbe, 19 April 1945.

cobbled streets of the country places was the wagons drawn by short, long-bodied unblinkered horses. Storks nested on the high roofs of the long farmhouses.

Enterprise went well. The immense fire plan fell on the foreshore, then the opposite escarpment, then on enemy forward positions and strong-points. At exactly 0200 hours the huge, black Buffaloes took the RSF and Royal Scots across, who quickly scaled the steep and sandy slopes. At about 0330 hours the Argylls and the KOSB crossed, as did the Seaforths on the Commando front. The only disaster occurred when three companies of Argylls assembled in a quarry – probably an enemy defensive fire target – and were heavily shelled, which inflicted about fifty casualties.

The historian of the Argylls wrote:

> Life down in the area of the crossing place was extremely dangerous. The enemy had the spot beautifully ranged and at very long range and he shelled it continuously, unaffected by the hectic counter-battery labours of the gunners. The enemy's jet-propelled aircraft began to strafe the same area. The AA guns got one or two and the Spitfires one or two more, but the Luftwaffe continued to machine-gun and drop light bombs all day. The courage of the Sappers who worked impassively on, building their pontoon bridge regardless of damage or casualties, was beyond all praise. It was trying to watch from the comparative safety of the cliff bank. As was the crossing of the HLI and the Gordons under the intermittent shower of high explosive.

The Recce, once across, sent patrols west to Hawarde, north to Kollow and Schwartzenbek (a railway and road junction on the main Hamburg–Berlin road). By 0800 hours the KOSB had captured the latter, with its garrison of 'Green' Police. The Commandos rapidly cleared Lauenburg and captured the bridge intact on the main road to the east over the Elbe–Trave Canal.

To expand the bridgehead further, 227 Brigade was pushing hard on the left towards Geesthacht six miles downstream, 44 Brigade in the centre was fighting for Krukow, Juliusburg and Gulzow, whilst 46 Brigade on the right was advancing towards Lutau, Basedow and Dalldorf. By nightfall on the 29th, 1,400 prisoners had been taken, a solid bridgehead and all objectives achieved. Col Foster's brave sappers had two Class 40 rafts working and had ferried more than thirty-five tanks across, a Class 9 ferry had put almost 100 vehicles across and a Class 9 FBE bridge. During the day divisional and Corps sappers suffered more than sixty casualties from constant Luftwaffe attacks (but thirteen planes had been shot down) and persistent long-range shelling.

Capt T.J. Stokes, 181st Field Regiment RA, reported: 'A ceaseless watch was kept on any enemy activity which could be observed on the other side. Eventually, almost every gun emplacement, infantry post and slit trench near the opposite bank was charted and drawn on large scale maps.' The artillery barrage had indeed been most effective for the assault crossings, but heavy guns firing possibly from casements five or more miles inland were difficult to pinpoint and neutralise. During the night of 29/30th, the divisional artillery crossed over the Elbe at the new Lauenburg bridge and by 0500 hours on the 30th the gunner advance parties arrived at Gulzow and other possible battery sites several miles inland. The second day resistance suddenly hardened on the right flank. The Cameronians were counter-attacked near Basedow by four determined enemy companies just before dawn. For four or five hours it was a close-quarter fight against *Panzerfaust* and Spandau teams. Despite defensive-fire targets fired by the divisional gunners, intense 2-inch mortar firing by the Cameronians and the arrival of Staffordshire Yeomanry tanks, the pitched battle continued until 1100 hours. However, the German infantry held its front strongly. By the end of the 30th the Cameronians had accounted for forty Germans and captured 142, but suffered forty casualties themselves. A wooded hill, Zucher Holz, a mile north, was also strongly held, and the Seaforths took four hours to clear it, accounting for seventy of the determined opposition. The Seaforths had thirty casualties in the wood-clearing action. Piper Fyffe Christie, 9th Cameronians, commented:

> Now the battle-weary soldiers were increasingly unwilling to take unnecessary risks – although the Cameronians continued to take punishing casualties at the River Elbe crossing. To replace them the reinforcements were no longer veteran Scots

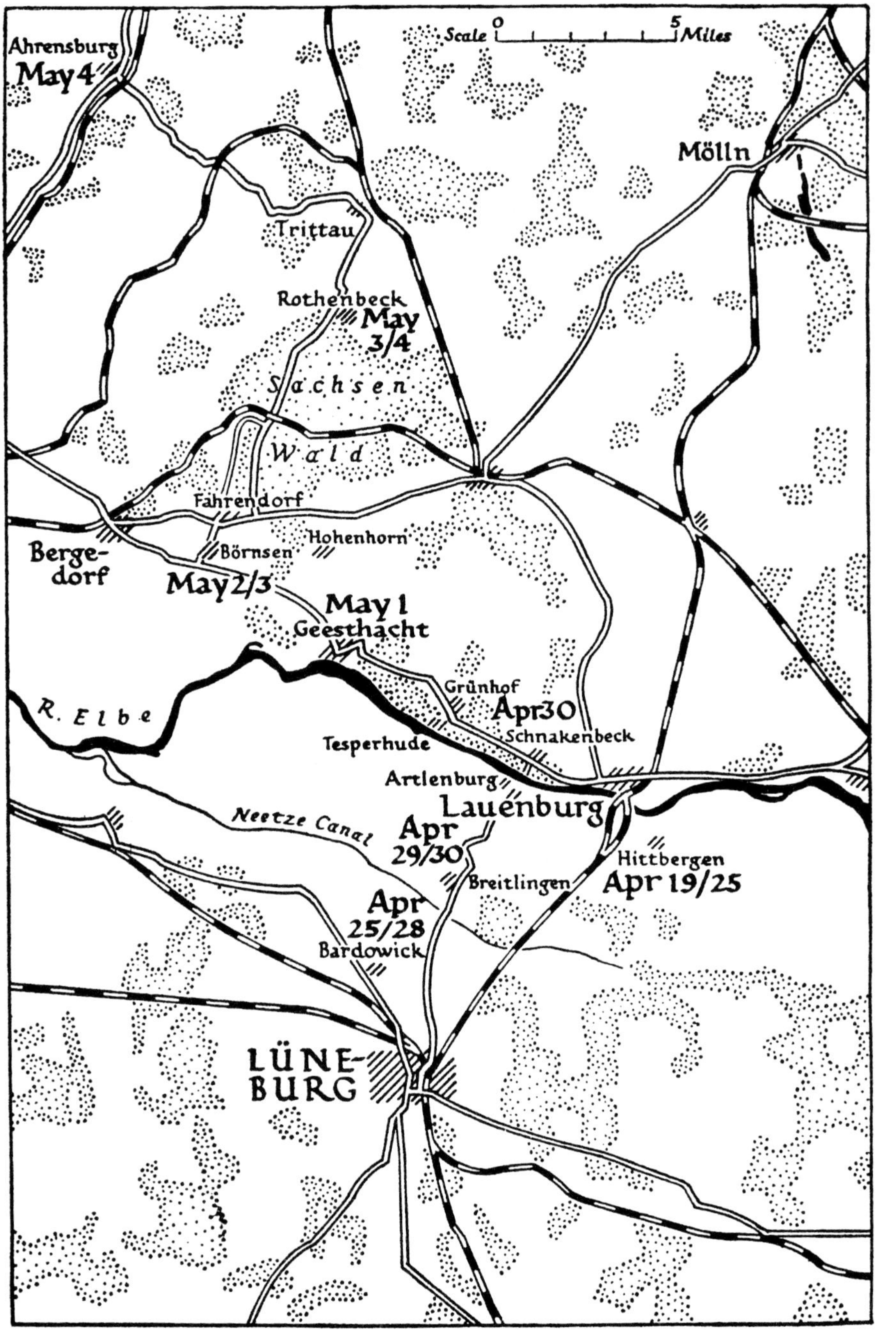

The final battlegrounds beyond the River Elbe.

> but a mixture of troops from other regiments, notably anti-aircraft gunners who had previously been defending British cities. As infantry they fought bravely, but the family structure of the Battalion which had stood them in good stead in past engagements was weakened.

And the Sassenachs in the new intakes did not appreciate the piping practice when 'resting' out of the line!

Just to the north-west of the Seaforths, the Glasgow Highlanders also had trouble clearing Lutau, which they eventually did, taking 100 prisoners and damaging many of the enemy. In the centre the Royal Scots encountered enemy SPs in Kollow, and the KOSB sent patrols into a large wood, Gulzower Holz, took lots of prisoners and found two long-range 12-inch guns which had obviously been used to shell the bridgehead. On the left flank resistance was crumbling, and Grunhof and Tesperhude were both occupied. During the day three enemy frogmen in full aquatic dress, with orders to blow up the Artlenburg bridge, were captured. By nightfall 227 Brigade had made progress – the HLI in Wiershop, Argylls in Krummel and the Gordons in Hamwarde. 15th Scottish Division was now across the river and the author's 11th Armoured Division was pouring over the bridges. On 1 May Brig Colville over the civil telephone completed negotiations for its surrender with the German garrison commander of Geesthacht, a town six miles west on the banks of the river. There was a store of V1 rocket fuel and munitions, and reputedly also of poison gas capable of destroying the whole countryside. Geesthacht was where XII Corps would bridge the Elbe for its advance on Hamburg. And the whole division started to move westwards to clear the huge forest of Sachsenwald, north-east of Hamburg and several miles inland from Geesthacht. Soon 53rd Welsh, 5th British (arriving from Italy) and 6th Airborne Divisions arrived on the scene, while 11th Armoured's new Comet tanks crashed through the cobbled towns of Bad Oldesloe and Reinfeld towards Lübeck.

Sgt Tiny Kirman, 'A' Squadron, 15th Recce, had an exciting day patrolling towards Bergedorf and Hamburg. He outflanked German positions, eliminated Spandau posts and gave valuable support. 'My car patrol going towards Hamburg came under heavy fire and we pulled back to allow the Argyll and Sutherland Highlanders and the Coldstream Guards tanks to attack. The battle was at its height when I noticed two German officers walking forward with a white flag. Thinking they wanted to surrender, I drove up to them with a sergeant major of the Highlanders, and the senior officer, a major, immediately asked to be taken to an officer.' Blindfolded, they were taken back to an HQ. 'They returned, and later two staff cars full of Germans were brought through. By now the rumour of peace negotiations had got around, but the battle continued, although people were coming and going all the time.'

The opening of surrender negotiations for Hamburg, by officers of the 2nd Argyll & Sutherland Highlanders. From left to right: Maj Vyvyan Cornwell (with flag), Maj McElwee, Lt-Col Russell Morgan and the Recce troop leader with the German colonel.

Sgt Kirman, who won the MM that day, started the chain of events via Brig Colville to the GOC, to the Corps Commander, and to the Army Commander, which led to the surrender of Hamburg. Although the city was a shambles, it could have been as well defended in its ruins, as Berlin and to a lesser extent Bremen had been. Meanwhile Sachsenwald forest was cleared and by the evening hundreds more prisoners went into the cages. The KOSB captured the Prince and Princess von Bismarck in the Schloss of Friedrichsruh. But a little *Götterdämmerung* remained. Marine cadets from the Flak school in Hamburg had a bitter battle with the HLI in Hohenhern and Neu Bornsen. The Argyll historian wrote:

> East of Bornsen there were deep gullies cutting into the side of the hill, filled with dense undergrowth well suited to ambushes and delaying tactics. The enemy were using their 20mm light anti-aircraft guns with good effect. Opposing the Battalion were tough youths of sixteen and upwards [from the same Marine Cadet School], thoroughly indoctrinated with Nazism and determined to kill at least one enemy apiece before the inevitable surrender. Their tactics were to sit back well concealed in the undergrowth and engage at point-blank range, throwing down their weapons and putting up their hands as soon as opposition became serious, if there were no ready means of escape. Only by accepting the risk of very heavy casualties was it possible to advance fast against such methods. Moreover the artillery had outrun their ammunition supplies.

Maj-Gen Barber, GOC 15th Scottish, and Intelligence Officer interview the German Chief of Staff of Marshal Busch, prelude to surrender of Hamburg, 2 May 1945.

Soon, however, white flags began to appear. The news spread that Adolf Hitler was dead, and the *Wehrmacht* (apart from the SS and *Hitlerjugend*) was disposed to give up. The Chief of Staff of Army Group Blumentritt agreed to go to VIII Corps HQ with Maj-Gen 'Tiny' Barber to arrange preliminaries to surrender. Hamburg then surrendered to the Desert Rats – 7th Armoured Division. The Baltic was reached by 11th Armoured and 6th Airborne Divisions. The German forces in Italy surrendered. Doenitz had announced Hitler's death on Hamburg radio.

On 3 May the division moved to a concentration area north-east of Hamburg, where north of the Elbe the whole land was crammed full with homeless refugees fleeing from the Russians to the comparative safety of the

British (or Americans). Nearly all were heading for Hamburg, not realising that it was a bombed-out shell. The Recce Regiment historian at Elmenhorst wrote:

> We were checking the amazing procession of the defeated German forces along the Hamburg road. They were coming from the east and the north. There were men on foot, men on bicycles and men in carts. There were wheezing, massive dilapidated lorries dragging three or four or five trailers, all piled high with passengers and baggage. When stopped, some of the lorries managed to start again. Many did not. Looking at this motley collection, one wondered how the German Army had managed to resist so long.

The endless stream of uniformed jetsam poured along every road: Luftwaffe, Flak units, Marines, Panzer Grenadiers, U-boat crews, town police, *Volksturm*, a few *Hitlerjugend*, a few SS (some were still fighting in the Forst Segeberg). But their fierce discipline and allegiance to their now dead Führer kept them going – indomitably. The Allied air forces ruled the skies. The Allied tanks and AFVs and artillery forces outnumbered the *Wehrmacht* by ten to one, and the writing was on the wall during Overlord and the irresistible Russian advances, but it was not until all the German towns were crammed with dead and wounded, with red crosses painted on the hospital roofs and the survivors penned into Schleswig-Holstein that there was a final surrender. And that was mainly due to the death of Hitler in a sordid Berlin bunker.

Admiral Doenitz flew to Field Marshal Montgomery's HQ at Luneburg, where he and Gen von Keitel signed the peace treaty – at 1820 hours on 4 May. 15th Scottish was concentrated north of the Hamburg–Lübeck autobahn, Divisional HQ at Hammoor, 44 Brigade in Bargteheide and Delingsdorf, 46 Brigade around Trittau, 227 Brigade in Ahrensburg; and the Recce Regiment seized bridges in the harbour area of Kiel, and over the Kiel Canal to control the German forces moving south from Denmark to surrender. On the 6th the HLI padre took a service for the whole of 227 Brigade – a simple and moving service where the massed pipers played 'Flowers o' the Forest' in the woods on the far side of the lake. Maj-Gen Barber briefly recalled the greatest fights of the campaign, and the division's appalling losses, a total casualty list of 669 officers and 11,422 ORs. And Monty stressed, 'And so let us embark on what lies ahead, full of joy and optimism. We have won the German war. Let us now win the peace.'

Nearly 12,000 casualties – mainly Scotsmen, Argylls, Cameronians, Gordons, Seaforths, Glasgow Highlanders, Highland Light Infantry, King's Own Scottish Borderers, Royal Scots Fusiliers, Royal Scots, Scottish Recce, Middlesex and certainly not least the brave sappers and gunners, all with the vital support of the RASC and Field Ambulances – yes, there were nearly 12,000 casualties in the eleven months of fighting. More than 1,500 of them are buried in the immaculate War Graves

The massed pipe bands of 15th Scottish Division at the German cavalry barracks in Luneburg, 17 April 1945. Left to right: Maj-Gen Barber, Lt-Gen Barker, Brig Bolton and Brig Colville.

Commission cemeteries along the divisional centre lines. In France, Belgium, Holland and finally in the Third Reich, the 'Crossing Sweepers' earned immortal fame for their four river and canal assault crossings. On 10 April 1946 15th Scottish Division was disbanded.

Bibliography

Barnes, B.S., *The Sign of the Double 'T'*, Sentinel Press, 1999
Bryant, Arthur, *The Turn of the Tide*, Wm Collins, 1958
Clay, E.W., *The Path of the 50th*, Gale & Polden, 1950
Churchill, Winston, *Triumph and Tragedy (Second World War)*, Cassell, 1951
Daglish, Ian, *Operation Bluecoat*, Pen and Sword, 2003
Delaforce, Patrick, *Smashing the Atlantic Wall*, Cassell, 2002
——, *Churchill's Secret Weapons (Hobart's Funnies)*, Hale, 2001
Doherty, Richard, *A Noble Crusade*, Spellmount, 1999
D'Este, Carlo, *Bitter Victory (Sicily)*, Wm Collins, 1985
Kemsley, Riesco, *Scottish Lion on Patrol*, White Swan Press, 1950
Kiln, Robert, *D-Day to Arnhem (Hertfordshire Gunners)*, Castlemead, 1993
MacLellan, C.R., *Wave an Arm, Follow Me*, Lancelot Press, 1993
Martin, H.G., *History of 15th Scottish Division*, Wm Blackwood, 1948
Moorehead, Alan, *Eclipse*, Hamish Hamilton, 1946
——, *African Trilogy*, Hamish Hamilton, 1946
McElwee, W.L., *Argyll & Sutherland Highlanders*, Thos Nelson, 1949
Picot, Geoffrey, *Accidental Warrior*, Penguin Books, 1993
Powell, Geoffrey, *History of the Green Howards*, London, 1992
Rissik, David, *The DLI at War*, DLI Depot, Co. Durham, 1952
Stokes, T.J., *Return to Europe*, Private Printing, 1945
Wilmot, Chester, *The Struggle for Europe*, Wordsworth, 1997
Woollcombe, Robert, *Lion Rampant*, Chatto & Windus, 1955

Index